Silverware
OF THE 20TH CENTURY

THE TOP 250 PATTERNS

Silverware

OF THE 20TH CENTURY

THE TOP 250 PATTERNS

Harry L. Rinker

HOUSE OF COLLECTIBLES

THE BALLANTINE PUBLISHING GROUP • NEW YORK

Important Notice. All of the information, including valuations,
in this book has been compiled from the most reliable sources,
and every effort has been made to eliminate errors
and questionable data. Nevertheless, the possibility of error, in a work of such
immense scope, always exists. The publisher will not
be held responsible for losses that may occur in the purchase,
sale, or other transaction of items
because of information contained herein. Readers
who feel they have discovered errors are invited
to *write* and inform us, so they may be corrected in
subsequent editions. Those seeking further information
on the topics covered in this book are advised
to refer to the complete line of *Official Price Guides*
published by the House of Collectibles.

Copyright © 1997 by Rinker Enterprises, Inc.

All rights reserved under International and Pan-American Copyright Conventions.

H This is a registered trademark of Random House, Inc.

Published by: House of Collectibles
The Ballantine Publishing Group
201 East 50th Street
New York, NY 10022

Distributed by The Ballantine Publishing Group, a division of Random House, Inc., New York, and
simultaneously in Canada by Random House of Canada Limited, Toronto.

http://www.randomhouse.com

Manufactured in the United States of America

ISSN: 1094-6063

ISBN: 0-676-60086-7

Text design by Debbie Glasserman
Cover design by Kristine V. Mills-Noble
Cover photo by George Kerrigan

First Edition: November 1997

10   9   8   7   6   5   4   3   2   1

Contents

Acknowledgments

The manuscript preparation for *Silverware of the 20th Century* and its companion volumes—*Dinnerware of the 20th Century* and *Stemware of the 20th Century*—provided ample proof that nothing is ever as simple as it first appears. Five months quickly became eight months. In the end, persistence prevailed over frustration, but at a cost. As a result, this acknowledgment begins with an apology to those individuals who experienced higher-than-normal stress levels because of my delays.

My name appears on the cover as the author. However, I am deeply grateful to a team of behind-the-scene individuals, whose expertise is utilized throughout this book.

I am certain that when Gary S. Corns, manager of the Imaging Services Design Team at Replacements, Ltd., agreed to serve as project liaison, he did not know what he was getting into. We optimistically believed that a few instructions to the computer were all that was needed to gain access to an orderly presentation of the information needed for this book. When this proved to be more complicated than we first thought, it was Gary's stick-to-itiveness that kept the project moving forward. Gary, my deepest thanks for staying the course, for seeing that all illustrations were photographed and all documents were scanned, and for answering numerous last-minute questions.

I love the "can-do" attitude at Replacements, Ltd. It reflects the leadership philosophy of Bob Page, Replacements' founder. Speaking to Bob about my research, about what was happening at Replacements, and about possible future projects was one of the high points of each of my visits to Greensboro.

I was ably assisted in my research by members of Replacements' curating staff. Kudos to Chris Kirkman, Jan Valentino, Jessica Whitehead, Jamie L. Robinson, and others who willingly shared their expertise.

Replacements operates on a team concept. Doug Anderson, Executive Vice President; Dale Frederiksen; Mark Klein, Director of Marketing; Mark Donahue, Media and Marketing Coordinator; and Todd Hall can play on my team anytime. Hopefully, they feel the same way about me.

Shortly after this project began, Pat Thompson, who served as Media and Marketing Coordinator; struck out on her own. Pat played an instrumental role in shaping this project and in securing Replacements' commitment to it. Best wishes for a highly successful career as an independent public relations consultant.

Dena George at Rinker Enterprises, Inc., was responsible for the price listings, for securing illustrations, and for proofing copy. Nancy Butt, reference librarian, also proofread. Additional support came from Dana Morykan, Kathy Williamson, Virginia Reinbold, and Richard Schmeltzle.

Cooperation from manufacturers and their agents was generously given. My sincere appreciation to: Bixler's Jewelers (Easton, Pa.), Sherry Davis; Hand Industries (The Dirilyte Line), Shelby Beam; W. J. Hagerty & Sons, Adam T. McMurry, National Sales Manager, Home Care Products Division; Lenox Brands (Dansk, Gorham, and Kirk-Stieff), Alice Kolator, Director of Public Relations, and Tracy Mitchell; Oneida, Sandra E. Finley, Public Relations Coordinator; Reed & Barton, Marci Karales, Public Relations Manager; Syratech Corporation (International, Towle, and Wallace), Cheryl Balian, Director of Public Relations; *Tableware Today*, Amy Stavis, Editor/Publisher; Tiffany & Company, Linda Buckley, Publicity; University Products, John A. Dunphy, Director of Marketing; and, WMF, Peter Braley. Special thanks to Christie Romero, author of *Warman's Jewelry*, for responding positively to my requests for information from her research library.

Randy Ladenheim-Gil, project coordinator and editor at House of Collectibles, wore the "good" and "bad" cop hats. In the course of our many conversations, she pointed out that while an author may view a book as finished once he or she submits a manuscript, the difficult and time-consuming process of publishing the book remains. It is a point well taken.

Individuals who are involved in the publication and sale of books often do not receive the recognition they deserve. Most are nameless, even to the author. While I am able to express my gratitude to Alex Klapwald, for coordinating the production of this book, and Simon Vukelj, for directing its sales, a note of general thanks is all I can offer to the copy editors, designers, paste-up artists, printers, and sales personnel. Once this book is published, I look forward to meeting many of them and thanking them personally.

I am deeply indebted to Timothy J. Kochuba, General Manager of House of Collectibles, for allowing me to author this book and for his unswerving commitment to and faith in the project.

Finally, my thanks to you, the purchaser of this book. I trust you will find it more than meets your expectations.

Introduction

I get excited about silverware. I love the color. In fact, I prefer it over gold. While precious, it is not so precious that I feel the need to lock it up in a bank vault rather than use it.

Many of my childhood memories are associated with silverware, from setting the dining room table for holiday meals with our "best" silver to the arrival of the first set of dishwasher-safe stainless steel. When the silver-plated candelabra was placed on the table, it signaled an important occasion was about to occur.

Although a few serving pieces matched these place-setting patterns, most did not. I grew up in a family of savers whose cultural tradition stressed handing things down from generation to generation. Silverware was always a treasured heirloom in my family. All of these "odd" pieces came with a family story. When a guest asked, "Where did you get this piece?" the answer became a piece of oral history and an important insight into my roots.

I began my research for this book in the kitchen and dining room drawers of my home. I gathered the "odd" serving pieces and examples of the daily and good silverware services and set about researching the patterns. Since Connie, my wife, and I had both been married previously and came from large families, the group of pieces I started with was quite large.

Connie had a bridal registry for her first marriage. To the best of my knowledge, I did not. Connie's sterling pattern is International's Prelude, chosen in part because her husband was the son of a jewelry store owner, and that was the pattern the store carried and the one his mother recommended. The pattern is listed in the Appendix in the Top 25. Connie's everyday flatware was stainless, as was mine.

All of the inherited silverware pieces that I assembled for research were silver plated. Connie and I came from families who earned a modest income; sterling was out of their price range.

Fortunately, a number of excellent reference books are available for pattern identification. They are listed in the bibliography at the end of this book. I will not bore you with the research results, except to say that my everyday stainless turned out to be Oneida's Debonair.

As an appraiser, I am used to the strange and the unusual. However, nothing prepares the appraiser for the variety of unusual circumstances encountered when dealing with flatware that has been handed down through the family. When an estate has multiple heirs but has only one set of flatware, the logical approach would be to divide the number of heirs into place settings, distribute them accordingly, and then evenly divide the serving pieces. For whatever reason, this is not the typical approach. Instead, one heir receives all of the forks, another all of the spoons, and so forth.

I once opened a woman's dining room buffet drawer and discovered over 200 spoons. She was the "spoon lady." Whenever a family service was broken up, this woman received the spoons. Another heir was given the forks, another the knives, and so on. I have encountered this phenomenon dozens of times. In fact, I need look no further than the flatware from my mother's estate. The initials and monograms allowed me to identify the owners of several dozen forks, knives, and spoons. In no instance did I find a full place setting.

It is impossible to undertake a project of this nature without having it become a major learning experience. Learning involves more than information. In this instance, my research on caring for silver led to a discussion with Connie about her Prelude flatware. We had used the pattern on an everyday basis when we first got together, but stopped after a few years. When I asked Connie why we no longer used the sterling, she noted that she was having trouble with spotting from the dishwasher. A few quick trials based on the information in chapter 3 identified the problem. Once again, Connie's Prelude is our everyday flatware. It goes surprisingly well with our California patio-style, solid-blue dinnerware. It also looks great with the Johnson Brothers Scenes from Constable blue transfer dinnerware we use for formal entertaining.

As I learned more about the history and use of my silverware, I challenge the reader to do the same. There is something about using silverware, either an inherited service or one selected recently, that causes one to pause and reflect. Perhaps it is the fact that making a commitment to using silverware tempers the casual focus of much of today's dining. Given today's fast-paced lifestyle, this may be just what the doctor ordered.

As an antiques and collectibles writer and appraiser, people frequently ask me to value their tableware services and to recommend someone, sometimes anyone, who will buy them. I always ask my clients if they have talked with their children to see if they would like them. The stock answer is, "They do not want them."

My response is twofold. First, be patient. The nostalgia gene is a late bloomer. Many young adults who said no to their parents' queries in their thirties have deep-seated regrets by their forties. Second, use your tableware, especially when your children and their families visit. It only takes a few meals to change how your children view your family heirlooms.

The true value of objects is not monetary, but the memories associated with them. Use creates those memories. Silverware, dinnerware, and stemware were not created to be displayed in a china cabinet or stored in a buffet. They were made and sold to be used. It is a point that should never be forgotten.

"Get out the silverware and set the table" usually means to get out the flatware and set the table with place settings. Silverware and flatware are not synonymous. Silverware describes objects made from silver, whether flat or hollow. Today, its generic use is even broader. When it comes to tabletop ware, silverware often means any item with a silver surface appearance. Although stainless has no silver in it, it does have a silverlike surface. In this book, silverware means sterling, silver plated, and stainless ware in their flat and hollowware forms.

Flatware refers to the forks, knives, and spoons that constitute a place setting and matching serving pieces. The term is used in this context throughout this book.

The flatware patterns in this book are divided into five basic groups: sterling, silver plated, stainless, Dirilyte, and gold accented. Sterling flatware is made from 925/1000 silver. If it does not say *sterling*, it is not sterling. There are exceptions, but very few. When the word *sterling* does not appear, assume the flatware is silver plated. Silver plating is the application of a thin layer of silver on a base metal. It served as the major alternative to sterling prior to World War II. Stainless is a steel alloy that contains a minimum of 13 percent chromium. The most common stainless is 18/8, a mixture that includes 18 percent chromium and 8 percent nickel. Dirilyte is a metal alloy that has a golden appearance. It contains no gold.

Some flatware patterns in this book are accented with gold plating. Since their numbers are small, the only reference to this is found in the brief pattern information appearing before the listing. Everything that is said about silver plating, from how it is done to proper care techniques, applies to gold plating.

How does one determine what constitutes the top 250 patterns of twentieth-century silverware? The most obvious approach is to research production and sales records and make a list. However, this information is not readily available. Manufacturers jealously guard such statistics. Making them public provides the competition with valuable information that could be used against them.

If sales and production statistics were the only criteria used to develop the top 250 patterns list, the result would be far different from the list that appears in this book—there would be more patterns from the first decades of the twentieth century and far fewer contemporary patterns. Such a list would reflect past, not present, tastes.

The top 250 patterns list that appears in this book, as well as the lists that appear in its companion dinnerware and stemware volumes, is based on today's market demand. The patterns listed are those most often requested by individuals who are seeking replacement pieces. They are the top 250 patterns currently in use.

An analysis of the top 250 pattern list reveals several key marketing and use trends. Many of the patterns are still in production, and many are over fifty years old, a testament to the ability of the silverware industry to produce pattern designs that endure through multiple generations. Because manufacturers and distributors often limit the number of retailers that are allowed to sell their products, many individuals have turned to mail-order catalogs and replacement services to replace or add pieces to their contemporary silverware service. The Replacements, Ltd., letterhead now indicates its ability to supply "Discontinued & Active" china, crystal, and flatware.

The list is just about evenly divided between patterns whose origin pre-dates and post-dates World War II. New design opportunities provided by stainless steel are a primary reason. Another is the continuing ability of flatware designers to create new patterns and adapt older ones to blend perfectly with emerging design styles.

The list is almost evenly balanced between sterling, silver-plated, and stainless patterns, which supports the theory that most families have a minimum of two flatware patterns, one for daily use and one for entertaining.

Silverware of the 20th Century: The Top 250 Patterns is designed to serve a number of purposes. There is more substance to this book than just a list of forms and their values. Use it to its full potential.

First, this book provides the basic guidelines needed to select, use, and care for silverware. As the old adage goes—the more one knows about something, the more one appreciates it. This book offers the opportunity to learn about silverware—its evolution, its use in the art of fine dining, the history of its makers, and the unique story behind some of the patterns.

Second, this book shows the tremendous variety of flatware patterns that are readily available to a decorator or those who wish to acquire new silverware. There are dozens of choices for most decorating styles. Every pattern is illustrated. Take a few minutes, flip through the pages, and marvel at the ingenuity of those who designed and manufactured the patterns.

Third, the checklist approach identifies which forms are available within each flatware pattern. When a flatware pattern has matching hollowware, these pieces also are listed. Although this book's principal focus is flatware, its overall focus is the tabletop. If the desire is only to acquire place settings, then every listed pattern is a possibility. If setting a table with matched place settings, serving pieces, and hollowware is the goal, the choice of patterns narrows.

The checklist also serves as a hunting list. Many individuals will be surprised at the number of forms in some patterns.

Fourth, this book answers the question: About how much will I have to pay to replace a piece or to expand my silverware? The pricing is retail and realistic. However, prices are not absolute. Price guides are exactly what their name implies—guides. Most individuals buy with a budget in mind. Realistic prices allow the user to determine which patterns are affordable and which are not.

Silverware of the 20th Century is one title from a series of three books focusing on tableware. If you find it helpful and informative, you may also be interested in its two companion titles—*Dinnerware of the 20th Century* and *Stemware of the 20th Century.*

I

GUIDELINES FOR SELECTING, USING, AND CARING FOR SILVERWARE

CHAPTER ONE

A Brief History of Silverware

Silver, one of the precious metals, is mined from the earth. It is found in subsoils all over the world, either in native form, veins or dendrites, silver sulfide or argyrose, double sulfide of silver and copper, double sulfide of silver and iron, or as argentiferous galena. Bolivia, Chile, Mexico, Peru, and the United States are the main producers of silver. Silver is refined into ingots. Gold, palladium, and platinum are by-products of silver refining.

Pure silver is too soft for functional use. Alloys, primarily copper, are added to give it hardness and strength. Over the years, individual countries have established silverware standards. German silver often conforms to an 800/1000 standard, that is, 800 parts silver per 1,000. Britain's sterling standard, 925/1000, and Britannia standard, 958/1000, are universally recognized.

Unlike their English counterparts, American silver manufacturers followed an independent course regarding silver purity standards during the eighteenth and nineteenth centuries. Between 1814 and 1830, Baltimore required that all silver made in the city be marked at a hall and identified by a letter date. An Assay Office was created to ensure a coin silver quality level equal to 917/1000. Between 1800 and 1814, Baltimore attempted to enforce a 925/1000 standard, an effort that met with mixed results. Maryland required an 896/1000 standard from the 1840s through the 1860s.

U.S. coins were minted to an 892/1000 standard between 1792 and 1837, and a 900/1000 standard after that date. While 900/1000 was the accepted standard for coin silver, some silversmiths and manufacturers increased the impurities to the point where coin silver ranged from 750/1000 to 900/1000.

In 1852, Tiffany adopted the English 925/1000 sterling standard for its silverware. Gorham, incorporating an English-style lion into its trademark to indicate purity, followed in 1868. Other manufacturers also developed trademarks as a guarantee of the quality of their products. Liberal use was made of the word *sterling*. Some late-nineteenth-century pieces marked "sterling" did not conform to the 925/1000 standard. Uniformity would not be achieved until federal legislation was passed.

Charles Lewis Tiffany and Charles Stieff, founder of the Baltimore Silver Company (later The Stieff Company), worked actively at the turn of the century to have America adopt the English sterling standard. Finally, the U.S. Federal Stamping Act of 1906 required that all silver marked "sterling" contain 925 parts pure silver per 1,000.

SILVER'S EARLY HISTORY

Silver is known as "the noblest metal" and the "Queen of Metals." Egyptian excavations at Beni Hassam, dating around 2500 B.C., have drawings depicting silversmithing. The earliest museum examples of silver decorative and utilitarian vessels date from around 1900 B.C. References to silver are found in the Bible; the Book of Genesis reports that Abram "was rich in gold, in silver and in cattle." In ancient Rome, Cicero wrote about "wrought and stamped silver," Horace described "homes that gleamed with silver," and Pliny attended "suppers served on pure and antique silver."

Silver was a sign of wealth, hence, it was restricted to ownership by royalty, the aristocracy, and the clergy. Instead of cups, dishes, platters, and other tableware made of silver, a family of modest means used implements made from pewter (the poor man's silver), gourds, or wood.

While it was necessary to add alloys to silver to give it strength, alloys were also added in larger quantities by unscrupulous silversmiths to debase the metal. Standards were required. In 1300, King Edward I of England decreed that "no manner of vessel or server part out of the maker's hand until it had been assayed by the warden of the craft and further that it be stamped with a leopard's head." This was the first hallmark. As it has for centuries, The Worshipful Company of Goldsmiths and Silversmiths continues to enforce sterling silver regulations on behalf of the Crown in England.

Silver was one of the many materials to benefit from the Italian Renaissance of the fourteenth century; silversmiths achieved the highest levels of craftsmanship. The desire for works of art made of silver quickly spread to France and England. Silverware manufacture was dominated by the guild system. Hallmarks identifying purity, location of manufacturer, maker, and date were used throughout Europe. By the seventeenth century, the Huguenots, French Protestants who fled to England in the middle of the century, were among the best silversmiths of any era.

Wars and numerous internal conflicts among and within the countries of Europe have resulted in the limited survival of silverware made before 1700. Pieces made after that date are in ample supply.

Elkington & Co., Birmingham, England, perfected the electroplating process in the 1830s. It was rapidly adopted throughout the world by the early 1840s. It was also during this period that German or nickel silver was developed. While this metal contains no silver, it has a silver-like appearance. Its use spread quickly, especially to America.

THE HISTORY OF SILVERWARE MANUFACTURING IN AMERICA

History records a Thomas Howard operating as a silversmith in Jamestown, Virginia, in 1620 and a John Mansfield working in Charlestown, Massachusetts, as early as 1634. The first American silversmiths offered a wide variety of services, from the manufacture of spoons and a few select hollowware pieces to repair services for everything from clocks and watches to firearms. Several also acted as general merchants and traders.

The English tradition of apprenticeship continued in the American colonies through the eighteenth century and into the first decades of the nineteenth century. An average apprenticeship lasted six to seven years. During that period, the master sought to teach the apprentice the skills of the trade, and the apprentice was supposed to serve the master, as directed. When the training period ended, the apprentice became a journeyman or freeman, working for day wages or by piece work. A journeyman became a master when he established his own shop.

The port cities of Boston, Newport, New York, Philadelphia, and Baltimore were the primary silverware manufacturing centers in the eighteenth century. However, many inland towns claimed one or more versatile silversmiths. Over 500 individuals are known to have worked as silversmiths in America before 1800. As respected members of their communities, many of these early silversmiths played leading roles in local and state governments and community institutions such as the church.

Much of the early silver used to manufacture flatware and hollowware in America came from melted-down coins and older pieces of silverware. Before banks, silverware represented a means of "saving" one's wealth. Further, disposing of a piece of recognizable silverware was much more difficult than selling stolen coins.

While American silversmiths used touchmarks to identify objects made by them, they did not use hallmarks. Silversmith guilds and assay houses were two institutions that were not transferred from Europe to America. Many silversmiths did not retail their own products. Retailers often overstruck the maker's mark with their own mark, or they added their mark alongside the maker's.

By the beginning of the nineteenth century, large silversmith shops, almost equivalent to factories, and small specialty shops, offering engraving and other decorating services, had emerged. However, it was mass production, the extensive use of German silver, and the advent of silver plating during the 1830s and 1840s that completely changed the direction and focus of the American silverware industry. The emergence of steam power made stamping operations possible. The corridor between Meriden and Wallingford, Connecticut, became the American center for the manufacture of silverware.

A few large companies such as Kirk and Tiffany continued to manufacture and sell primarily handcrafted products. The small, independent silversmith survived as a studio craftsman, enjoying a brief renaissance during the Arts and Crafts movement of the first two decades of the twentieth century. By the post–World War II period, most of these silversmiths made more jewelry than they did hollowware or flatware.

The period following the Civil War was marked by the continued introduction of new machinery and techniques, a rapid market expansion that took advantage of transportation and print media advances, and a continuing merger of smaller firms into larger ones. The 1876 Centennial Exposition in Philadelphia provided American silver manufacturers the chance to showcase their work to the world.

The last quarter of the nineteenth century was America's Gilded Age. During this period, the dining rituals of the wealthy required enormous dinnerware, stemware, and flatware services. Hundreds of specialized flatware and serving pieces evolved. Excess was the order of the day.

By the 1880s, the American public as a whole wanted their share of the good life. Sales for silver-plated ware, because it was durable and inexpensive, exceeded those for sterling silver. Manufacturers responded with silver-plated services whose individual piece count easily exceeded fifty-plus forms.

Recognizing the need to encourage the sale of sterling silverware, seven silver manufacturers—The Alvin Corporation, The Gorham Company, International Silver Company, Lunt Silversmiths, Reed & Barton, The Towle Silversmith, and R. Wallace & Sons Mfg. Co.—organized The Sterling Silversmiths Guild of America in 1917. It remained active through the early 1950s.

Oneida's success in promoting its products through celebrity spokespersons and print advertising, heavily concentrated on women's magazines, was quickly copied by other silverware manufacturers. The bridal market became a major advertising focus in the 1920s, with retailers promoting their bridal registries. Bridal sales reached their peak in the 1950s.

Open stock, the sales concept that a flatware pattern would remain in production for an extended period, was initiated by a number of manufacturers. This was designed to encourage individuals to buy a starter set, usually four to six place settings, and to add to it over time. Advertisements touted the purchase of additional pieces for anniversary, birthday, and holiday gifts.

IDENTIFYING MARKS

of

Members of the Sterling Silversmiths Guild of America

- **THE ALVIN CORPORATION**

ALVIN STERLING   ALVIN STERLING   ALVIN STERLING

- **THE GORHAM COMPANY**

GORHAM STERLING   GORHAM STERLING

- **INTERNATIONAL SILVER COMPANY**

Sterling   INTERNATIONAL STERLING   Sterling

- **LUNT SILVERSMITHS**

LUNT STERLING   R&L   Treasure

- **REED & BARTON**

D.H   R STERLING

- **THE TOWLE SILVERSMITHS**

STERLING   TOWLE STERLING

- **R. WALLACE & SONS MFG. CO.**

STERLING   WALLACE STERLING   WALLACE   RW&S STERLING

A wide variety of manufacturers, especially those in the food industry, and institutions such as banks and grocery stores, used silverware as incentive premiums. A 1950s box of Mother's Oats, a product of the Quaker Oats Company, included a free piece of Oneida's stainless steel Fortune pattern flatware. A full place setting could be ordered for $1.25, plus two Mother's Oats box tops. Matching Fortune pattern crystal glassware also was available.

General Mills's Betty Crocker Catalog Program continues this tradition today. It offers twenty-four Oneida Community flatware patterns—ten 18/8 stainless patterns (exclusive to Oneida), four gold electroplate patterns, six silver plate patterns, four gold accent 18/8 stainless patterns—and four Oneidaware® patterns. The catalog claims, "We've been the largest supplier of quality Oneida Community flatware since the 1930s. In fact, there's a good chance your mother and grandmother got their Oneida flatware from Betty Crocker." The catalog also includes storage bags, storage chests, and care supplies.

Towle encouraged its retailers to offer a Silver Club Plan, whereby purchasers could take their silver home the same day and pay for it later. Companies such as Easterling, Empire Crafts, and Home Decorators focused on the direct sale of tabletop items, including flatware, to consumers. Today, these companies have been replaced by direct mail catalog firms such as Barrons, Michael C. Fina, and Ross-Simons. All three offer bridal registry services. Fina has a ninety-day payment plan.

Following World War II, the Big Two—sterling and silver-plated flatware—became the Big Three, with the arrival of stainless steel flatware. The period between 1945 and the end of the 1960s was a post-war golden age for silverware manufacturers. Dozens of new flatware patterns were introduced to satisfy consumer tastes that ranged from traditional to modern. As in the early part of the century, world-famous industrial designers contributed their talents to the flatware market.

Beginning in the 1970s and continuing today, a new round of mergers reduced the number of major silverware manufacturers. Many flatware patterns were discontinued. The sales concept of open stock was dropped. The positive side of these mergers is that many silverware manufacturers became divisions of large conglomerates, whose sales focus remains on a full range of tabletop wares. Silverware supplements and supports their dinnerware, stemware, and giftware lines. The end result is a smaller, but much revitalized, silverware market.

THE EVOLUTION AND MANUFACTURING OF FLATWARE

One achieves a far better appreciation for something by understanding how it evolves and how it is manufactured. A piece of modern flatware is not the product of a single hand, but involves the skills of dozens of designers, modelers, die makers, factory workers, salespeople, wholesalers, and retailers.

The Design Process

Balance, design, harmony, rhythm, and unity are the cardinal rules governing pattern design. The process begins with a design team, often consisting of two dozen or more individuals. Research is a continuous process. After reviewing the files, preliminary drawings are made and evaluated. A new pattern must address a wide range of issues, ranging from reflecting current consumer tastes to ease of manufacture. This creative stage usually takes several months.

A skilled craftsperson makes a carved and hand-chased example of the final design or top finalists, which is carefully reviewed for its aesthetic qualities and marketability. When a final selection is made, the carved and hand-chased example becomes the design prototype for all of the pieces in the service.

A large-scale model, three times the actual size of a pattern handle, is made in wax, which is used to refine the details of the new pattern. The decorative motif of the pattern must be of sufficient thickness to be practical when reduced in size, yet delicate enough to accomplish the desired effect. A mold is cast in plaster of paris in reverse from the wax model. This mold is used to make a working bronze cast. After correcting any final defects, this bronze cast becomes the master mold for the pattern.

The next step is to create the stamping or forming dies. A separate top and bottom steel die must be made for each form. Their creation demands great skill. Perfection is required. A device, similar to an artist's pantograph, partially cuts out the steel dies. Today, much of this work is achieved through CAD/CAM computer technology. Before the final dies are hardened, they are hand worked to correct and bring into relief the finer parts of the pattern. When finished, dies are polished to a high degree. A complete modern service requires 100 or more dies.

The Manufacturing Process

In the factory, sheets of sterling silver, base metal, or stainless steel from which the initial blank will be cut are prepared. Sheets of predetermined thickness and width are cut into blanks. A properly sized blank reduces waste. Blanks are next rolled to achieve proper grade; thickness varies throughout the piece.

A process known as "cutting out" creates the base outline of the form. The piece is still flat and without shape, and there is no ornamentation. At this point, blanks for forks are sent for tining, an operation that cuts out the tines, except for a narrow strip joining the points. This strip stays in place until the stamping process is completed.

Because the metal has hardened during these steps, blanks are sent for annealing. Once reheated, the blanks are ready for stamping, a process that transfers the design to the piece and forms it to the proper shape.

When the dies are completed, they are mounted in a stamping press. Blanks are placed on the bottom die. The top die is forced down onto the bottom die with tremendous force. This stamps the design into the blank. It is common for an individual piece to be stamped several times. Restamping ensures maximum depth and sharpness of detail.

Clipping, an operation that removes the thin flash or fin that occurs around the handle during the stamping process, occurs next. The narrow strip connecting the fork tines is also removed.

The manufacturing process concludes with a series of finishing operations. Trimming, preliminary finishing, is done with an assortment of abrasive belts and wheels that revolve at a high speed on specially devised lathes. Sandbuffing follows the trimming operations. It involves bringing the piece into contact with a variety of lathes using specially prepared leather bobs or wheels of varying sizes and shapes. Pumice serves as a polishing abrasive. The piece is now in a semi-finished condition.

The polishing process varies for silver, silver plate, and stainless. The silver polishing process is the most elaborate. Cloth buffs on high-speed lathes are used for the polishing operation. Ornate pieces are put through an oxidizing program to highlight the pattern details. A final polishing process involves a number of different types of polishing wheels and materials.

When the polishing process is completed, pieces are washed, dried, inspected, and packaged for shipment. There are also several inspection points during the manufacturing process. Pieces that fail to pass inspection are remelted.

Electroplating involves an additional step between clipping and polishing. A base metal sheet, rather than a sterling silver sheet, is used for silver-plated ware. A layer of silver is applied to the base metal blank through an electrolytic process known as electroplating.

The piece that is to be plated is immersed in a tank with two silver anodes. A negative charge is applied to the base metal blank and a positive charge to the anodes. The silver anodes release minute particles of silver that travel through the solution in the tank and adhere to the base metal blank.

The amount of silver deposited on a piece is determined by two things—time spent in the tank and the rate of electrical charge. Because of these variants, there are several grades of silver plating. A quality, silver-plated piece will have enough plating to last one to two generations.

SILVERWARE'S DESIGN ELEMENTS

Silverware closely mirrors the design style elements found in architecture and furniture. Since it is designed to complement both, this comes as no surprise.

The ability of a design style to endure for centuries is one of the most fascinating aspects of silverware. In fact, once a style such as Baroque or Bauhaus has entered the design vocabulary, it never seems to go out of fashion.

Design motifs are used over and over again. Today it is possible to purchase flatware that incorporates the following design styles: Egyptian, Greek, Roman, Gothic, English, French, or Italian Renaissance, Louis XIV, XV, or XVI, William and Mary, Queen Anne, Georgian, Empire, a host of Victorian Revival, such as Rococo, Renaissance, and Neo-Gothic (Eastlake), Art Nouveau, Arts and Crafts, Art Deco, Streamline Modern, and Post-War Modern. What is surprising is how adaptive all of these design motifs are. Is it the design style or the elegance of the silver that makes it so? The argument has strong supporters on each side.

THE EVOLUTION OF KIRK STIEFF

The 1979 merger of Samuel Kirk & Sons, Inc., and The Stieff Company consolidated under one roof Baltimore's two great silverware manufacturers. Each had a long and distinguished history.

Samuel Kirk & Sons, Inc.

Samuel Kirk was born in Doylestown, Pennsylvania, in 1793. Samuel's Quaker heritage included connections with English silversmithing and banking; Jonah Kirk was registered with London's Goldsmiths' Hall from 1696 to 1697; Sir Francis Child served as Lord Mayor of London in 1699 and was a founder of the Child Banking House.

At age seventeen, Samuel Kirk was apprenticed to James Howell, a Philadelphia silversmith. After completing his apprenticeship, he moved to Baltimore, where he entered into a partnership with John Smith in 1815. The partnership lasted five years.

Baltimore was the only American city with a formal system for the assay of silver. Maryland law stipulated that silver made between 1814 and 1830 had to contain a minimum of 900 parts pure silver. Baltimore's links were more southern than northern, and Kirk considered himself a southern silversmith.

Samuel Kirk established his own business in 1820. His reputation spread quickly. Lafayette ordered a pair of goblets from Kirk during his triumphal tour. Clients included members of famous southern families such as the Carrolls and Lees.

Kirk began crafting pieces in the highly ornamental Repoussé style in the late 1820s. This revival is often referred to as "Baltimore Silver." Unfortunately, many of Kirk's early pieces were lost during the Civil War.

In 1846, Henry Child Kirk, Samuel's son, became a partner, and the company was renamed Samuel Kirk & Son. When Charles D. and Clarence E. Kirk joined the firm, the name was again changed to Samuel Kirk & Sons.

Charles and Clarence left the firm in 1868. The company reverted back to its old name, Samuel Kirk & Son. Samuel Kirk died in 1872, and Henry Kirk continued alone. In 1890, Henry Child Kirk Jr. joined his father. When a reorganization occurred in 1896, the firm became Samuel Kirk & Son Company. Henry Sr. continued to head the company until his death in 1914. Henry Jr. then became president.

Kirk produced many famous trophies and presentation pieces. The forty-eight-piece dinner service made for the Cruiser *Maryland* in 1905 is one of the most ambitious. The service contains over 200 scenes and pictures illustrating Maryland's history and is on display today at the Maryland State House in Annapolis.

Kirk incorporated in 1924 as Samuel Kirk & Sons, Inc. In 1961, Kirk issued its

Carrollton pattern in honor of Charles Carroll of Carrollton, a signer of the Declaration of Independence.

The company prided itself on its commitment to making handcrafted pieces. Kirk added a line of silver-plated giftware in 1972 and also expanded into jewelry, both 14K gold and sterling silver, decorative and utilitarian pewter pieces, and sculptures cast by the lost wax process.

The Stieff Company

Charles C. Stieff founded the Baltimore Silver Company in 1892 on Cider Alley near Redwood Street in downtown Baltimore. Following its incorporation in 1904, the firm became The Stieff Company.

Stieff was a leader in introducing the English sterling 925/1000 standard in Maryland. Once adopted, he urged strict enforcement. Stieff was a stickler for quality. He operated out of a single shop, because he felt expanding would compromise the quality of his product. Stieff was also an aggressive marketer, especially in newspaper advertising.

Stieff's expansion took place when Gideon Stieff, Charles's son, assumed control of the company in 1914. After expanding the company's manufacturing capabilities, Gideon launched a national advertising campaign. In 1925, Stieff's Wyman Park facility was built. By the mid-1930s, Stieff had opened a number of retail stores. A franchise system ensured that stores maintained the level of quality that Stieff desired. Over 400 retailers sold Stieff by the mid-1940s.

Colonial Williamsburg chose Stieff to manufacture its silver reproductions in 1939, expanding to pewter reproductions in 1951. Based on its success with Colonial Williamsburg, Stieff reached reproduction agreements with a number of leading American historic sites and museums, including Historic Newport, Monticello, the Museum of Fine Arts in Boston, Old Sturbridge Village, and the Smithsonian.

In 1967, Stieff purchased the Scofield Company, a sterling manufacturer, and in 1970 he bought Colonial miniatures. Descendants of the Stieff family continue to play key management roles in the company today.

The Kirk Stieff Company

The Stieff Company acquired Samuel Kirk & Sons, Inc., in 1979, creating a new entity—Kirk Stieff. Kirk Stieff manufactures products under the Kirk and Stieff trademarks as well as the new joint trademark of Kirk Stieff. Stieff introduced a new line of silver-plated hollowware in 1982. Kirk Stieff launched its Dancing Surf flatware pattern in 1986 and its Paramount flatware pattern in 1987.

Today, Kirk Stieff is a division of Lenox Brands.

CHAPTER TWO

Silverware Finesse—Selecting and Using the Silverware That Is Right for You

How did you acquire your silverware—through inheritance, a bridal registry, or necessity? Passing down silverware from one generation to the next is a well-established tradition. Silverware is simply "too good to throw out." If the recipient loves the pattern, the family association is a definite value enhancement. Unfortunately, many individuals who are less than pleased with their parents' or grandparents' pattern kept their mouths shut and graciously accepted it. This silverware languishes in cabinets, closets, or drawers—unused and unloved.

First-time brides, especially if they are having a large wedding, frequently register their silverware, dinnerware, and stemware patterns. Many brides are young and their aesthetic tastes and decorating skills are far from mature. Previously, a wide range of retailers and silverware counselors were available to assist brides in pattern choices. Today, the decision is usually made by the bride, with minimal assistance. Ideally, the bride will choose well, and the pattern she selects will bring continuing pleasure. Realistically, as individuals grow and their tastes mature, much of what was pleasing in the past is no longer appealing.

In today's highly mobile society, many individuals buy their silverware when they first set up housekeeping. Budgets are tight, and time is precious. A selection is made after a quick trip to one or two retail sources. Each person makes a commitment to purchase "good" silverware later, when income level and time allow for a more thorough look at what is available. Unfortunately, the two seldom occur simultaneously. People continue to use what they have available, whether they like it or not.

Take this simple two-question quiz: (1) Name your daily and good silverware patterns;

(2) When was the last time you used your "good" silverware? If you do not know the name of your patterns or several months have passed since you last used your "good" silverware, it is time to make some changes.

Explore the many different retail sources for sterling, silver-plated, and stainless silverware. You will be amazed at the affordability and wide variety of choices—the more you see, the more excited you will become.

Now comes the hard part: replacing your current silverware with a pattern that reflects your present tastes and decor. Individuals surround themselves with the things they love. Since you use your silverware almost every day, it makes perfectly good sense to own patterns that bring pleasure each time they are used.

STERLING VERSUS SILVER PLATED AND STAINLESS

Today's manufacturers accept the fact that most individuals own several silverware services, a sterling or silver-plated service for formal dining and one or more silver-plated or stainless services for everyday use. Several manufacturers offer patterns in all three compositions.

Between 1900 and the end of the 1950s, the situation was nowhere near as harmonious as today. Most individuals owned only one silverware service. Sterling and silver plate competed with each other. Manufacturers of sterling aggressively marketed their products as being far superior to silver-plated products.

Sterling manufacturers argued that their products combined beauty, durability, and craftsmanship. The concept of permanence, that is, a product with lasting quality that extended for generations, was heavily stressed. Silver was often referred to as "the ageless metal." While not specifically stated, owning sterling was seen as an indication of a person's proper social status, which was hinted at through touting sterling as a reflection of quality and a product that added authority and dignity to the table. It was a subtle hint that sterling was about class and social standing. Surprisingly, today's advertisements and sales brochures are practically devoid of any mention of the investment quality of silver. Occasionally, references are made to silver being one of the precious metals or a "pure" metal.

The following excerpt from a Towle Silversmiths' sales brochure demonstrates this marketing approach: "Sterling is unmistakable; it has a depth, a color, a patina that nothing can successfully imitate. It adjusts instantly to temperature changes. It does not give off substances which affect the taste of or stain foods. Sterling gives the impression of warmth and sensuous softness, which is more appropriate even than gold or platinum for the subtle elegance of fine tableware."

In the 1990s, a sterling flatware place setting costs three to five times more, depending on the pattern, than a comparable silver-plated or stainless flatware place setting. Given the length of time a silverware service will be used, many modern buyers do not see a big difference between spending $120 to $200 or $40 a place setting. During the early part of the twentieth century, the ratio was 8:1 or 10:1. The difference between $14 and $1.25 was viewed as being a far greater gap by buyers of the past than today's buyers.

SELECTING YOUR SILVERWARE

While the silverware industry's literature urges individuals to select their silverware first, then match their dinnerware and stemware, reality suggests that individuals almost always choose their dinnerware and stemware prior to selecting their silverware. Silverware's versatility is the primary reason. Many silverware patterns work well with several different design styles.

Members of today's Me and X generations trust themselves more than they do their elders. They view asking for advice as indicative of their failings, not their wisdom. Just the opposite is true when selecting a silverware pattern. Solicit advice from decorators, retailers, parents, relatives, and friends whose entertaining talents are admired. The selection of a silverware pattern should never be rushed, but should be slow and deliberate.

Silverware reflects the personality of the user. You are the most important person your silverware needs to please. You will know you have found the right pattern when you fall in love with it. The heart plays a critical role in the selection process for silverware, perhaps even more so than for dinnerware and stemware.

When selecting silverware, use five criteria—use, design, craftsmanship, availability, and cost. While all silverware is designed for daily use, a silver-plated or stainless pattern is far more likely to be selected for everyday use than a sterling pattern. Select a pattern that is durable and versatile, because it will be used with a wide range of dinnerware, from ceramic to plastic. A good rule is to keep the pattern simple.

Most individuals reserve their sterling for holiday use and formal entertaining. While manufacturers encourage everyday use, the reality is that this rarely happens. When selecting a sterling service, choose a pattern that complements your formal dinnerware and stemware. One way to achieve this goal is to select a silverware pattern that has an identical or similar design element that is found in your dinnerware pattern.

Many manufacturers, for example, Lenox Brands, offer a full range of tabletop wares. These companies design and manufacture silverware, dinnerware, and stemware patterns that fully coordinate. Consider this option first. If you do not find a combination that pleases you, expand your search.

Design consists of three categories—pattern, proportion, and balance. While some individuals want a pattern that reflects the very latest in modern design, most prefer a pattern with lasting quality, that is, one that is always tasteful.

• • •

SALLY JESSY RAPHAEL ON SILVERWARE

Talk-show host extraordinaire Sally Jessy Raphael fell in love with her silver when she was a bride in Puerto Rico twenty-five years ago. "In St. Thomas, I met a man called Claude Carón—he was Leslie's father—and he had a store there. And I told him I loved this silver, but I was a poor struggling broadcaster. And he said, 'Well, why don't I have it made for you and when you can afford it, you buy it from me piece by piece.' Now he put out a lot of money, and every trip I went over, I bought one spoon or one knife. Over twenty-five years. A spoon, fork, and knife at a time. He was just a divine, divine man. And then he passed away, but not till I had the whole set bought from him.

"The price, from the time he bought it, quadrupled. It was handmade, a two-year order. And my silver has my silver mark on it. We've got the mark of the company, the mark of the man who made it, and then my own silver mark. And it quadrupled in price, and I still got it at the price he paid. Today I cherish that."

Beauty is in the eye of the beholder. Yet there are certain lines that harmonize in such a way that they evoke almost universal agreement that the result is beautiful. Every silverware manufacturer strives to create such designs.

When someone indicates that a person or thing is a "10," everyone knows what is meant. This is how you should feel about the daily and good silverware patterns you select. Each time you use it, you should fall in love again with the design.

Think of the pattern design as the dressing on a silverware shape or body. The greatest pattern design cannot save a poorly proportioned shape. Examine the contour of the body shape. It should create as much pleasure as the pattern design.

Pick up forms and hold them in your hands. The pattern you select should have a nice fit, feel, and balance. It should be extremely comfortable. Test the cutting combination of the knife and fork. Do they act as a natural extension of your hands?

Handle serving as well as place-setting pieces. Balance is extremely important. Also evaluate the design and form line of the serving pieces. Think of your silverware service in its totality. If you like the pattern and form of the place-setting pieces but are not enamored with the form of the serving pieces, reject the pattern and continue your search.

Craftsmanship is about quality of workmanship, which is why brand name is a major factor in purchasing silverware. The market is flooded with cheap imitations. Avoid them. Make your silverware selection from a major manufacturer.

If the silverware pattern you select is in current production, buying a pattern produced by a major manufacturer is not only your assurance of a high-quality product, but also increases the chance that the pattern you select will remain in production for an extended period of time. All manufacturers guarantee their products. Buying an established brand-name product means someone will be available to solve any problems you may unexpectedly encounter.

Even if your silverware pattern is no longer in production, it still makes sense to select a pattern from a brand-name manufacturer. These manufacturers strongly marketed and sold their patterns, increasing the chances that enough examples survived so you can readily acquire the forms you seek. The variety of serving pieces also tends to be more numerous in patterns made by major manufacturers.

Even the major manufacturers marketed patterns that were not successful. Before making your final selection, carefully check a pattern's availability, especially if it is no longer being made and must be purchased in the secondary market.

Silverware of the 20th Century provides you with a working list of the most readily available and popular patterns. Public tastes shift over time. Patterns will be added and deleted in subsequent editions of this book. However, their number will be small. An overwhelming number of the patterns in this book have stood the test of time. They have a proven endurance record.

While manufacturers no longer emphasize the concept of open stock, that is, a commitment to keeping the pattern in production for decades, occasionally it will appear in a company's promotional literature and advertisements. Open stock provides a set of fixed prices for comparison shopping. If you are able to locate forms on sale or on the secondary market at less than full retail, take advantage of the situation. However, many consider the ability to buy a form in an open-stock pattern at full retail to be far more preferable than having to wait for it to become available on the secondary market.

Individuals will more readily change their dinnerware and stemware services than they will their silverware services. For this reason, buying the best you can afford, even pushing a little beyond your budget, makes sense when purchasing silverware.

Keep price in the forefront of your mind. Do not frustrate yourself by selecting a pattern only to find you cannot afford it. Most manufacturers practice group pricing flatware, that is, patterns are divided into four to six groups with the same price applying to a form from a pattern within the group. Retailers are glad to make this information available to assist you in the selection process.

Most individuals begin by purchasing a starter set, consisting of four, six, or eight place settings, a few basic serving pieces, and a storage chest. Realizing this, many manufacturers offer a starter set, often referred to as a bride's set, at a bargain price. A 1965 International forty-four-piece bride's set contained sixteen teaspoons, eight place forks, eight place knives, eight salad forks, a sugar spoon, butter knife, tablespoon, pierced tablespoon, and chest. A deluxe serving set, consisting of a gravy ladle, flat server, large cold meat fork, and large salad or serving spoon also was offered at a discount.

Systematically adding to your silverware service is a wonderful way to keep acquisition costs affordable. Considering anniversaries, birthdays, and holidays, it will take only a few years to reach a well-rounded service for eight or twelve.

Prior to the 1950s, many individuals had their initials engraved on their sterling or silver-plated service. This changed in the 1960s, 1970s, and 1980s, due in part to the growing popularity of stainless steel, the emphasis on casual dining, and the increasing frequency of divorce.

Many older patterns were designed to allow space for a large initial or three-letter monogram. In fact, an engraved initial or monogram actually enhanced the pattern. If you have inherited a pre-1940 set of silverware, chances are it is initialed or monogrammed. Do not hesitate, especially if your inherited pattern is sterling, to have the old initial or monogram removed.

With the return of more formal, traditionalist entertaining in the 1990s, individuals are once again having their silverware initialed or monogrammed. Many restoration services will remove old initials and monograms. Engraving services must still be found locally; however, a few major manufacturers do offer engraving services for current production patterns.

SILVERWARE'S PROPER PLACE

Silverware belongs where you are. Its use is just as appropriate for casual and everyday dining as it is for the most formal dinner party.

Use begins with the place setting. A four-piece place setting consists of a teaspoon, place knife, place fork, and salad fork. A place spoon, allowing for the serving of cereal, soup, or dessert, increases the service to five. The addition of a butter spreader increases the service to six, the traditional place-setting count for formal dining.

Creating the proper table setting utilizing your silverware involves following a few simple rules, which are based on convenience and common sense. Do not be afraid to bend the rules when the occasion warrants. Today's casual elegance is a far cry from the structured formality of the 1930s.

- All forks go to the left, the single exception the oyster or cocktail fork.
- Spoons and knives go to the right.
- Pieces are placed in the order of their use, from the outside in.
- Do not have more than three pieces of silver on either side of the dinner plate. The exception is the oyster fork, which is placed at the right of the plate, on the outside, beside the soup spoon.
- Knives are placed with the cutting edge toward the plate.
- Forks are placed tines up.

- Spoons are placed bowls up.
- Butter spreaders are placed horizontally across the bread and butter plate, to the upper-left-hand side of the dinner plate.
- Flatware should be spaced equidistant from each other and in a line approximately one inch in from the edge of the table.
- A single glass is placed to the right, just above the point of the knife. When more than one glass is used, they are set on an angle or in a triangular formation.
- Individual salts and peppers are placed at the top center of the dinner plate.
- A folded or sculptured napkin is laid on the place plate. If convenience requires that the first course be on the table when guests are seated, the napkin is placed to the left of silverware located to the left of the plate. Do not place silverware on top of the napkin.
- When serving coffee or tea, teaspoons are placed on the saucers with the cups.
- Dessert silver is served with the course.
- Silverware should be laid flat in a tasteful grouping when serving a buffet. Do not rack.

THERE IS NOTHING WRONG WITH CHANGE

Do not hesitate to change your silverware service. As your personal tastes change or you acquire new dinnerware and stemware, your silverware pattern may no longer be appropriate. When this occurs, buy new silverware.

What about the cost? Put the issue into perspective. How much do you spend every three to five years for a new car or every ten years for a new television set? These costs can easily exceed the cost of a new silverware service. Further, consider the percentage of the original purchase price you receive when you trade or sell your five-year-old car. The depreciation in the value of your silverware service, assuming you purchased it new, is likely to be less.

Your old silverware service has value—but how much? Begin your research by reading this book. Writing to a replacement service and requesting a quote provides a second opinion.

But not all value is monetary. Since silverware is designed to serve several generations, consider passing along your old silverware to your children or your friends' children as a starter set. If no one wants it, consider selling it.

To sum up, silverware should not reside in storage. Nothing is gained by keeping it in a chest or drawer. Its beauty, more than dinnerware and stemware, is enhanced through use. Silverware can add a touch of elegance to your life.

UNDERSTANDING SILVER PLATE

Silver plating is the application of a thin coat of pure silver onto a base metal. Today, that amount is measured in microns. In the first quarter of the twentieth century, the following standards applied.

Flatware

The federal government required a thickness of 0.00125 inch, the equivalent of 1 troy ounce per square foot, for all general surfaces. The tines of forks and backs of spoon bowls were to be reinforced to a thickness of 0.00180.

Federal Specification Plate	9 troy ounces per gross of teaspoons (0.00125 inch)
Half Plate	1 troy ounce per gross of teaspoons (0.00015 inch)
Standard Plate	2 troy ounces per gross of teaspoons
Double Plate	4 troy ounces per gross of teaspoons
Triple Plate	6 troy ounces per gross of teaspoons
Quadruple Plate	8 troy ounces per gross of teaspoons

Hollowware

The federal government required 0.00125, the same thickness as for flatware.

Federal Specification Plate	20 dwt. per square foot (0.00125 inch)
Extra Heavy Hotel Plate	15 dwt. per square foot
Heavy Hotel Plate	10 dwt. per square foot
Medium Plate	5 dwt. per square foot
Light Plate	2 dwt. per square foot (0.000125 inch)

1 pound = 12 ounces = 240 pennyweight (dwts.)

The following excerpt from Württembergische Metallwarenfabrik's (WMF's) *WMF Cutlery Production Information* data sheets provides a 1990s look at the modern silver-plating process.

WMF "Perfect" Hard Silver-Plated Cutlery

"WMF 'Perfect' hard silver-plated cutlery is characterized by its particularly high utility value, combined with the sparkle of silver. A cutlery entirely suitable for day-to-day use (silver does not tarnish if used daily), which retains its attractive appearance for many years.

"Thanks to the WMF 'Perfect' hard silver-plating process, the surface of the cutlery is extremely durable. In the WMF 'Perfect' hard silver-plating process, a specialty of the makers, the most heavily stressed parts of the principal cutlery pieces, such as bowl points and contact areas of handles, receive a layer of silver, which is increased by 100 percent. This constitutes an enormous advantage over conventional plating methods.

"In addition, the silver layer on all parts of the cutlery pieces is hardened by a special WMF process in the silver bath. This achieves double the hardness of normal plating. WMF 'Perfect' hard silver-plated cutlery is therefore less sensitive to scratching and wear and tear."

90 Gram Silverplating

"In Germany, 90 gram silverplating is the commonest type of coating. This means that 90 grams of pure silver are deposited in the galvanic process on 24dm^2 cutlery surface (1dm^2 = 10 × 10cm). In 90 gram silverplating, 24 tablespoons are more or less equivalent to the prescribed area of 24dm^2."

How Does Silverplating Work?

"In the silver bath (electrolyte), a current flows from the plus pole, in this case the pure silver anode (silver bar), to the minus pole, the cutlery piece. This electrical current (direct current) takes fine particles from the silver anode and deposits them on the cutlery piece. On the principal WMF cutlery pieces, the flow of silver is guided by a covering device, so that heavily stressed points receive a silver coating which is 100 percent thicker than elsewhere. A uniformly applied 90 gram silver coating has a thickness of 36 microns. The special WMF 'Perfect' silver-plating process results in a thickness of 72 microns to be found on the reinforced cutlery areas. Thus the plating on WMF 'Perfect' hard silver-plated cutlery will last much longer than that on uniformly plated cutlery of other manufacturers. 1 micron = 1/1000 mm. WMF 'Perfect' hard silver-plated cutlery is dishwasher-safe."

SILVERWARE PATTERNS AND THE DESIGN STYLES THEY COMPLEMENT

Selecting the right silverware pattern is critical to creating an ambiance you desire. Choices abound. Throughout this book, you will find pattern groupings designed to assist you in the selection process.

These pattern suggestions are only the beginning of the selection process. Review all the patterns in this book and add or subtract additional patterns to create your working list. Once you have assembled your list, it is easy to choose the pattern that works best for you.

You probably noted during your review that some patterns appear quite similar. Popular patterns were offered with slight variations by a number of manufacturers. You also observed that there is a wide variety of pattern interpretations within a single shape or pattern theme, which is why silverware is so exciting and offers so much. There is a pattern that is just right for everyone's taste.

Baroque/Renaissance, Federal, Modern, and Traditional were the four pattern categories selected for listing purposes. Each category is subdivided into sterling, silver plated, and stainless. The listings include only those patterns found in this book. In a few instances, the temptation to include current production patterns not found in this book was strong, especially for the Federal category.

Many of these group listings could easily be expanded to include a dozen or more patterns. Since the desire to limit is implicit in these suggestions, five patterns were selected as the ideal. There are fewer than five patterns in the Federal silver plate and stainless categories. The primary reason is that Traditional patterns, especially plain pieces with a fiddle back handle, also work well in a Federal setting.

There is no right or wrong choice. The choice that counts is the one that pleases you. Further, who said you had to limit your choice to one? There is nothing wrong with owning two or three sets of silverware.

CHAPTER THREE

Caring for Your Silverware

Keeping silver, silver-plated, and stainless flatware bright and shiny is the principal goal of flatware care. It requires far less effort than most people think.

The key is to use your flatware every day; then only minimal maintenance or polishing is needed. If unused and exposed to sulfur and other chemicals in the air, silver will tarnish (oxidize). Proper storage lessens the effect, but nothing works as well as daily use.

Patina is a finish or surface texture acquired by silver and silver-plated silverware with years of usage. It is achieved through a series of tiny microscopic lines that develop over time as silver comes into contact with other silver objects. This is why the soft, glowing finish of silver seems to increase with use. To ensure a uniform patina, alternate the use of silver and silver-plated pieces.

A 1984 Towle sales brochure notes, "Incidentally, all silver takes on tiny scratches which are more noticeable when the silver is new. But, you'll find these blend together with use and actually beautify the surface. This 'patina,' or soft, lustrous finish that is acquired after years of usage, is one of the most attractive characteristics of sterling flatware."

STORING SILVERWARE

A silver or storage chest, flannel rolls or bags, or drawer pads are recommended for storing flatware. They can be purchased from a variety of sources.

Gorham, Oneida, and Eureka Manufacturing Company, a division of Reed & Barton, are three silverware manufacturers that offer a full range of storage supplies. Hinged lid storage chests with one, two, or no drawers are available in cherry, oak, and walnut. A typical storage chest holds about 130 to 150 pieces. A drawer increases that number by approximately fifty pieces. Storage chests have an anti-tarnish liner. Designs vary, from a simple rectangular box to the more elaborate Chippendale-style chest. If the chest will be stored out of sight, a simple box will suffice. If it will be displayed openly, the design style and finish should harmonize with the other furniture in the room.

Flannel rolls and flap-style bags come in a variety of sizes, determined by the number of pieces to be held, traditionally six, eight, or twelve, and the form. For example, Eureka offers tarnish-resistant flannel rolls for seven spoon forms—coffee spoon, cream soup spoons, dessert spoons, iced teaspoons, soup spoons, tablespoons, and teaspoons or salad forks (the same size fits both).

Numerous-sized tarnish-resistant flannel bags are available for storing hollowware. Store each piece in a separate bag. While the bags provide some protection, they should not be viewed as providing sufficient protection for pieces to be stored inside or on top of each other. Store pieces in their upright position. Allow ample space between each piece. Do not jam pieces into a storage space so they touch each other.

Some individuals place small camphor squares in their silver storage chests and drawers to prevent tarnish. If you use them, make sure they do not come into direct contact with the silver. Using an anti-tarnish protecting strip, such as those made by W. J. Hagerty & Sons, South Bend, Indiana, makes more sense. Protection strips are effective for up to one year.

Standard anti-tarnish flannel is available for sale by the yard. Use it to line any proposed storage area in a piece of furniture or cabinet. Zippered and non-zippered drawer liners are another option. Gorham also custom makes individually designed drawer pads. Contact your local Gorham retailer for details.

University Products, Holyoke, Massachusetts, offers a product called Corrosion Intercept, a polyethylene material featuring bonded copper particles that react, then neutralize, corrosive gases. The 1mm thick material can protect for up to ten years and turns black to indicate that it is time to change the bag. The company claims it provides effective tarnish protection for silver and other metals.

While rubber and plastic flatware kitchen drawer storage units can be used for stainless steel flatware, avoid their use for silver and silver plate. When selecting a kitchen drawer storage unit, purchase one with an individual storage section for each piece. When salad forks are stored in the same section as dinner forks, the possibility of damage increases. The same is true for butter and dinner knives or soup, tea, and serving spoons that are thrown together into a single storage bin.

Never store silverware in a plastic bag. First, the chemical composition of the plastic may be harmful. Second, moisture trapped inside the bag has the potential to cause damage. Third, plastic that sticks to silver is difficult to remove and almost always leaves a nasty mark.

Never use rubber around silver, and never store near heat. Securing silverware pieces with a rubber band is a bad idea. Rubber and heating sources—coal, gas, and oil—oxidize silver.

Many latex paints contain rubber and sulfur compounds. Check with the retailer or manufacturer regarding a paint's ingredients before applying it to any area where silver is stored. One testing method is to put a paint sample and a piece of silver into a plastic bag and observe the result over several weeks.

Finally, never wrap silver in felt, chamois leather, or newspaper. Felt and chamois leather are sources of hydrogen sulfide, a chemical compound that can cause tarnish. Printer's ink residue left on silver plate will eventually eat it away.

WASHING SILVERWARE

Flatware can be washed either by hand or in a dishwasher. Hand washing is recommended for silver and silver-plated flatware. It is mandatory for silver and silver-plated hollowware. Automatic dishwashers have a tendency to cause pitting and discoloration in hollowware. Further, never immerse a weighted piece (filled base) of hollowware in water. These pieces should be cleaned by hand polishing.

Some older flatware knives have their handles filled with pitch or tar. Extremely hot water and the drying temperature of the dishwasher can loosen blades or cause the handles to split, due to expansion. Modern knives are dishwasher-safe. However, double check with the manufacturer to make certain. Never wash any flatware with bone, ivory, mother-of-pearl, or wood handles in the dishwasher.

Before washing a piece of flatware, rinse it thoroughly immediately after use to remove any food residue, especially coffee, mayonnaise, mustard, piquant sauces, tea, vinegar, and so on. Avoid prolonged soaking, especially for stainless, as the corrosive effects of water may cause pitting or staining. W. J. Hagerty & Sons makes a product called Hagerty Fork Clean, a dip-and-rinse solution designed to clean silver and silver plate fork tines without scrubbing. It is not recommended for use on stainless steel.

Watch out for the garbage disposal. Flatware and garbage disposals do not mix. If a piece of silver or stainless flatware is damaged in a fight with a garbage disposal, consider having it restored before relegating it to the garbage can.

Hand Washing

Wash flatware in hot, sudsy water, separately. Do not place it in the sink with the dinnerware, crystal, and/or pots and pans. Never use an abrasive cleaner or scouring pad.

Do not overload the sink or dishpan. Crowding the pieces can create deep scratches, which are not the same as the microscopic scratches associated with patina.

Rinse flatware with clean, hot water immediately after washing. A double sink, one side with wash water, the other side with rinse water, is ideal. If a second sink is not available, use a rubber or plastic tub.

Dry flatware immediately with a soft cloth to remove any excess moisture and to avoid spotting. Do not air dry, as spots will result. Drying also ensures the removal of any chemicals in tap water. Chloride and other chemicals added to some urban water systems are mildly corrosive.

Using a Dishwasher

Most silver, silver-plated, and stainless flatware is dishwasher-safe. While hand washing remains the preferred approach, today most individuals wash their flatware in the dishwasher. Follow these simple tips when using a dishwasher:

- Use a reputable brand of dish-washing detergent, ideally one that is recommended by the manufacturer of the machine. Avoid detergents with phosphorus and sulfur compounds, if possible.
- Check your water for hardness. If it is too hard, add a water softener to your water supply. However, if your softener requires salt, you may wish to reconsider, as salt is extremely corrosive.
- Place flatware in the plastic basket that comes with the machine so the water jets are able to reach all of the surfaces.
- Arrange flatware in the plastic basket, according to size. Knife blades, fork tines, and spoon bowls should always point upward.
- Do not wash sterling and silver-plated flatware with stainless flatware.
- Do not wash any iron or steel articles prone to rusting with stainless steel flatware.
- Check coated wire racks to ensure that the protective coating is intact. If a rack is damaged, replace it.
- Remove the basket of flatware immediately after the dishwasher has completed its cycle; the goal is to prevent the flatware from being exposed to trapped moisture.

Small, dark spots may appear on knife blades—these are extraneous rust deposits. They can be caused by the transfer of rust from articles that are not made from stainless steel, damaged plastic coating on dishwasher racks that allows portions of the basket to oxidize, rust deposits from old or damaged water pipes, chips in enameled cookware that allow the steel to oxidize and rust, and water with a high iron content. You can remove these dark spots with vinegar, lemon juice, or cleaning agents such as WMF Purargan®.

Occasionally, pale spots appear on cutlery after rinsing, which are caused by the incomplete removal of the cleaning and/or rinsing agent used in the dishwasher or by failure to empty the dishwasher promptly, thus allowing for steam and moisture retention. If the problem persists, have your dishwasher serviced. Discipline yourself to not leave flatware in the dishwasher once the cycle is completed. Some pale spots, if you find them in time, can be removed by using a soft, dry cloth.

POLISHING SILVER AND STAINLESS

While the procedures for washing silver, silver-plated, and stainless steel flatware are basically the same, they diverge when it comes to polishing. The simple rule is: Do not use silver care products on stainless and do not use stainless care products on silver. There are *no* exceptions.

Silver

Silver is chemically inactive. Tarnishing results from environmental pollutants and prolonged contact with some foods. If pollution is a problem, an air filtering and air conditioning system will lessen its impact.

Polishing is a process that each time removes dirt and tarnish as well as a microscopic amount of the metal. This is the primary reason most manufacturers recommend polishing silver no more than once or twice a year and relying on daily use, rotation, and washing to best preserve the shine in the interim. Too-frequent polishing of silver-plated flatware will expose the base metal. Excessive buffing of silver and silver-plated flatware will lessen the depth of ornate designs and remove delicate engraving.

Many manufacturers, for example, Gorham, have developed a full line of silver care products that they recommend for use with their silverware. Ask your flatware retailer for a list.

Use a non-abrasive, anti-tarnish polish. W. J. Hagerty & Sons and Goddard's™ are two commercial companies whose products come highly recommended. Hagerty's Silver Care Package includes 8-oz. Hagerty's Silversmith's Polish for hollowware, 7-oz. Hagerty Silver Foam for flatware, a horsehair brush, and a polishing cloth. Firms that specialize in providing conservation supplies to museums also offer precious metal care products. University Products (P.O. Box 101, Holyoke, MA 01041) and Talas (213 W. 35th Street, New York, NY 10001) are two examples.

Many commercial polishes contain abrasives like silica. Do not use them. Also avoid any all-purpose metal cleaner, as the formula is too harsh. Use a polish made specifically for polishing silver. Check the contents of any polish you plan to use. Some silver polishes contain

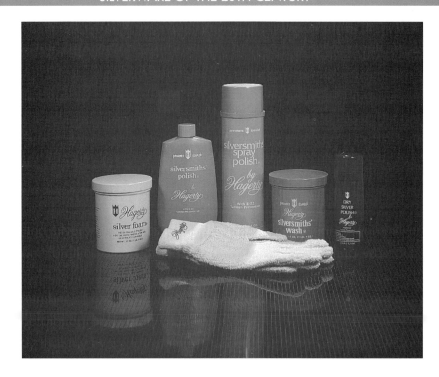

ethanol and sulfur compounds, which have been linked to cancer. Do not inhale the fumes, wear rubber gloves when using them, and better yet, avoid any polish that contains these compounds—there are many alternatives.

Do not apply more polish than you need—better too little than too much. Excessive polish makes a piece slippery and difficult to handle. W. J. Hagerty & Sons manufactures a sponge applicator. Many individuals prefer working with a pair of gloves or a mitt to keep hands dry and free of polish. After several uses they can be laundered to remove excess polish. A quick spray with a dry silver polish restores their effectiveness.

Since polish is acidic, it is important to remove all polish residue when polishing is completed. Wash polished pieces in soap and water; rinse thoroughly. If polish residue remains in hard-to-reach places, a common problem with ornate patterns, brush lightly with a jeweler's silver brush, horsehair brush, or a worn, soft, natural-bristle toothbrush.

When polishing or drying silver, use a very soft cloth. A linen dish towel is too coarse and will scratch a silver surface. Surprisingly enough, cloth diapers and T-shirts are two possibilities.

Do not use dips and other tarnish-removal solutions. Especially avoid the products touted in infomercials and on television home shopping channels. Most of these will remove the oxidation that truly enhances a flatware pattern's detail. Never, never, use a dip on stainless steel!

Use a towel or gloves to handle silver and silver-plated ware when putting them into storage. How many times have you removed a piece of silverware from storage and found one or more fingerprints? The oil and dirt in your fingertips and hands leaves an unwanted deposit. Given enough time, this oil and dirt will become visible. Take a minute to do a final wipe before storing pieces for a lengthy period of time.

Stainless Steel

W. J. Hagerty & Sons makes two stainless steel products. The first is a gentle and safe polish for stainless steel and chrome. It imparts a brilliant mirror-bright shine and is entirely non-abrasive. The second is Hagerty 18/8 Stainless Steel Wash, a product designed to remove water deposits and soap residues. It restores luster and brightens any gold accents.

DUSTING SILVER

Dust is an abrasive; it can scratch. When allowed to accumulate on a surface, it becomes greasy. This surface dust can act like a lubricant, causing a piece to slip from your grasp.

Gently dust any displayed silver or silver-plated flatware once a month. W. J. Hagerty & Sons offers a silver duster, a two-piece cloth that removes light tarnish from silver between polishings. Conservation Materials (100 Standing Rock Circle, Reno, NV 89511) produces "Dust Bunny," a 17" × 17" white cloth that attracts and holds dust particles, but it is not chemically treated. The synthetic fiber acquires a high-static charge during wiping that attracts the dust particles. The cloth can be washed and reused. The Toy Tender, available from Jim Tolliver (900 Country Road, A099, Edgewood, MN 87015), consists of a set of three 100 percent Australian lamb wool dusters. They work great for toys as well as silverware. Fluffing out the wool loads it with static electricity. When soiled, one need only swirl it in sudsy water, rinse thoroughly, and dry.

RESTORATION SERVICES

"It is too good to throw out" is a concept that certainly applies to flatware. When a piece of flatware has dulled with age, is damaged, shows signs of heavy use, or has a blade that needs replacing, owners may want to have it polished, restored, or repaired. These services are offered by some manufacturers (only for their own products), jewelry shops, replacement services, and private individuals.

Restoration and cleaning services available from Replacements, Ltd., (P.O. Box 6029, Greensboro, NC 27420) is one example. Only select restoration services are offered, for example, monogram removal on sterling silver and blade replacement for sterling and stainless flatware. Cleaning and machine buffing is available for sterling, silver plate, stainless, gold electroplate, and pewter.

If your silver-plated ware needs replating, contact a jewelry store in your area that offers this service. Your local jeweler will subcontract the work to a national firm that deals only with retail stores, not individual customers. Flatware is sent back to its original manufacturer if the company is still in business. Otherwise, it and all hollowware is sent to a national firm.

Request an estimate before authorizing any replating work. If the estimate seems high, seek a second opinion. Many replating firms also offer repair services such as removing dents, resoldering, and repitching a weighted base. If additional work is needed beyond replating, make sure there is a clear understanding of what will be done and what it will it cost before proceeding.

Plating depth is measured in microns. Request a plating in the 20 to 30 micron range for pieces that will experience heavy use, such as a platter. A coating between 10 and 15 microns is all that is required for larger hollowware pieces, such as coffeepots. Assuming daily use, replating should last fifteen to twenty years, longer if gentle cleaning solutions are used.

PACKING AND SHIPPING FLATWARE AND HOLLOWWARE

When preparing flatware and hollowware for shipping, take the time to do it right. Wrap flatware pieces individually, first in a piece of white tissue paper and then in a layer of newspaper or bubble wrap. Do not use newspaper as the initial wrap; the ink used to print newspapers can rub off onto the flatware.

If you insist on shipping your flatware in its storage chest, crumple up tissue or paper towels and jam them into all open areas. Continue until any movement by the pieces is prevented. Shake the closed storage chest. If you feel the slightest movement or hear any noise, open the chest and begin the process again.

When packing hollowware, stuff crumpled tissue or paper towels inside the piece. Wrap paper around finials, necks, standards, collars, and so on, until you have created a cylinder equal in diameter to the widest measurement of the piece. Do one final wrap with tissue before encasing it in newspaper or bubble wrap. If a hollowware piece has multiple parts, for example, a lidded sugar, wrap each piece separately.

When shipping flatware and hollowware, use the double-box method. Place one box inside of another, packing at least two inches of crushed paper between all six sides of the outer carton. Keep shipping boxes uniform and manageable. There is a correlation between box size and potential damage—the larger the container, the more possibility of damage.

Place heavier pieces in the bottom of the carton. Separate pieces with cardboard, bubble wrap, or foam. Even when pieces are individually wrapped, it is critical to prevent them from bumping into each other during shipment. If possible, avoid using plastic peanuts; they do not always prevent pieces from shifting and knocking into each other. Pad the top and sides as fully as possible to avoid air pockets. Once again, apply the shake test; there should be no movement when you shake the box.

Before sealing a carton, insert a paper with your full name, address, and telephone number. Seal the box with 2″ × 3″ sealing tape; do not use masking tape. Mark the outside of the box "Fragile." Make sure your name and return address and the recipient's are clearly visible.

When shipping flatware or hollowware, check the levels of insurance coverage provided by the carrier you selected. It pays to shop around. Insurance practices and rates vary. Insist on a return receipt. This is your record that your shipment arrived, and it provides a contact name if trouble should arise.

INSURING YOUR SILVERWARE

Silver flatware is a prime target for thieves. It is difficult to trace because it is mass-produced. It is impossible to identify a specific piece with a specific owner. All pieces in a pattern look alike. Unfortunately, most stolen silver is sold for its melt or scrap value. Buyers of scrap metal rarely ask about the origin of the material they are buying.

Most household insurance policies provide only a limited amount of precious metals coverage, usually no more than $2,500. Additional insurance must be purchased through a fine arts rider. Contact your insurance agent for quotes.

Fine arts insurance covers two basic areas: loss (generally meaning theft or fire) and breakage. Some companies provide separate quotes for each; others offer only a single quote. Unless you are extremely careless, you do not need breakage coverage for your silverware. Make it clear to your insurance agent that you want extended coverage only for loss, and ask what the quote specifically encompasses.

Many different types of insurance coverage are available. Insist on full replacement coverage, that is, what you would have to pay today to replace your silverware if purchased from a retailer or replacement service.

Assume you will have a loss. Make a complete list of all of your silverware. Describe each piece. Record the form, pattern name, name of the manufacturer, and any other pertinent information. Keep purchase records with your list. Make a second copy and store it outside your home, preferably at your office or with your heir or executor. Do not use a safety deposit box.

Revisit the value issue every three to five years. If you are still insuring your silverware based on its value during the Hunts' manipulation of the silver market in the early 1980s, it is overvalued and consequently you are paying far too much insurance. An insurance company pays based on value at the time of loss, not necessarily the amount for which it is insured. The metal value of silver fluctuates, as does the price of silverware on the secondary market. Use *Silverware of the 20th Century* as your first step in understanding the value of your silverware in today's market.

If your silverware is antique and/or you own other antiques in addition to your silverware, you may wish to consider the coverage offered by the National Association of Collectors' insurance program. This program requires no written inventory for objects valued under $2,500, it is based on replacement costs, and it extends coverage automatically as you add to your service. For information about the insurance program and its rates, write to the NAC, P.O. Box 2782, Huntersville, NC 28070, or call 1-800-287-7127.

CHECK THE INTERNET

If you are computer literate and connected to the Internet, check out www.hagerty-polish.com. In fact, perform a directory search using the name of the manufacturer of your silverware. Chances are you will find that the company is on the Internet.

In summary, your silverware was designed and manufactured to be used, not to reside in a drawer or storage chest. Treated with the respect it deserves, it will last for generations.

Silver, silver-plated, and stainless flatware, especially when it is a family heirloom, adds an aura of elegance to even the simplest meal. It is appropriate and welcome for every meal.

CHAPTER FOUR

Expanding or Replacing Pieces from Your Silverware Service

Are you looking to expand the number of place settings in your silverware service? After using your silverware, have you decided to expand your service to include hollowware pieces? Has a piece been accidentally damaged beyond repair? What should you do?

The answer is simple. Take advantage of the wide range of opportunities—from antiques and collectibles periodicals to replacement services—that are available for expanding or replacing your silverware.

There is a direct correlation between the amount you will pay and the time you are willing to spend on the hunt. The hunt has costs, however. If you spend two or three hours of your time and several dollars in postage and telephone calls and save only five dollars, you need to rethink your approach. Even though the cost may be slightly higher, finding a source that can immediately supply what you are searching for often is the most economical approach.

DOCUMENTING YOUR PATTERN

You know the manufacturer, the name of your pattern, and what it looks like. Many of the people you contact will also recognize the manufacturer and pattern name, but they may have trouble visualizing it. You need to help them.

Making a photocopy of several pieces of flatware is the simplest way to document your pattern. Use a dinner knife, dinner fork, and teaspoon. Concentrate on two key pieces of information: the pattern on the handles and the shape of the knife blade.

You do not have to photocopy each piece separately. Do all three on a single sheet. Close the lid so you have a white background behind the pieces. Do not be afraid to apply slight pressure to make a tight seal. Light leakage creates unwanted shadowing over some of the surface. If this is a problem, drape a piece of paper over the side to prevent the light from entering.

Silver reflects light. Expect some surface shading, even if the copier lid is tightly sealed. If you are not happy with the initial copy, experiment by adjusting the dark-to-light setting until you obtain a good, sharp image.

If your handle pattern is ornate and the photocopy machine you are using has the ability, consider enlarging the image. If you do this, note on the photocopy the enlargement percentage that was used. Also, photocopy the knife at 100 percent to provide an exact tracing to match the knife blade.

If a photocopy machine is not available, use thin paper and do a pencil tracing of your pattern. Lay the knife flat and draw the outline of the handle and blade. A few patterns, for example, Reed & Barton's Old English Antique, are available in more than one handle style. Knife blade styles have changed over time. The tracing allows the seller to make sure the match is exact.

After having gone to all of this trouble, make several photocopies of the final results. This prevents having to repeat the process later. Keep two or more copies on file.

If you retained a copy of the manufacturer's catalog or sales brochure that came with your silverware, photocopy it. A magazine advertisement featuring the pattern also provides valuable reference information.

Because of its reflective qualities, silver, especially hollowware, is difficult to photograph. Even professional photographers have trouble capturing an unblemished silver surface color. The best advice is to not attempt it.

If you insist on photographing silver hollowware, you need a good 35mm camera, a photographic tent, and several good light sources. A photographic tent is a half-dome cloth form supported by an exterior wire frame. The piece to be photographed is placed inside the tent. The slit opening into the dome can be closed around the camera lens. Light sources are placed around the tent. The cloth diffuses the light, thus preventing hot spots on the image. Photographic tents are expensive; the cheapest one costs over $100.

A second approach is to create a shelf using a large piece of opaque white plastic. The piece of silverware is placed on top of the shelf near the front edge. A light source is placed beneath, thus the shot is bottom lit. The image is shot in a dark environment. With the light streaming up from below, the shadow and reflection are minimized.

Use a telephoto lens and position yourself as far away from the object as is practical. Test several different photographic angles to reduce reflection. Bracket your exposure a full stop in either direction.

Photograph hollowware from an angle that is slightly above the piece. In other words, shoot down on it a little. This provides a sense of depth for the item in the finished photograph. If you have the capability, photograph details such as the pattern or handle. Place a ruler beside the piece to provide size information.

It is critical that the picture be in focus. Photograph details with a close-up or telephoto lens. Make sure you have enough depth of field when photographing hollowware pieces.

Photograph flatware using a copy stand. Light from both sides, preferably at a 45° angle. Light balance across the entire image surface is critical. This can be checked with a spot light meter.

Include with the photograph a card with your name, address, and telephone number. This enables individuals searching on your behalf to contact you upon finding a match.

Given the difficulties involved in photographing silverware, consider calling several local photographers to determine the cost to have your pieces done professionally. If the cost is within your budget, this is a quick and painless solution.

Of course, the documenting solution that makes the most sense, provided your pattern is included in this book, is to make an enlarged photocopy of that illustration.

KNOW EXACTLY WHAT YOU ARE SEEKING

Lack of adequate information is one of the primary reasons individuals do not respond to want requests. You must be specific—the more information you provide, the better.

If your goal is to expand your silverware service or purchase hollowware accessories, send the person a list of the pieces you already own, as well as a list of those you are seeking. The seller may have pieces that are not on your list, and you will certainly want to know about these.

Clearly indicate the condition level at which you wish to buy. If you want to purchase the piece in excellent condition, that is, virtually free of any defects, state this specifically. Indicate whether you are willing to accept a piece that has had restoration work. The more emphasis you place on "like new" condition, the more difficult it will be to locate the pieces you desire.

The standard approach is to ask for quotes. Some individuals prefer to indicate on their want list what they are willing to pay, usually noting that this is a maximum price and that they hope to receive lower quotes. The reality is that virtually every quote will be at the willing-to-pay price.

Indicate your full name, address, and day and evening telephone numbers on any request you distribute. Today, sellers are far more likely to telephone than to write.

BUYING OPTIONS

You have more buying options than you realize. Utilizing a replacement service is the most obvious choice. However, before exploring that sales venue, eight additional possibilities are discussed next. Using your imagination, you probably can add to this list.

Auctions. Auctioneers almost always sell silverware in lots. Putting a full service on the block as a unit is quite common. If you are willing to pay a little above melt value, you will be an active competitor on all sterling pieces. Silver plate and stainless flatware are real bargains, selling for pennies on the dollar in most cases.

While auctioneers selling via catalog have learned from experience that polishing silverware enhances its salability, most general auctioneers do not bother to do this. Often sterling and silver-plated hollowware is included in the same lot, but the auctioneer simply did not take the time to separate the pieces. If you love the hunt and take the time to carefully inspect objects before they are auctioned, you will bag more than your fair share of silverware trophies.

Garage sale circuit. This is not as crazy as it sounds, especially if you are seeking a silver-plated or stainless pattern and frequently attend garage sales. This is the cheapest buying source you will find.

In most cases, the seller wants to sell the pieces as a lot, rather than individually. Buy all of the pieces, as spares provide an inexpensive backup in case you break a piece. If you try to buy only a few pieces, do not be surprised if the seller asks a price almost equal to the entire lot. Sellers know that what remains will be worth considerably less because the service has been split.

Do not be afraid to hand out your list of wants to individuals who appear to be garage sale regulars. You cannot be everywhere at once. Many eyes searching on your behalf are better than two.

Friends and neighbors. If you have a friend or neighbor who has a silverware service that matches your pattern, do not hesitate to say, "If you ever tire of that service and want to get rid of it, call me." Never underestimate the power of positive suggestion.

When using your silverware for a party or family gathering, mention your desire to expand your service or find replacement pieces. You will be amazed at what people remember. Again, your chances for success increase proportionally to the number of people who are looking on your behalf.

Post your want list on church, grocery store, or service club bulletin boards. Make sure you attach a photocopy of the handle pattern to this list to help catch an individual's attention.

Antiques malls. Antiques malls are becoming increasingly aware of the importance of securing want lists and passing them on to their dealers. Many have bulletin boards and are more than willing to post buyers' want lists.

A lot of antiques malls allow their dealers to place business cards in their booths. As you walk through the malls, collect the cards from those dealers who feature silverware for sale and send each a copy of your want list. If the booth is devoted to replacement dinnerware, stemware, and/or silverware, consider calling the dealer and talking with him or her directly.

Antiques shows. Many antiques shows include dealers who specialize in the replacement of silverware and stemware. They often will have several dozen or more of the most popular patterns. Even if they do not have your pattern, take the time to talk with them about your specific needs. These dealers are heavily networked. It may take them only a few telephone calls to locate the pieces you are seeking.

Talk with any generalist dealer who has a few pieces of silverware for sale. Antiques show dealers only bring a small portion of their merchandise to the show. They may have exactly what you are seeking at home. Practice the old adage, "It never hurts to ask."

Antiques and collectibles trade periodicals. Most antiques and collectibles trade periodicals have a classified advertisement section. Many also offer business card classifieds, an advertisement measuring $3^1/2'' \times 2''$, the standard business card size. Follow a traditional business card approach when designing your advertisement.

Place a "want" or "seeker" advertisement. Keep it short and simple, for example, "WANTED. Quotes on serving pieces for Reed & Barton's Francis I pattern. Name, telephone number with area code." You should have no difficulty limiting your request to twenty-five words or less.

There are over fifty antiques and collectibles trade periodicals. In addition to using a strong regional paper, consider placing your advertisement in one or more of the following national publications:

AntiqueWeek, P.O. Box 90, Knightstown, IN 46148
Warman's Today's Collector, 700 East State Street, Iola, WI 54990
Antique Trader Weekly, P.O. Box 1050, Dubuque, IA 52004
Maine Antique Digest, P.O. Box 1429, Waldoboro, ME 04572
Collectors News, 506 Second Street, Grundy Center, IA 50638

Manufacturer. Some patterns remain in production for decades. Before assuming that the pattern you inherited or purchased has been discontinued, check with the manufacturer. While some forms may no longer be available, others may.

Some manufacturers maintain a small inventory of out-of-production pieces. Write to request a list of available pieces. Others offer a "made-to-order" program, primarily for sterling flatware. Orders are collected for a specific period of time, usually one year. At a fixed point, the old dies are retrieved from a warehouse and enough pieces are manufactured to fill orders on hand. While the per piece price may appear high, consider the costs involved in going back into limited production. Utilize this approach only after exhausting all other avenues.

Mail-order catalogs. If your pattern is still in production but the manufacturer does not sell direct and you cannot find a source within reasonable driving distance, consider contacting a mail-order catalog firm specializing in the sale of silverware, other tabletop wares, and giftware. Barrons (P.O. Box 994, Novi, MI 48376), Michael C. Fina (508 Fifth Avenue, New York, NY 10036), and Ross-Simons (9 Ross-Simons Drive, Cranston, RI 02920) are three examples.

Mail-order catalogs generally sell at full retail. In addition, you pay a shipping and handling charge. Surprisingly, many replacement services sell current production material at a slight discount. Comparison shop before ordering.

REPLACEMENT SERVICE

Ordering from a replacement service is the quickest and easiest way to expand or replace silverware. Today's replacement services are very customer-oriented.

Most replacement services have a staff of skilled researchers who are more than willing to assist you in identifying any silverware pattern. Send them a set of your photocopies. Within a few weeks, you should receive a letter providing you with the name of the pattern and a list of pieces available. If the service's research efforts prove negative, you will be informed of this as well.

Most replacement services automatically add your name to their records. If they do not have the pieces you need, they will contact you when they find them. A few services offer a "call collect" program. You provide a number that can be called collect within a few hours of their entering a piece in their sales inventory.

Replacement services acquire material in a variety of conditions. When reviewing a quote, pay close attention to the condition of the piece being offered. If you are uncertain about a piece's condition, call for clarification.

You may find the same piece in identical condition listed at two separate prices. When you find a bargain price, take advantage of it.

Many replacement services also offer repair services. If a piece of your silverware needs restoration, request a quote. Repairs are done with the assumption that the piece will be put back into use. The restoration cost may be less than buying a replacement. Also, if the piece is scarce, you have a piece to use until an unbroken piece is available.

Finally, only order from a replacement service that offers a money-back guarantee, no questions asked. This is the most important aspect of doing business by mail. If you have a problem, call immediately. As indicated previously, complete customer satisfaction is the goal.

Replacements, Ltd. (P.O. Box 26029, Greensboro, NC 27420 / 1-800-737-5223) worked closely with the House of Collectibles and me in the preparation of this book. I have visited its warehouse and used its curating library and strongly recommend contacting them whenever you are exploring replacement-service options.

FINDING A REPLACEMENT SERVICE

You will find advertisements for replacement services in a wide range of periodicals—from magazines such as *Family Circle*, to Sunday newspaper supplements such as *Parade*, to antiques and collectibles trade newspapers such as *AntiqueWeek* (P.O. Box 90, Knightstown, IN 46148). Check several publications. Begin your search with a list of a half dozen or more possibilities.

Read replacement service advertisements carefully. Some specialize only in patterns from one or two companies. Others offer an extremely wide range of replacement services that also can include silverware, dinnerware, stemware, tabletop accessories, and contemporary collectibles.

David J. Maloney Jr.'s *Maloney's Antiques & Collectibles Resource Directory, 3rd Edition* (Dubuque, Iowa: Antique Trader Books: 1995) contains the most comprehensive list of replacement (matching) services. Look under his Dinnerware, Glass, and Flatware general headings. Maloney provides a full mailing address, telephone number, and a brief description of each firm's specialties. He also provides a list of firms that repair dinnerware.

Do not hesitate to ask family or friends who have used a replacement service about their experiences. Personal recommendations often are the best.

CHAPTER FIVE

Keys to Using This Book

This book has three specific goals: (1) to assist you in the selection and care of the silverware patterns you decide are right for you; (2) to provide a checklist of forms that were manufactured as part of or in conjunction with those silverware patterns; and (3) to enhance your appreciation of your silverware selections by providing historical information about their manufacturers and occasionally about the patterns themselves.

Do not ignore the previous chapters as they contain a wealth of information. Chapter 3 is a must-read. Even the most experienced silverware user will learn something new.

ORGANIZATION

This book is organized in two sections. The first section, the first six chapters, provide information about the historical evolution of silverware and the processes used to make it, identifying patterns that please you, use and care tips, how to add to your patterns or replace pieces, maximizing use of this book, and silverware terminology.

The heart of the book is an alphabetical listing—first by manufacturer, then by composition, and finally by pattern—of 250 of the most-requested patterns from replacement services. A brief history introduces each manufacturer.

Pattern names are those used by the manufacturer. To maintain consistency, the fork has been selected as the form of choice for illustration. Illustrations contain the details necessary for pattern identification.

An alphabetical approach also is used within the listings. Listings are by form; shape is a qualifying adjective of a form.

A pattern name index is provided. The same pattern name was sometimes used by different manufacturers. In every case, the pattern designs differ significantly. If you own a pattern, know its name, and want to locate it quickly, use the pattern name index.

UNDERSTANDING THE CHECKLIST FORMAT

Pattern listings are based on a checklist approach. The goal is to provide a list of the basic forms for each pattern and extended lists for some patterns. Every pattern includes the basic place setting pieces, plus several serving pieces. With most patterns containing fifty or more forms, an encyclopedic list of every available form in every pattern would more than double the size of this book.

If you find a serving form and want to determine its value, but the form is not included in the listings in this book, look through the book for a similar pattern in terms of composition, ornateness of design, maker, and price that includes a listing for the form. It is safe to assume that the value will not differ by more than a few dollars.

Not all manufacturers use the same terminology for the same form. This book does. The same form terms are used consistently from pattern to pattern. The following five abbreviations are used:

FH	Flat Handle	SP	Silver Plated
HH	Hollow Handle	SS	Sterling
		ST	Stainless

Understanding the method used for listing forms is essential in locating the correct price. Some forms were manufactured with variations. A sterling pie server may be made entirely of sterling or it may have a sterling handle and stainless blade. When the latter occurs, it is noted as "Server, pie, ST blade." Pay particular attention to the composition of salad sets. Salad serving spoons and forks may be found with bowls and tines made from sterling, silver plate, stainless, plastic, or wood.

Forms may be found individually priced, such as "Carving Fork" or "Carving Knife," or as a unit, such as "Carving Set, two pieces." Discrepancies sometimes exist between the price of the set and the sum of its pieces. As a rule, it is less expensive to buy as a set than to buy individual pieces.

The silverware industry has generous manufacturing tolerances. A 9" serving spoon can range from $8\frac{7}{8}$" to $9\frac{1}{8}$". Because many individuals wish to purchase exact replacement matches for their silverware, known size variations are listed separately. In most instances, there is no difference in price, nor should there be. The issue is not value, but knowing the degree of variation within the form.

The size of each piece has been included when available. Sizes included in this book are measured in either diameter/length or height. The following chart will help determine which dimension applies:

Size in Diameter/Length		Size in Height	
Ashtray	Plate	Candelabra	Pitcher
Cleaver	Scoop	Candle Holder	Shaker
Dish	Server	Candlestick	Sifter
Food Pusher	Sharpener	Coffeepot	Sugar
Fork	Slicer	Compote	Tumbler
Knife	Spoon	Creamer	
Ladle	Spreader		
Opener	Tea Strainer		
Pick	Tongs		
Pizza Cutter	Tray		
Plane			

SEEKING A PRECISE PATTERN MATCH

Close does not count when seeking replacement or additional pieces for a silverware pattern. The match must be exact.

There are three areas to check to be sure a replacement piece matches your silverware pattern. These are the pattern; the shape of the fork's tines, the knife's blade, and the spoon's bowl; and the way the handle is formed, that is, flat, hollow, pistol grip, turned up, turned down, and so on.

When a manufacturer creates a silverware pattern that has proven to be extremely popular, other manufacturers then produce their own version of the original pattern. Though the two pieces may appear identical at first glance, a close inspection will reveal subtle variations. There has to be, as designs are patented, and an exact copy represents a patent infringement. Design patents expire. In the past, rival manufacturers made exact copies of a competitor's patent once the patent no longer protected the design. Today, this is rarely done.

Mergers, shifts in production location, and subtle shifts in the weight of pieces occur constantly. Durgin introduced the Fairfax pattern. When Gorham purchased Durgin, it kept Fairfax in production. Eventually, Gorham used its own backstamp on Fairfax. Matching backstamps are important to some buyers, which is why there are two listings for Fairfax in this book, one for pieces with the Durgin backstamp and the other with the Gorham backstamp. WMF initially manufactured its Line pattern in Germany. Later, production was moved to the Far East. Again, the pattern is listed twice in this book, one for pieces with the Germany backstamp and the other with a backstamp devoid of the country of origin.

The weight of a piece, especially in some sterling silver patterns, does vary in some forms. Even a minuscule reduction in size can result in tremendous cost savings. Further, different-style knife blades affect weight. Buyers appear extremely understanding regarding this issue—almost none insist on a match by weight.

A precise match occurs only when every design element is identical. Begin by holding the two pieces at arm's length. Then bring them forward for a closer inspection. A noticeable difference means the pieces are not an exact match.

PRICING NOTES

The prices that appear in this book are based on what one would pay to purchase a specific piece of silverware from a seller specializing in silverware replacement. They are price guidelines, not price absolutes. Price is of the moment, contingent on supply and demand and a host of other variables.

Prices are based on the assumption that a piece is in fine condition, that is, it shows no visible damage at arm's length and only minor defects upon close inspection. Visible defects such as deep surface scratches and dents lower a piece's value significantly, often by 50 percent or more.

The silverware patterns that appear in this book are mass-produced. As a result, it pays to comparison shop. Replacement services are price-competitive. Further, each brings its own interpretation of value to the patterns it sells. The interpretation can differ significantly from seller to seller.

A number of patterns included in this book are currently in production. They are sold at authorized sales centers and through mail-order catalogs, usually at the manufacturer's suggested retail price. Before buying from these sources, check prices for these patterns from replacement services. Replacement service prices occasionally may be lower than the manufacturer's suggested retail prices. Replacement services buy a large portion of their inventory on the secondary market. When they buy at favorable prices, they are in a position to pass along these savings to their customers. However, replacement services charge premium prices for pieces from discontinued patterns or discontinued forms from a current production pattern.

Individuals who remember or still retain the price lists that show what they initially paid for their pieces sometimes have difficulty accepting the price quotes they receive from replacement services. While they may need only a piece or two, the replacement service probably bought an entire service to be in a position to make these pieces available. When considered in this light, replacement service prices are not out of line.

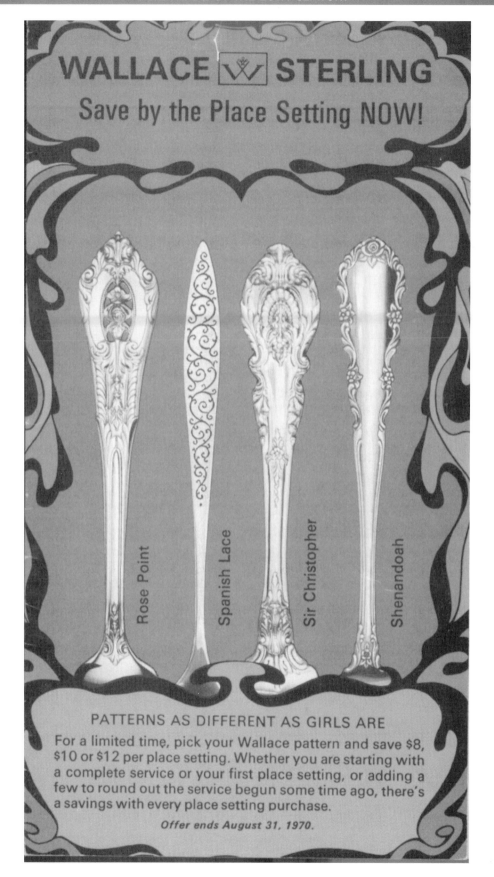

A REQUEST FOR YOUR HELP

As much as I would like it to be, this book is not comprehensive. Silverware manufacturers do not maintain reference archives. Last year's advertisements, catalogs, and price lists are discarded when the current year's sales materials arrive. Design and production records are kept for a few years, then trashed. Historical records are lost when one company acquires another. Contemporary manufacturers focus on the future, not on the past.

Over a decade ago, Replacements, Ltd., in Greensboro, North Carolina, began assembling a dinnerware, stemware, silverware, and collectibles reference library. Today, its holdings are the best research source on the subject in the United States. Replacements, Ltd., generously made its library available. However, even in this great collection, there are gaps.

You can help fill them. If you have information to add to what appears in this book about a pattern, please share it. Here are a few possibilities: (1) promotional literature about your pattern, for example, a pamphlet describing how it was made, its designer, and/or special features; (2) a brochure and/or price list of available forms and shapes; (3) pieces in your service that do not appear on the checklist; and (4) manufacturers' promotional literature on how to care for your silverware.

While I would love to have the original copy, you can send me a photocopy. First, appropriate information will be incorporated into the next edition of this book. Second, I will make a duplicate copy and send it to the Replacements, Ltd., library. Finally, although I tried to make this book error-free, I am certain some errors slipped through the cracks. I cannot correct them if you do not point them out to me.

Send any information you have that expands my research database and your comments, positive or negative, to: Silverware Pattern Research, Rinker Enterprises, Inc., 5093 Vera Cruz Road, Emmaus, PA 18049. Your assistance will be most appreciated.

Flatware Piece Type Guide

Flatware pieces are measured by length in inches.

Shown below is a representative view of many common flatware pieces.
Actual shapes and sizes of pieces will vary based on manufacturer and pattern.

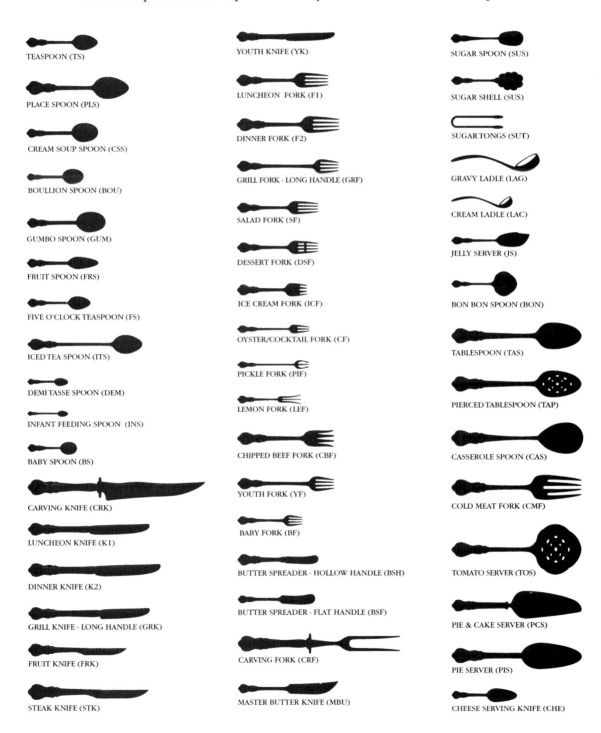

TEASPOON (TS)

PLACE SPOON (PLS)

CREAM SOUP SPOON (CSS)

BOULLION SPOON (BOU)

GUMBO SPOON (GUM)

FRUIT SPOON (FRS)

FIVE O'CLOCK TEASPOON (FS)

ICED TEA SPOON (ITS)

DEMI TASSE SPOON (DEM)

INFANT FEEDING SPOON (INS)

BABY SPOON (BS)

CARVING KNIFE (CRK)

LUNCHEON KNIFE (K1)

DINNER KNIFE (K2)

GRILL KNIFE - LONG HANDLE (GRK)

FRUIT KNIFE (FRK)

STEAK KNIFE (STK)

YOUTH KNIFE (YK)

LUNCHEON FORK (F1)

DINNER FORK (F2)

GRILL FORK - LONG HANDLE (GRF)

SALAD FORK (SF)

DESSERT FORK (DSF)

ICE CREAM FORK (ICF)

OYSTER/COCKTAIL FORK (CF)

PICKLE FORK (PIF)

LEMON FORK (LEF)

CHIPPED BEEF FORK (CBF)

YOUTH FORK (YF)

BABY FORK (BF)

BUTTER SPREADER - HOLLOW HANDLE (BSH)

BUTTER SPREADER - FLAT HANDLE (BSF)

CARVING FORK (CRF)

MASTER BUTTER KNIFE (MBU)

SUGAR SPOON (SUS)

SUGAR SHELL (SUS)

SUGAR TONGS (SUT)

GRAVY LADLE (LAG)

CREAM LADLE (LAC)

JELLY SERVER (JS)

BON BON SPOON (BON)

TABLESPOON (TAS)

PIERCED TABLESPOON (TAP)

CASSEROLE SPOON (CAS)

COLD MEAT FORK (CMF)

TOMATO SERVER (TOS)

PIE & CAKE SERVER (PCS)

PIE SERVER (PIS)

CHEESE SERVING KNIFE (CHE)

CHAPTER SIX

Silverware Glossary

This glossary is designed to help you understand the terminology used to describe the shapes, method of decoration, types of silverware forms, and manufacturing and aging terms encountered when reading about silverware. Take a few minutes to review it.

Although this book's primary focus is flatware, hollowware accessory pieces are included in the listings for those patterns that had complementary hollowware. Since manufacturer and retail literature usually includes terms relating to both, this glossary does so as well.

Terminology and the meaning of terms change over time. Some terms have become obsolete, for example, bright-cut. Others have acquired a generic meaning, while their initial meaning also is retained, for example, silverware. Several are synonymous with each other, for example, German silver and nickel silver.

Acanthus: A Mediterranean broad-leaved, spiny shrublike plant that serves as the inspiration for foliate decoration.

Alloy: A substance comprising two or more metals, usually intermixed through heating. Sterling is an alloy of silver, copper, and several other metals.

Annealing: A manufacturing process whereby silver is softened by heat to be worked. Silver becomes work hardened after one or two operations. To keep the material malleable, it is passed through an annealing furnace. The temperature of a flatware annealing furnace is about 1,300°F.

Applied: The technique of taking an object made separately and adding it to the body of a piece.

Apprentice: A person bound by indentures to serve another person, usually for the purpose of learning a trade. A typical apprenticeship lasted seven years. Once the apprenticeship was completed, the person became a journeyman.

Assay: A test made of metal to determine its quality and purity.

Baltimore Assay Mark: Between 1814 and 1830, Baltimore required that silverware made within the city conform to the coin standard of 900/1000. Pieces were assayed at a hall and an assay mark was applied.

Base Metal: An alloy or metal to which a coating or plating is applied.

Beaded: A decorative motif consisting of a narrow band of adjacent beadlike balls.

Bleeding: A technical term applied to pieces of plate when the base metal, usually copper, is exposed.

Border, applied: A cast, rolled wire, or other type of edge that is soldered onto an article.

Border, stamped: A border created when the metal is struck with a die. Once struck, the product is trimmed and finished.

Boss: A raised area, usually circular or oval, on the surface of an object.

Bright-cut: An engraving produced by short, repetitive strokes of a beveled cutting tool.

Bright Finish: A highly polished finish, almost mirrorlike in quality, achieved by using a jeweler's rouge on a polishing wheel.

Britannia: A silver-white alloy, consisting of tin, copper, antimony, and small quantities of bismuth and zinc, that resembles pewter. It has a higher proportion of tin than pewter and no lead, as does pewter. A typical formula consists of 140 parts tin, 3 parts copper, and 10 parts antimony.

Buffing: A polish finish achieved by using a flexible, rotating abrasive wheel.

Burnishing: A polishing process for electroplated pieces involving the use of a highly polished steel tool or bloodstone that is rubbed over an object's surface. Burnishing hardens the silver. Burnished silver plating tends to last twice as long as regular silver plating.

Chafing Dish: A serving piece where one dish or vessel fits inside the other; the outer vessel is filled with hot water and helps keep the food in the inner vessel warm.

Cartouche: An oval or oblong figure surrounded by decoration, often used as the location to monogram a piece.

Casting: A manufacturing process involving the pouring of molten metal into molds; also used to describe the products from these molds.

Chasing: A method of ornamentation done by hand. The metal is shaped by using small tools and punches that are struck with a hammer. When the design is impressed into the surface, the process is called *chasing*. When the design is made by driving out the metal from the inside and then molded back into detailed form, the process is called *repoussé chasing*.

Coin Silver: See *Silver, Coin.*

Collar: A narrow decorative flange applied around the rim or pedestal of a vessel.

Compote: A footed or stemmed dish of varying bowl shape, height, and size. Often used for serving bonbons, candy, nuts, and so on. Also known as a *comport.*

Cutlery: Any knife with a cutting edge.

Dessert Knives: Trade name for knives that are *luncheon size.*

Die Cutting: A manufacturing process whereby a design or pattern is cut out of a piece of steel to form a die, from which a quantity of similar articles can be stamped out or impressed.

Die Stamping: A manufacturing process in which a sheet of metal is stamped in a press, used to make individual pieces as well as applied ornamentation; synonymous with *stamping.*

Dinner Size: Flatware that is slightly larger than *place size,* also called *European size.* It is used primarily for luxurious formal dining.

Dinnerware: General term used to describe bowls, dishes, plates, tea sets, and other accessory and hollowware pieces as distinguished from flatware.

Dirilyte: An extremely hard, solid bronze alloy developed in Sweden in the early 1900s. Although it is gold in appearance, it contains no gold.

Electroplating: A manufacturing process, introduced in the early 1840s, which electrically applies a thin layer of silver onto a base metal. The general term for the process is *plating.*

Embossing: A manufacturing process that creates a raised surface design from the reverse by rolling the piece between an embossing plate and a roller. No metal is removed in this process.

Engine Turning: A decorative technique in which lines are cut into the surface of an object using a machine.

Engraving: A manufacturing process that involves cutting lines into the metal to create a design; metal is removed during this process.

EP: Electroplate on copper.

EPBM: Electroplate on Britannia metal.

EPNS: Electroplate on nickel silver.

EPWM: Electroplate on white metal.

Etching: A manufacturing process in which the piece is covered with a protective coating; the design is created by removing a portion of the coating and immersing the piece in a nitric acid bath.

Ferrule: A thin element, often ivory or wood, inserted between the body of a hollowware piece and its handle to prevent heat transfer; synonymous with *insulator.*

Finial: The topmost portion of an object, usually referring to the knob on a lid.

Finish, Butler: A finish applied to give sterling hollowware a distinct luster. Patented by James

H. Reilly of the Brooklyn Silver Company, it is produced by revolving wheels of wire that produce tiny scratches on the piece.

Finish, Satin: A matte finish obtained by raising up a metal's surface with a long hair steel wire brush. The effect also can be achieved by a sandblasting process.

Flat Handle: Silverware handle made of one solid piece.

Flatware: When used with respect to silver, silver plate, and stainless steel, the term refers to forks, knives, serving pieces, and spoons. When applied to dinnerware and stemware, the term means any flat pieces, for example, a plate or platter.

Fluted: Decorated with parallel vertical grooves.

Forged: Metal that is shaped by heating and hammering.

French Plating: A manufacturing technique in which a heated iron is used to apply a thin foil of silver to a brass or copper object.

Gadrooning: A decorative motif consisting of narrow, parallel, vertical panels, usually tapered.

Gallery: A pierced ornamental border used on the top of vessels; often resembles a fence.

German Silver: An alloy containing approximately 50 percent copper, 40 percent zinc, and 10 percent nickel, developed in Germany in the nineteenth century in an attempt to imitate Patkong, a Chinese alloy. It contains no silver. The term was dropped during World War I in favor of nickel silver; synonymous with *Nickel Silver*.

Gilding: A manufacturing process used to describe the electroplating of a layer of pure gold onto another metal.

Hallmark: Mark(s) required by law to be placed on silver to indicate the maker, date, place of manufacture, and/or purity of silver.

Hammered Silver: A method of decoration achieved from repeated taps on the surface of the metal with a light hammer.

Hollow Handle: Handles made by soldering two halves together.

Hollowware: A generic term for any hollow vessel, for example, a bowl, creamer, pitcher, sugar, teapot, and so on; objects from which one serves.

Hundredweight: One-twentieth of a troy ounce; used to weigh gold, jewels, and silver. Also known as a *pennyweight*.

Insulators: Heat-resisting substances inserted between the handles and body of large hollowware pieces, for example, coffeepots and teapots, often comprised of an ivory-colored substance. Insulators prevent heat from traveling from the body of the piece to the handle; synonymous with *ferrule*.

Luncheon Size: Flatware that is slightly smaller in size than *place size*.

Martelé: A specific type of handwrought silver developed by Gorham in 1895, its pieces were made from 950/1000 silver, a higher standard than sterling.

Motif: The dominant feature of a design.

Mounts: Pieces of ornamental metal, such as a casting, stamped, or wire object, soldered onto a piece as a decorative element.

Nibbled Edge: An edge that is filed or nibbled to follow the exact design of the mount, for example, a gadroon border; a technique used on the highest-quality hollowware.

Nickel Silver: An alloy that is silverlike in color and contains approximately 50 percent copper, 40 percent zinc, and 10 percent nickel. It is often used to electroplate objects and contains no silver; synonymous with *German silver*.

Non-Tarnishing Silver: An alloy of silver and cadmium; also used to describe a piece of plated ware with a thin palladium or rhodium plating.

NS: Nickel silver.

Onslow Pattern: Flatware that is shaped as a volute scroll.

Oxidizing: A decorative process in which an oxide is applied to darken a metal, used to accentuate and enhance a design. Excessive polishing may remove oxidizing. Some stamped pieces acquire a natural oxidizing in low places. Polishing only the surface and allowing some of the natural oxidation to remain also enhances the overall decoration.

Patina: A soft, lustrous finish or surface texture acquired by silver from years of use.

Pewter: An alloy of tin, copper, and antimony. Initially a dull silvery gray, it can be polished to a bright high shine or dull satin. Often used to reproduce Early American pieces such as bowls, candlesticks, and plates.

Piercing: A decorative motif achieved by cutting away parts of the metal, achieved through cutting dies, punching tools, or a thin, fine-toothed steel blade, the last technique referred to as hand piercing.

Place Setting: Used to describe the number of pieces in a basic flatware setting. A four-piece place setting includes a knife, fork, salad fork, and teaspoon. A cream soup or second spoon expands the count to five. A six-piece place setting includes a butter knife.

Place Size: The most common size in which sterling flatware place-setting pieces are made today; originated after World War II, when most households had one, not two, sets of sterling silver flatware.

Plate: A term used in England and on the Continent to refer to pieces made from precious metals.

Pseudo-Hallmarks: Marks found on base metal, silver plate, and some American silver, imitating English and European marks. These marks are not required by law and frequently do not have the same significance as true hallmarks.

Reeded: A decorative motif of narrow, parallel, convex panels that resemble a bundle of reeds.

Repoussé: A French term meaning *raised decoration*, used to describe a decorating technique in which the metal is driven out from the inside and then detailed by molding it back; also known as *raised chasing*.

Reserve: The plain area in the center of a cartouche or decorative panel, usually meant as the place for engraving a name, initials, or presentation.

Service: The number of forms in a specific pattern; also used to indicate the number of place settings belonging to an individual, for example, service for six, eight, and twelve.

Sheffield Plate: A substance made by fusing, with intense heat, a thin sheet of silver to both sides of a thick sheet of copper, this product was rolled to proper thickness for fabrication. It was developed around 1743 by Thomas Boulsover and often was called "Old Sheffield Plate" to distinguish it from mid-nineteenth-century and later Sheffield electroplated pieces.

Silver, Coin: Silver that assays at approximately 900 parts silver per 1,000, the standard adopted for U.S. coins. Eighteenth- and early nineteenth-century coin silver may have a silver count as low as 700 parts per 1,000; also known as coin, dollar, standard, premium, "C," or "D" silver.

Silver, Pure: Pure or fine silver consists of 1,000 parts silver. No silverware today is made from fine silver, as it is too soft. The malleability of 100 percent silver would cause any piece of flatware made from it to bend and break.

Silver, Solid: A synonymous term for *sterling silver*.

Silver, Sterling: Silver consisting of 925 parts silver per 1,000. The remaining seventy-five parts consist of copper and other metals that are added to give silver strength; often synonymous with *solid silver*. The sterling silver standard was set by the 1906 Federal Stamping Act.

Silver Plate: The product resulting from electroplating a thin layer of pure silver on a base metal such as brass or nickel silver.

Silversmithing: A general term used to describe the manufacturing techniques and methods used to make silver articles.

Solder: A technique used to join two pieces of metal by melting another kind of metal between them.

Spinning: A manufacturing method to form and shape silver hollowware that involves revolving a flat disk of silver over a wood or steel chuck in the shape of the finished piece. A tool is then used to spread the silver over the rotating form.

Stainless Steel: Stainless steel contains three basic ingredients—chromium, nickel, and steel. Steel with a content level of 13 percent chromium or higher is considered stainless. The standard 18/8 mixture contains 18 percent chromium for strength and stain resistance and 8 percent nickel for a high luster and long-lasting finish. WMF's Cromargan® mixture is based on an 18/10 mix.

Stamping: A manufacturing technique in which a design is impressed into the metal using a die and a heavy press.

Sterling II: Flatware whose handles are sterling silver but whose blades, tines, and bowls are made from stainless steel; developed by Wallace Silversmiths.

Touchmark: The name, initials, or symbol of a craftsman or company.

Trademark: Symbol or trade name used by a manufacturer, widely used in the United States as a guarantee of quality. It is different from a hallmark. Because the United States never adopted a system of guild halls, there are no true hallmarks on American silverware.

Troy Measure: The measure used to weigh gold, jewels, and silver. One troy pound is equivalent to 12 ounces avoirdupois.

Turn: Placing an object on a lathe to scrape and/or shape it or to sharpen its decorative detail.

Vermeil: A gold electroplating process.

Weight Value: The price assigned to a troy ounce of gold or silver. Also used to describe the metal value of a piece, as opposed to the aesthetic value.

White Metal: An alloy consisting of two or more metals, for example, antimony, bismuth, copper, lead, and/or tin. The color depends on whether the lead or tin is dominant; the higher the level of tin, the whiter the color.

II

SILVERWARE
PATTERNS

CHAPTER SEVEN

The Patterns

DANSK

Dansk Designs, a conglomerate established by Jens H. Quistgaard of Denmark and Ted Nierenberg of the United States in 1954, began as an export sales group for Danish applied arts. The firm developed a reputation for marketing a select group of small glass, stainless steel, textile, and wood objects.

Objects exported by Dansk International Designs featured trendy, exquisitely crafted, practical designs. Wood objects included end grain-block carving boards, pepper mills with salt shaker tops, and Jens Quistgaard's teak ice bucket. Quistgaard also designed several flatware patterns for Dansk Designs. He referred to his work as "tabletop sculpture." Gunnar Cyrén and Torun Vivianna Bülow Hübe also designed flatware patterns for Dansk International Designs in the 1970s.

Quistgaard and Nierenberg led Dansk International Designs until 1984. In 1989, Dansk International Designs purchased Gorham from Textron, Inc., a conglomerate. In July 1990, Dansk was purchased by Brown-Forman Corporation in Louisville, Kentucky. Today, Dansk is a division of Lenox Brands.

JENS H. QUISTGAARD

Jens H. Quistgaard, born in 1919, is a Danish glassware, metalwork, and wood designer. He received his training as a carpenter, ceramist, draftsperson, silversmith, and sculptor over a ten-year period, beginning in the mid-1930s. Quistgaard served his silversmith apprenticeship with Georg Jensen Sølvsmedie.

After World War II, Quistgaard established his own design studio. His association with Dansk began in 1954. Quistgaard was the company's principal designer. His designs, highly sculptural in nature, influenced the full range of Dansk's production—ceramics, cookware, cutlery, glassware, silverware, and wooden tableware.

Quistgaard won the 1954 Lunning Prize. He received gold and silver medals at the 1954 Triennale di Milano for an enamel cast iron cooking pot designed for De Forenede Jerstøberier and for his flatware.

THE TOP FIVE PATTERNS

MODERN—STAINLESS

DANSK, FJORD

INTERNATIONAL, NEW CHARM

ONEIDA, OMNI

TOWLE, DESIGN 2

WMF, LINE

Dansk, Fjord, Stainless

Bottle Opener, 7 1/4″	$50.00
Butter Spreader, HH, paddled ST blade, 6 5/8″	32.00
Carving Set, two pieces, ST blade	250.00
Fork	40.00
Fork, salad, 6 1/2″	35.00
Knife	40.00
Knife, steak, 8 3/8″	45.00
Serving Fork, 9 1/8″	90.00
Serving Spoon, 9 1/8″	70.00
Spoon, iced tea, 9 1/2″	35.00
Spoon, soup, oval bowl, 7 1/8″	35.00
Spoon, teaspoon	30.00

Dansk, Thistle, Stainless

Butter Spreader	$22.00
Fork	25.00
Fork, salad	22.00
Knife	25.00
Serving Fork	60.00
Serving Spoon	50.00
Spoon, iced tea	25.00
Spoon, soup, oval bowl, 7 7/8″	15.00
Spoon, teaspoon	22.00

Dirilyte was originally created as Dirigold. Carl Molin, a Swedish metallurgist, first produced Dirigold, an extremely hard, solid bronze alloy in 1914. An exhibition of Dirigold objects in New York resulted in substantial orders. Upon Molin's return to Sweden, Oscar Von Malmborg joined the company to assist in the production and distribution of the Dirigold line.

A Dirigold display at the 1923 Gohlenburg Exposition also received a favorable response. A group of visiting Swedish Americans approached Molin about marketing Dirigold products in the United States. Von Malmborg left Sweden and came to Minneapolis, Minnesota, where he established a distribution company. Molin stayed behind to supervise the Swedish factory.

Within a short period of time, the decision was made to manufacture Dirigold in the United

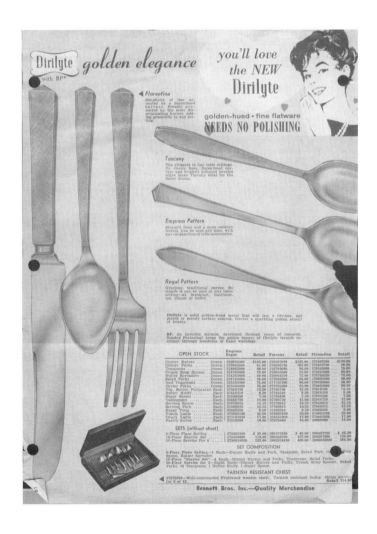

States. Molin and six of his employees and their families moved to Kokomo, Indiana, in 1926. Manufacturing of Dirigold in the United States commenced shortly after their arrival. The depression had a negative effect on the company; it was forced into receivership in 1930, though it managed to continue its manufacturing operations.

In 1935, a group of Kokomo businessmen purchased the company's assets—its formula, dies, and patent rights. They formed American Art Alloys and continued to market flatware and hollowware under the Dirigold name.

In 1935, the Federal Trade Commission brought suit against the company, charging that the name Dirigold misled the public because the alloy did not contain any gold. A decision was made to change the name of the product and the company. In 1937, Dirigold became Dirilyte, and the company became the Dirilyte Company of America.

Empress and Regal were the company's first two flatware patterns. Two additional patterns, Florentina and Tuscany, were later added. In addition to flatware, Dirilyte also made hollowware, ranging from an 18 1/4" × 14" large oval platter to an eight-cup coffee server.

Eleanor Roosevelt was a great admirer of Dirilyte, presenting it as gifts. George Bush used Dirilyte plates etched with the vice presidential seal as gifts for those who helped in his first presidential election campaign. The Shah of Iran placed an order for 200 place settings.

Beginning in 1961, Dirilyte offered an optional Bonded Protectant coating, BP for short, which helped eliminate the need for polishing. The BP coating was not a permanent finish, but would last for years. It came with a one-year warranty to ensure against defects in the application process. However, if Dirilyte containing the BP coating was washed in the dishwasher, its BP warranty was considered void. In 1994, Dirilyte had to discontinue offering the BP coating on all of its products, because the chemical company providing the coating ceased manufacturing it. The company also developed Dirilyte Polish, which proved to be effective in removing tarnish from Dirilyte pieces that did not have the BP coating.

In November 1971, the Dirilyte Company became a division of Hand Industries of Warsaw, Indiana. Production of Dirilyte flatware and hollowware ended in 1986. A retired employee returns to Hand Industries several times a week to answer questions about Dirilyte, available in back stock, Dirilyte Polish, and the company's polishing services. Address any inquiries you may have to Hand Industries, 315 S. Hand Drive, Warsaw, IN 46580.

Dirilyte Company of America, Regal, Dirilyte

Ashtray, 2 7/8″	$20.00
Butter Serving Knife, FH, 7 1/4″	25.00
Butter Spreader, FH, 5 5/8″	17.00
Candlestick, 10 1/2″	80.00
Carving Set, two pieces, ST blade	150.00
Creamer and Sugar, open, mini, 3 7/8″	200.00
Fork, 7″	22.00
Fork, 7 1/8″	22.00
Fork, 7 1/4″	22.00
Fork, 7 1/2″	22.00
Fork, 7 3/4″	22.00
Fork, cocktail, 6″	20.00
Fork, fish, 7 1/4″	25.00
Fork, pickle, short handle, 6 1/2″	25.00
Fork, salad, 6 1/4″	20.00
Fork, strawberry, 5″	30.00
Fork, youth, 6 5/8″	25.00
Knife, baby, 5 1/8″	25.00
Knife, HH, New French blade, 8 3/4″	25.00
Knife, HH, New French blade, 9 1/4″	25.00
Knife, HH, Old French blade, 8″	25.00
Knife, New French blade, 9 1/8″	25.00
Knife, Old French blade, 9″	25.00
Ladle, gravy, 6 3/4″	50.00
Lobster Pick, 7 3/4″	25.00
Pepper Shaker, 4 1/2″	80.00
Plate, bread and butter, 6 1/4″	35.00
Plate, dinner, 10 1/2″	50.00
Salt and Pepper Shakers, pair, 4 1/2″	140.00
Salt Shaker, 4 1/2″	80.00
Server, pie, 8 7/8″	90.00
Server, pie, 9 1/2″	90.00
Server, pie/cake, 10″	90.00
Serving Fork, cold meat, 8 5/8″	50.00
Serving Spoon, casserole, 9 5/8″	50.00
Serving Spoon, tablespoon, 8 3/8″	35.00
Spoon, baby, straight handle, 4 3/8″	25.00
Spoon, bonbon, 5 3/4″	25.00

DIRILYTE CARE AND STORAGE TIPS

Dirilyte without the BP coating may tarnish with repeated exposure to alcohol. The BP coating is resistant to the effects of alcohol.

Do not polish Dirilyte that contains the BP coating; its finish may be damaged if abrasives are used. Uncoated Dirilyte should only be polished with Dirilyte Polish.

Wash Dirilyte immediately after each use to reduce exposure to foods like salad dressing, eggs, mustard, butter, and so on. Wash by hand in warm water using a mild detergent, rinse well, and dry thoroughly. Handle each piece separately to reduce scratches. Hard water may shorten the life span of the BP coating.

Store Dirilyte in untreated flannel wraps. *Special chests or cloths to prevent tarnish on silver may have an adverse effect on Dirilyte.* Do not store Dirilyte products in plastic, as this increases the probability of tarnishing, and it may have an adverse effect on the optional BP coating.

Spoon, bouillon, round bowl, 5″	20.00	Spoon, soup, oval bowl, 7″	22.00
Spoon, cream soup, round bowl, 5 ⅞″	20.00	Spoon, sugar, 5 ⅝″	27.00
Spoon, demitasse, 4 ⅜″	15.00	Spoon, sugar, 5 ⅞″	27.00
Spoon, grapefruit, round bowl, 7″	20.00	Spoon, teaspoon, 6″	15.00
Spoon, iced tea, 8 ⅜″	22.00	Spoon, teaspoon, 5 o'clock, 5″	15.00
Spoon, jelly, 5 ¾″	27.00	Sugar Tongs, 4 ½″	60.00
Spoon, jelly, 6 ¾″	27.00	Tray, bread, 11 ⅝″	70.00
Spoon, sherbet, 4 ⅞″	17.00	Tray, round, 11 ⅞″	90.00

Les Hedge, Jack Luhn, and Glenn Olmstead started the Easterling Company in 1944, specializing in the direct sale of tabletop ware to consumers. Its catalog included cook-and-serve ware, dinnerware, sterling silver flatware, stemware, and other accessories.

Gorham Manufacturing Company made six patterns of sterling silver flatware for Easterling. In 1974, the design patents and sterling silver inventory were sold to the Westerling Company in Chicago, Illinois. Gorham continued to make the same six patterns for Westerling.

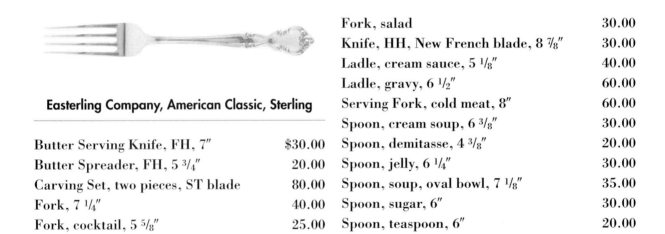

Easterling Company, American Classic, Sterling

Butter Serving Knife, FH, 7″	$30.00
Butter Spreader, FH, 5 3/4″	20.00
Carving Set, two pieces, ST blade	80.00
Fork, 7 1/4″	40.00
Fork, cocktail, 5 5/8″	25.00

Fork, salad	30.00
Knife, HH, New French blade, 8 7/8″	30.00
Ladle, cream sauce, 5 1/8″	40.00
Ladle, gravy, 6 1/2″	60.00
Serving Fork, cold meat, 8″	60.00
Spoon, cream soup, 6 3/8″	30.00
Spoon, demitasse, 4 3/8″	20.00
Spoon, jelly, 6 1/4″	30.00
Spoon, soup, oval bowl, 7 1/8″	35.00
Spoon, sugar, 6″	30.00
Spoon, teaspoon, 6″	20.00

GENSE

AB Gense, Eskilstuna, Sweden, is a manufacturer of stainless steel flatware. When World War II limited the supply of precious metals, Swedish silverware manufacturers began experimenting with stainless steel. Enhancing this effort was a cadre of designers and architects who had been actively working with Swedish manufacturers since the mid-1930s.

Folke Arström, born in 1907, opened his own design studio in 1934. In 1940, he became head designer of Gense. Initially, Arström worked exclusively in pewter and silver. He shifted his efforts exclusively to stainless steel in the early 1940s.

Arström's 1944 Thebe line of stainless steel flatware was designed in an effort to overcome prejudice against the material. His Facette pattern won a Gold Medal at the 1951 Triennale International Exhibition in Milan. In addition to Facette, Arström's 1956 Focus Deluxe flatware pattern with its softly shaped black nylon handles enjoyed great popularity in the United States and helped establish the use of stainless steel flatware for formal dining. In 1961, he received the Gregor Paulsson trophy.

Pierre Forsell is another Gense designer who has achieved world recognition. He is best known for his three-in-one fork. This two-pronged fork has a near rectangular shape with a straight edge that can be used for cutting and a bowl-like spoon that can be used for small foods and sauces. It was designed for use during buffets, where multiple eating utensils are impractical.

ESKILSTUNA, SWEDEN

Eskilstuna, "Town of Smiths," was established in the early sixteenth century using a block-grid plan. Eskilstuna became a Free Town in 1771. Single-story timber houses with high mansard roofs were a village hallmark. Many of these structures are preserved today in a historic district known as "Rademacher Smithies."

In eighteenth-century Sweden, almost every town had its own silversmith, pewter, and cabinetmaker guild. These groups often occupied a specific section of town, such as "Rademacher Smithies" in Eskilstuna. After visiting the historic district, visitors to Eskilstuna can also tour the Gense factory.

Gense, Facette, Stainless

Butter Spreader, FH, 6 1/4″	$10.00
Cheese Plane, ST blade, 8 5/8″	22.00
Cheese Plane, ST blade, 9″	22.00
Fork, 7 5/8″	12.00
Fork, cocktail, 4 3/4″	7.00
Fork, dessert, 5 5/8″	15.00
Fork, pickle, short handle, 6 3/4″	12.00
Fork, pie, 5 5/8″	10.00
Fork, salad, 7″	10.00
Knife, dessert, ST blade, 7 1/4″	17.00

Knife, fruit, ST blade, 6″	17.00
Knife, modern blade, 7 7/8″	12.00
Knife, steak, 8″	17.00
Ladle, gravy, 7 5/8″	22.00
Ladle, soup, 10 5/8″	27.00
Salad Set, two pieces, 10 3/4″	35.00
Server, pie, 10 1/4″	17.00
Serving Fork, 8 7/8″	20.00
Serving Fork, cold meat, 10 3/4″	22.00
Serving Fork, salad, 10 3/4″	32.00
Serving Spoon, tablespoon, 7 1/2″	12.00
Spoon, demitasse, 4 3/4″	7.00
Spoon, iced tea, 7 1/2″	12.00
Spoon, soup, oval bowl, 7″	10.00
Spoon, sugar, 5 5/8″	15.00
Spoon, teaspoon, 5 5/8″	7.00
Spoon, teaspoon, 5 o'clock, 5 1/8″	12.00

This sales brochure dates from 1960.

GORHAM CORPORATION

Jabez Gorham, founder of Gorham, served a seven-year apprenticeship with Nehemiah Dodge, an early American silversmith. In the mid-1810s, he became partners with Christopher Burr, George C. Clark, William Hadwen, and Harvey G. Mumford. The partnership manufactured jewelry and smalls. During that period, Jabez Gorham developed his high-quality "Gorham chain." In the 1820s, Gorham worked with Stanton Bebe, another silversmith of note.

In 1831, Jabez Gorham and Henry L. Webster formed Gorham & Webster, the result of a desire on Gorham's part to add silver spoons to his inventory. The firm became Gorham, Webster & Price in 1837 and J. Gorham & Son in 1841, when John Gorham, Jabez's son, joined the firm.

Gorham was one of the first silver manufacturers to recognize the advantages of using machinery in the silver-making process. John Gorham designed much of the early steam-powered machinery used by the company. By the late 1840s, Gorham was producing silverware in a modern factory environment.

Jabez Gorham retired in 1847. In 1850, the company became Gorham & Thurber, and two years later, in 1852, it was called Gorham & Company. After receiving a charter from the Rhode Island Legislature in 1863, Gorham Manufacturing Company was organized in 1865.

In 1863, Gorham made a decision to manufacture nickel silver electroplated ware. The company used the same molds and assembling methods it had used for silverware as it had for its electroplated ware. Tooling and die work took two years. The first electroplated ware appeared in 1865. After a hiatus of over a half century, Gorham reintroduced electroplating in the early 1960s. While Gorham discontinued production of electroplated flatware in 1962, it continued to make electroplated hollowware.

Two important events occurred in 1868. First, the company adopted the English 925/1000 sterling standard for its silverware and, second, its famous lion (the English hallmark for silver), anchor (symbol of the State of Rhode Island), and "G" mark for its sterling pieces.

Gorham recognized the importance of working with designers, such as William Christmas Codman, Erik Manussen, Thomas J. Pairpoint, and George Wilkinson. Wilkinson designed many of the early Gorham patterns. Codman's Art Nouveau designs were marketed under the Martelé label at the turn of the century.

Gorham introduced Chantilly in 1895. The Buttercup, Medallion, and Versailles patterns also achieved widespread popularity. Though not as ornate, patterns designed in the middle part of the nineteenth century should not be overlooked.

Gorham actively acquired other silverware manufacturers, creating two holding companies, Silversmiths Stocks Company (1906) and The Silversmiths Company (1907), for the purpose of acquiring the Durgin, Kerr, and Whiting companies. They acquired a financial interest in each of these firms. When Gorham Manufacturing Company reorganized in 1924, it purchased the assets of The Silversmiths Company and dissolved it. William B. Durgin Company, William B. Kerr Company, and Whiting Manufacturing Company operated as subsidiaries. Eventually, the operations of all three moved to Providence, Rhode Island—Whiting in 1925, Kerr in 1927, and Durgin in 1931.

Around 1913, Gorham acquired the Mt. Vernon Silversmiths, Inc., a company that resulted from the merger of Hayes & McFarland (New York, New York), Mauser Manufacturing (Mt. Vernon, New York), and the Roger Williams Silver Company (Providence, Rhode Island). Gorham purchased The Alvin Silver Company in 1928, the McChesney Company (Newark, New Jersey) in 1931, the Quaker Silver Company (North Attleboro, Massachusetts) in 1959, the Friedman Company (Brooklyn, New York) in 1960, and Graff, Washbourne & Dunn (New York, New York) in 1961.

The Gorham Manufacturing Company became The Gorham Corporation in 1961. In 1967, Textron, Inc., a conglomerate, purchased Gorham, selling it in 1989 to Dansk International Designs. Several years earlier, Gorham opened a state-of-the-art plant in Smithfield, Rhode Island. Dansk continued the use of the Gorham name. Brown-Forman Corporation of Louisville, Kentucky, purchased Dansk in July 1990. Brown-Forman Corporation is the parent company for Jack Daniel's, Canadian Mist, and Southern Comfort. Many older Gorham patterns were removed from current inventory and available only by special order.

Today, Gorham is part of Lenox Brands. Gorham's company archives are housed in Brown University's John Hay Library in Providence, Rhode Island.

THE GORHAM TRADEMARK

The Gorham trademark of the lion, anchor, and "G" was registered on December 19, 1899, as #33,902. Gorham's application indicated that the mark had been in use since January 1, 1853.

Today, Gorham claims 1848 as the earliest date for the mark. The lion faced left, not right, between 1848 and 1865.

WILLIAM B. DURGIN

William B. Durgin is one of the many companies that became part of The Gorham Manufacturing Company.

After serving an apprenticeship with Newell Harding & Co. in Boston, Durgin became a journeyman silversmith. He would make a quantity of silver spoons, then sell them throughout New England, traveling by horse and wagon, taking old silver in barter. In the early 1850s, he opened his own shop in Concord, New Hampshire.

New England responded positively to the simple designs of "Durgin's spoons." Durgin created new designs as the public's taste changed. George F. Durgin, William's son, joined the firm in 1880, introducing the manufacture of hollowware and novelties. The company was incorporated in 1898 as the William B. Durgin Company. After numerous expansions, Durgin built a new silverware factory between 1903 and 1904.

William B. and George F. died in 1905. The Silversmiths Company, a Gorham holding firm, purchased the business. In 1931, Gorham moved the company and its production from Concord to Providence, Rhode Island. Gorham continued to produce patterns using the Durgin name until the late 1930s.

STERLING

Gorham Corporation, Andante, Sterling Silver
(Introduced in 1963)

Butter Serving Knife, HH, 7″	$40.00
Fork, 7 1/8″	55.00
Fork, cocktail, 5 3/4″	35.00
Knife, HH, modern blade, 9″	40.00
Ladle, gravy, 6 3/8″	100.00
Spoon, soup, oval bowl, 6 1/2″	65.00
Spoon, sugar, 5 7/8″	45.00
Spoon, teaspoon, 6″	30.00

Gorham Corporation, Buttercup, Sterling Silver
(Introduced in 1899)

Butter Serving Knife, FH, 6 7/8″	$40.00
Butter Spreader, HH, modern ST blade, 6 1/4″	35.00
Fork, 7″	45.00
Fork, 7 1/2″	60.00
Fork, baby, 4 3/8″	45.00
Fork, ice cream, 5 3/8″	55.00
Fork, salad, 6 3/8″	50.00
Ice Cream Slicer, 10″	140.00
Knife, HH, blunt blade, 9 5/8″	55.00
Knife, HH, modern blade, 8 1/2″	40.00
Knife, HH, modern blade, 8 3/4″	40.00

Spoon, fruit, 5 5/8″	45.00
Spoon, ice cream, 5 5/8″	55.00
Spoon, iced tea, 7 1/2″	50.00
Spoon, jelly, 6 1/4″	40.00
Spoon, soup, oval bowl, 6 1/2″	50.00
Spoon, soup, oval bowl, 6 7/8″	50.00
Spoon, sugar, 6″	45.00
Spoon, teaspoon, 5 7/8″	25.00
Sugar Tongs, 4 5/8″	65.00

Photo courtesy of Lenox, Inc.

Gorham Corporation, Camellia, Sterling Silver
(Introduced in 1942)

Butter Serving Knife, FH, 7 1/8″	$32.00
Butter Serving Knife, HH, 6 5/8″	32.00
Butter Spreader, FH, 5 3/4″	20.00
Butter Spreader, HH, modern ST blade, 6 1/4″	22.00
Butter Spreader, HH, paddled ST blade, 6 1/8″	22.00
Carving Fork, ST tines, 8 7/8″	50.00
Carving Set, two pieces, ST blade	95.00
Fork, 7 1/4″	40.00
Fork, 7 7/8″	50.00
Fork, cocktail, 5 5/8″	25.00
Fork, pickle, short handle, 5 5/8″	25.00
Fork, salad, 6 1/2″	30.00
Knife, HH, modern blade, 8 7/8″	30.00
Knife, HH, modern blade, 9 5/8″	40.00
Knife, HH, New French blade, 8 7/8″	30.00
Knife, HH, New French blade, 9 5/8″	40.00
Knife, steak, 9 1/2″	45.00
Knife, youth, 7 1/2″	35.00
Ladle, cream sauce, 5 1/4″	35.00
Ladle, gravy, 6 1/2″	70.00
Server, cheese, ST blade, 6 1/2″	40.00

Knife, HH, modern blade, 9 1/8″	40.00
Knife, HH, modern blade, 9 5/8″	55.00
Knife, HH, New French blade, 8 3/4″	40.00
Knife, HH, New French blade, 9 5/8″	55.00
Knife, youth, 7 5/8″	45.00
Ladle, gravy, 6 1/8″	120.00
Ladle, punch, 13 1/2″	200.00
Ladle, punch, ST bowl, 13 1/2″	70.00
Salad Set, two pieces, 8 7/8″	250.00
Server, cheese, ST blade, 7″	50.00
Serving Fork, cold meat, 8 1/8″	130.00
Serving Fork, fish, 8 5/8″	145.00
Serving Spoon, salad, 7 7/8″	120.00
Serving Spoon, salad, ST bowl, 11 1/4″	45.00
Serving Spoon, tablespoon, 8 3/8″	85.00
Serving Spoon, vegetable, 10″	150.00
Spoon, baby, straight handle, 4 1/2″	45.00
Spoon, bouillon, round bowl, 5 1/4″	45.00
Spoon, cream soup, round bowl, 6 1/4″	50.00
Spoon, demitasse, 4 1/8″	25.00

Server, pie, ST blade, 10″	50.00
Server, pie, ST blade, 10 1/4″	50.00
Serving Spoon, tablespoon, 8 1/2″	60.00
Serving Spoon, tablespoon, pierced, 8 1/2″	75.00
Spoon, cream soup, round bowl, 6 1/4″	30.00
Spoon, demitasse, 4 1/4″	20.00
Spoon, iced tea, 7 1/2″	35.00
Spoon, sugar, 6 1/8″	32.00
Spoon, teaspoon, 5 7/8″	20.00
Spoon, teaspoon, 5 o'clock, 5 5/8″	20.00
Sugar Tongs, 4″	55.00

Spoon, bonbon, 4 1/4″	32.00
Spoon, iced tea, 7 1/2″	35.00
Spoon, jelly, 6 1/4″	30.00
Spoon, soup, oval bowl, 7 1/8″	35.00
Spoon, sugar, 6 1/4″	32.00
Spoon, teaspoon	22.00

Gorham Corporation, Chantilly, Sterling Silver
(Introduced in 1895)

Bowl, vegetable, footed, round, 12 1/2″	$1,200.00
Butter Serving Knife, HH, 6 3/4″	40.00
Butter Spreader, FH, 5 7/8″	30.00
Butter Spreader, HH, modern ST blade, 6 1/4″	30.00
Candelabra, triple light, 13″	800.00
Candlestick, 9 1/2″	260.00
Carving Set, two pieces, ST blade	130.00
Compote, 4″	400.00
Compote, 4 1/2″	800.00
Creamer and Sugar, open, mini	400.00
Fork, 7″	45.00
Fork, 7 1/2″	65.00
Fork, cocktail, 5 1/2″	30.00
Fork, fruit, ST tines, 7 1/4″	35.00
Fork, ice cream, 5 1/2″	55.00
Fork, lemon, 4 3/8″	30.00
Fork, lettuce, 9 3/8″	100.00
Fork, pickle, short handle, 5 7/8″	30.00
Fork, salad, 5 3/4″	50.00
Fork, salad, 6 1/2″	50.00
Knife, fish, ST blade, 8 1/2″	45.00
Knife, HH, blunt blade, 8 1/2″	40.00
Knife, HH, modern blade, 8 7/8″	40.00
Knife, HH, modern blade, 9 1/4″	40.00

Gorham Corporation, Celeste, Sterling Silver

Butter Serving Knife, HH, 7″	$30.00
Butter Spreader, HH, modern ST blade, 6 1/2″	20.00
Carving Knife, ST blade, 10 3/4″	60.00
Carving Set, two pieces, ST blade	120.00
Fork, 7 5/8″	50.00
Fork, cocktail, 5 3/4″	25.00
Fork, ice cream, 5 1/2″	35.00
Fork, lemon, 4″	25.00
Fork, pickle, short handle, 5 7/8″	25.00
Fork, salad, 7″	30.00
Knife, cheese, ST blade, 7 1/2″	35.00
Knife, HH, modern blade, 9 3/8″	25.00
Ladle, cream, 5 1/4″	40.00
Ladle, gravy, 6 3/4″	70.00
Salt and Pepper Shakers, pair, 3″	200.00
Server, cheese, ST blade, 7″	40.00
Server, pastry, 7″	120.00
Server, pie, ST blade, 10″	50.00
Server, pie/cake, ST blade, 10 3/4″	50.00
Serving Fork, cold meat, 8 5/8″	70.00
Serving Spoon, tablespoon, 8 5/8″	65.00

Knife, HH, modern blade, 9 5/8″	55.00	Spoon, soup, oval bowl, 6 3/4″	50.00
Knife, HH, New French blade, 8 3/8″	40.00	Spoon, soup, oval bowl, 7″	50.00
Knife, HH, New French blade, 8 7/8″	40.00	Spoon, sugar, 6″	45.00
Knife, HH, New French blade, 9 1/8″	40.00	Spoon, sugar, shell-shaped bowl, 6″	45.00
Knife, HH, New French blade, 9 5/8″	55.00	Spoon, teaspoon, 5 3/4″	25.00
Knife, HH, Old French blade, 8 5/8″	40.00	Sugar, open, mini, 3 3/4″	200.00
Knife, HH, Old French blade, 9 5/8″	55.00	Sugar Tongs, 4 1/4″	60.00
Knife, steak, 8 5/8″	50.00	Teapot	2,000.00
Knife, steak, 9 1/8″	50.00	Tray, bread, SP, 12 1/2″	35.00
Ladle, cream sauce, 5 3/8″	50.00		
Ladle, gravy, 6 5/8″	110.00		
Ladle, punch, 14″	200.00		
Ladle, punch, ST bowl, 14″	80.00		
Salad Set, two pieces, 8 7/8″	250.00		
Salad Set, two pieces, plastic bowl	80.00		
Salad Set, two pieces, oversize, 10 3/8″	300.00		
Server, macaroni, 8 7/8″	130.00	**Gorham Corporation, Chapel Bells, Sterling Silver**	
Server, pastry, ST bowl, 11 3/8″	45.00		
Serving Fork, cold meat, 6 3/8″	85.00	Butter Serving Knife, FH, 7″	$35.00
Serving Fork, cold meat, 7 1/8″	85.00	Butter Spreader, FH, 5 3/4″	22.00
Serving Fork, cold meat, 8 1/2″	100.00	Butter Spreader, HH, paddled ST blade, 6 1/8″	27.00
Serving Fork, salad, ST tines, 11 3/8″	45.00	Carving Knife, ST blade, 10 3/8″	65.00
Serving Spoon, dressing, 12 1/2″	240.00	Carving Set, two pieces, ST blade	120.00
Serving Spoon, salad, 8 7/8″	110.00	Fork, 7 1/4″	45.00
Serving Spoon, tablespoon, 8 1/2″	85.00	Fork, 8″	55.00
Serving Spoon, tablespoon, pierced, 8 3/8″	115.00	Fork, cocktail, 5 3/8″	25.00
Serving Spoon, vegetable, 9 5/8″	160.00	Fork, ice cream, 5 5/8″	45.00
Serving Spoon, vegetable, round bowl, 10 1/2″	600.00	Fork, pickle, short handle, 5 3/4″	32.00
		Fork, salad, 6 1/2″	40.00
Serving Spoon, vegetable, round bowl, 12 5/8″	700.00	Knife, HH, modern blade, 8 7/8″	32.00
Spoon, bonbon, 4 5/8″	45.00	Knife, HH, modern blade, 9 1/2″	45.00
Spoon, bouillon, round bowl, 5″	40.00	Knife, HH, New French blade, 8 7/8″	32.00
Spoon, chocolate muddler, long handle, 8 3/8″	70.00	Knife, HH, New French blade, 9 1/2″	45.00
		Ladle, cream sauce, 5 1/4″	50.00
Spoon, cream soup, round bowl, 6 1/4″	50.00	Ladle, gravy, 5 3/4″	80.00
Spoon, fruit, 5 3/4″	40.00	Server, cheese, ST blade, 6 5/8″	50.00
Spoon, grapefruit, round bowl, 6 5/8″	60.00	Server, pie, ST blade, 10″	60.00
Spoon, iced tea, 7 1/2″	40.00	Serving Fork, cold meat, 7 3/8″	70.00
Spoon, olive, 5 7/8″	90.00	Serving Spoon, casserole, 9″	100.00
		Serving Spoon, tablespoon, 8 1/2″	80.00

Serving Spoon, tablespoon,
    pierced, 8 ½″   90.00
Spoon, bonbon, 4 ⅝″   40.00
Spoon, cream soup, round bowl, 6 ¼″   35.00
Spoon, demitasse, 4 ¼″   20.00
Spoon, iced tea, 7 ½″   40.00
Spoon, jelly, 6 ⅛″   35.00
Spoon, soup, oval bowl, 6 ¾″   45.00
Spoon, sugar, 6″   35.00
Spoon, teaspoon, 6″   25.00
Sugar Tongs, 4″   60.00

Gorham Corporation, Chateau Rose, Sterling Silver

Butter Serving Knife, FH, 7 ⅛″ $37.00
Butter Spreader, FH, 5 ¾″   20.00
Butter Spreader, HH,
    paddled ST blade, 6 ⅛″   27.00
Fork, 7 ¼″   40.00
Fork, 7 ⅞″   55.00
Fork, cocktail, 5 ⅝″   30.00
Fork, salad   35.00
Knife, HH, modern blade, 9 ⅝″   50.00
Knife, HH, New French blade, 9″   40.00
Knife, HH, New French blade, 9 ½″   50.00
Ladle, gravy, 6″   85.00
Serving Fork, cold meat, 7 ⅜″   70.00
Serving Spoon, tablespoon, 8 ½″   70.00
Spoon, cream soup, round bowl, 6 ¼″   35.00
Spoon, demitasse, 4 ¼″   25.00
Spoon, iced tea, 7 ½″   35.00
Spoon, jelly, 6 ¼″   40.00
Spoon, soup, oval bowl, 6 ¾″   40.00
Spoon, sugar, 6″   40.00
Spoon, teaspoon, 6″   22.00

Gorham Corporation, Decor, Sterling Silver

Butter Spreader, HH,
    modern ST blade, 6 ¼″ $40.00
Fork, 7 ¼″   80.00
Fork, salad, 6 ½″   80.00
Knife, HH, modern blade, 9″   60.00
Knife, HH, modern blade, 9 ⅝″   75.00
Serving Fork, cold meat, 8 ⅛″   155.00
Serving Spoon, tablespoon, 8 ½″   140.00
Spoon, cream soup, round bowl, 6 ½″   80.00
Spoon, demitasse, 4 ⅜″   45.00
Spoon, fruit, 5 ⅞″   70.00
Spoon, iced tea, 7 ⅝″   75.00
Spoon, sugar, shell shaped bowl, 6″   75.00
Spoon, teaspoon, 6″   45.00

Gorham Corporation, English Gadroon, Sterling Silver

Butter Spreader, HH,
    modern ST blade, 6 ¼″ $25.00
Carving Set, two pieces, ST blade   130.00
Fork, 7 ⅛″   50.00
Fork, 7 ⅝″   65.00
Fork, cocktail, 5 ⅜″   27.00
Fork, ice cream, 5 ½″   55.00
Fork, lemon, 4 ⅜″   35.00
Fork, salad, 6 ¼″   50.00
Knife, HH, modern blade, 8 ⅞″   35.00
Knife, HH, New French blade, 8 ⅞″   35.00
Knife, HH, New French blade, 9 ⅝″   50.00

Ladle, gravy, 6 1/4″	90.00	Spoon, iced tea, 7 1/2″	45.00
Server, cheese, ST blade, 6 5/8″	50.00	Spoon, jelly, 5 1/2″	30.00
Serving Fork, cold meat, 8″	95.00	Spoon, relish, 5 3/4″	40.00
Serving Spoon, tablespoon, 8 1/2″	80.00	Spoon, sugar, 5 7/8″	40.00
Spoon, bonbon, 4 3/4″	45.00	Spoon, teaspoon, 5 3/4″	20.00
Spoon, cream soup, round bowl, 6 1/4″	40.00	Spoon, teaspoon, 5 o'clock, 5 3/8″	20.00
Spoon, iced tea, 7 1/2″	40.00	Sugar Tongs, 4 1/4″	60.00
Spoon, sugar, shell-shaped bowl, 6 1/4″	45.00		
Spoon, teaspoon, 5 7/8″	27.00		
Spoon, teaspoon, 5 o'clock, 5 5/8″	25.00		

Gorham Corporation, Etruscan, Sterling Silver

**Gorham Corporation, Fairfax,
Sterling Silver, Durgin backstamp**
(Introduced in 1910)

Butter Serving Knife, FH, 7″	$40.00	Butter Serving Knife, HH, 6 3/4″	$40.00
Butter Spreader, FH, 5 3/4″	25.00	Butter Spreader, FH, 5 1/2″	30.00
Butter Spreader, HH, modern ST blade, 6 1/4″	25.00	Butter Spreader, HH, modern ST blade, 6 1/8″	30.00
Carving Fork, ST tines, 8 3/4″	50.00	Carving Fork, ST tines, 8 3/4″	65.00
Fork, 7″	45.00	Carving Knife, ST blade, 9 7/8″	65.00
Fork, 7 5/8″	60.00	Carving Set, two pieces, ST blade	130.00
Fork, cocktail, 5 3/8″	30.00	Creamer	700.00
Fork, lemon, 4 7/8″	30.00	Fork, 7 1/4″	45.00
Fork, pastry, 6″	50.00	Fork, 7 1/2″	65.00
Fork, pickle, short handle, 5 5/8″	30.00	Fork, fruit, ST tines, 7″	35.00
Knife, HH, modern blade, 8 1/2″	40.00	Fork, salad, 6 1/4″	45.00
Knife, HH, Old French blade, 8 1/2″	40.00	Knife, HH, Old French blade, 8 5/8″	35.00
Ladle, gravy, 7″	90.00	Knife, HH, Old French blade, 9 5/8″	50.00
Server, cheese, SP blade, 6 1/8″	50.00	Knife, steak, 8 1/4″	50.00
Server, pie, SP blade, 10″	60.00	Nut Dish, 3 3/8″	75.00
Serving Fork, cold meat, 6 1/4″	80.00	Serving Fork, cold meat, 8 5/8″	110.00
Serving Fork, cold meat, 8 5/8″	90.00	Serving Spoon, salad, ST bowl, 11 1/4″	45.00
Serving Spoon, tablespoon, 8 3/8″	75.00	Spoon, bouillon, round bowl, 5 5/8″	40.00
Spoon, baby, straight handle, 4 5/8″	40.00	Spoon, cream soup, round bowl, 6 1/4″	45.00
Spoon, bouillon, round bowl, 5 1/4″	35.00	Spoon, infant feeding, 5 5/8″	40.00
Spoon, cream soup, round bowl, 6 1/4″	40.00	Spoon, soup, oval bowl, 7 1/8″	50.00
Spoon, fruit, 5 7/8″	35.00	Spoon, sugar, 5 7/8″	40.00
Spoon, grapefruit, round bowl, 6 5/8″	45.00	Spoon, teaspoon, 5 3/4″	25.00

Gorham Corporation, Fairfax, Sterling Silver, Gorham backstamp

Butter Serving Knife, FH, 6 ⅞″	$32.00
Butter Spreader, FH, 5 ⅛″	25.00
Butter Spreader, FH, 5 ½″	25.00
Carving Fork, ST tines, 9″	50.00
Carving Knife, ST blade, 10″	50.00
Carving Set, two pieces, ST blade	100.00
Creamer	850.00
Fork, 7 ¼″	45.00
Fork, 7 ⅞″	60.00
Fork, lemon, 5″	25.00
Fork, salad, 6 ½″	32.00
Knife, HH, Old French blade, 8 ⅝″	32.00
Ladle, cream sauce, 5 ⅛″	40.00
Ladle, gravy, 5 ⅞″	75.00
Salad Set, two pieces	190.00
Server, tomato, SP blade, 8 ¾″	80.00
Serving Fork, cold meat, 7 ½″	70.00
Serving Fork, cold meat, 8 ⅝″	80.00
Serving Spoon, casserole, 7 ¼″	95.00
Serving Spoon, casserole, 9″	95.00
Serving Spoon, salad, 8 ⅝″	95.00
Serving Spoon, tablespoon, 8 ½″	65.00
Spoon, bouillon, round bowl, 5 ¼″	30.00
Spoon, cream soup, round bowl, 5 ⅝″	35.00
Spoon, grapefruit, round bowl, 6 ⅞″	35.00
Spoon, iced tea, 7 ½″	35.00
Spoon, soup, oval bowl, 7 ⅛″	35.00
Spoon, sugar, 5 ⅞″	35.00
Spoon, teaspoon, 5 ¾″	22.00
Spoon, teaspoon, 5 o'clock, 5″	20.00
Sugar Tongs, 3 ½″	55.00
Sugar Tongs, 4 ½″	55.00

Gorham Corporation, French Scroll, Sterling Silver

Butter Serving Knife, FH, 7″	$37.00
Fork, 7 ¼″	45.00
Fork, 8″	60.00
Fork, cocktail, 5 ¾″	25.00
Fork, salad, 6 ½″	40.00
Knife, HH, modern blade, 8 ⅞″	32.00
Knife, HH, modern blade, 9 ⅝″	45.00
Ladle, gravy, 6 ⅛″	80.00
Serving Spoon, tablespoon, 8 ⅜″	85.00
Spoon, cream soup, round bowl, 6 ⅜″	37.00
Spoon, fruit, 5 ⅞″	35.00
Spoon, jelly, 6 ¼″	32.00
Spoon, sugar, 6″	40.00
Spoon, teaspoon, 5 ⅞″	25.00

Gorham Corporation, Greenbrier, Sterling Silver
(Introduced in 1938)

Butter Spreader, FH, 5 ⅞″	$22.00
Butter Spreader, HH, modern ST blade, 6 ¼″	25.00
Butter Spreader, HH, paddled ST blade, 6 ⅛″	22.00
Carving Fork, ST tines, 8 ⅝″	55.00
Carving Fork, ST tines, 9″	55.00
Carving Set, two pieces, ST blade	110.00
Fork, 7 ⅜″	45.00
Fork, 8″	60.00
Fork, baby, 4 ⅜″	37.00
Fork, ice cream, 5 ½″	45.00

Fork, pickle, short handle, 5 7/8″	30.00
Fork, salad, 6 3/4″	35.00
Knife, HH, modern blade, 8 7/8″	35.00
Knife, HH, modern blade, 9 5/8″	45.00
Knife, HH, New French blade, 8 7/8″	35.00
Knife, HH, New French blade, 9 5/8″	45.00
Ladle, cream sauce, 5 1/4″	45.00
Ladle, gravy, 6 1/4″	80.00
Server, pie, ST blade, 10″	60.00
Server, pie, ST blade, 10 1/4″	60.00
Serving Fork, cold meat, 8 1/8″	80.00
Serving Spoon, tablespoon, 8 1/2″	70.00
Spoon, baby, straight handle, 4 1/2″	37.00
Spoon, cream soup, round bowl, 6 3/8″	30.00
Spoon, iced tea, 7 5/8″	40.00
Spoon, jelly, 6 1/4″	35.00
Spoon, sugar, 6″	40.00
Spoon, teaspoon, 5 7/8″	25.00
Spoon, teaspoon, 5 o'clock, 5 5/8″	22.00

Gorham Corporation, Hispana/Sovereign, Sterling Silver
(Introduced in 1967)

Butter Serving Knife, HH, 7 3/8″	$50.00
Fork, 7 1/2″	70.00
Fork, pickle, short handle, 5 7/8″	40.00
Fork, salad, 6 7/8″	60.00
Knife, cheese, ST blade, 7 3/4″	55.00
Knife, HH, modern blade, 9″	50.00
Salad Set, wooden bowl	50.00
Server, pie/cake, ST blade, 11″	80.00
Serving Fork, cold meat, 8 1/2″	115.00
Serving Spoon, tablespoon, 8 1/2″	100.00
Spoon, bonbon, 4 7/8″	60.00
Spoon, sugar, 6 1/8″	45.00
Spoon, teaspoon, 6″	35.00

Gorham Corporation, King Edward, Sterling Silver
(Introduced in 1936)

Butter Serving Knife, HH, 6 1/2″	$40.00
Butter Spreader, FH, 5 3/4″	30.00
Butter Spreader, HH, modern ST blade, 6 1/4″	25.00
Carving Fork, ST tines, 8 5/8″	65.00
Carving Set, two pieces, ST blade	130.00
Fork, 7 1/8″	40.00
Fork, 7 5/8″	60.00
Fork, ice cream, 5 1/2″	50.00
Fork, lemon, 4 3/8″	30.00
Fork, salad, 6 1/4″	45.00
Knife, HH, modern blade, 9″	35.00
Knife, HH, modern blade, 9 3/4″	45.00
Knife, HH, New French blade, 8 7/8″	35.00

Photo courtesy of Lenox, Inc.

Knife, HH, New French blade, 9 5/8″	45.00
Knife, steak, 8 1/2″	50.00
Ladle, gravy, ST bowl, 6 3/8″	90.00
Server, cheese, ST blade, 6 1/2″	50.00
Serving Fork, cold meat, ST blade, 8 1/8″	90.00
Serving Spoon, tablespoon, 8 3/8″	90.00
Spoon, bonbon, 4 3/4″	45.00
Spoon, cream soup, round bowl, 6 1/4″	45.00
Spoon, demitasse, 4 1/8″	22.00
Spoon, iced tea, 7 1/2″	40.00
Spoon, jelly, 6 1/8″	35.00
Spoon, soup, oval bowl, 6 3/4″	45.00
Spoon, sugar, 5 3/4″	40.00
Spoon, teaspoon, 6″	22.00

Gorham Corporation, Lancaster, Sterling Silver

Fork, 7″	$40.00
Fork, 7 5/8″	60.00
Fork, chipped beef, 5 3/4″	65.00
Fork, cocktail, 5 1/2″	30.00
Fork, lettuce, 9 1/4″	100.00
Fork, salad	45.00
Fork, strawberry, 4 5/8″	40.00
Knife	45.00
Ladle, soup, 10 1/8″	300.00
Serving Fork, cold meat, 7 1/8″	80.00
Serving Spoon, tablespoon, 8 1/2″	70.00
Spoon, bouillon, round bowl, 5 1/8″	40.00
Spoon, demitasse, 3 7/8″	25.00
Spoon, grapefruit, round bowl, 6 7/8″	50.00
Spoon, soup, oval bowl, 7″	35.00
Spoon, sugar, shell-shaped bowl, 6″	40.00
Spoon, teaspoon	25.00
Spoon, teaspoon, 5 o'clock, 5 1/4″	20.00
Sugar Tongs, 4 1/8″	60.00

Gorham Corporation, La Scala, Sterling Silver
(Introduced in 1964)

Butter Serving Knife, HH, 7″	$45.00
Butter Spreader, HH, modern ST blade, 6 1/2″	30.00
Fork, 7 1/2″	50.00
Fork, 8″	70.00
Fork, cocktail, 5 3/4″	35.00
Fork, salad, 6 3/8″	50.00
Knife, HH, modern blade, 9 1/8″	40.00
Knife, HH, modern blade, 9 3/4″	50.00
Knife, wedding cake, ST blade, 13 1/4″	90.00
Serving Spoon, tablespoon, 8 7/8″	100.00
Spoon, bonbon, 5 1/8″	50.00
Spoon, demitasse, 4 3/8″	30.00
Spoon, iced tea, 7 5/8″	45.00
Spoon, soup, oval bowl, 6 3/4″	50.00
Spoon, sugar, 6 3/8″	45.00
Spoon, teaspoon, 6 1/4″	30.00

Gorham Corporation, Lily of the Valley, Sterling Silver

Butter Serving Knife, FH, 7 1/8″	$40.00
Butter Serving Knife, HH, 6 3/4″	40.00
Butter Spreader, FH, 5 3/4″	30.00
Butter Spreader, HH, modern ST blade, 6 3/8″	30.00
Butter Spreader, HH, paddled ST blade, 6 1/8″	30.00

FORMS AVAILABLE IN GORHAM'S LANCASTER PATTERN

Forks

Asparagus
Beef
Beef, Small
Berry
Cheese
Cold Meat, Extra
Cold Meat, Large
Cold Meat, Small
Dessert
Fish, Large
Fish, Small
Ice Cream, Large
Ice Cream, Small
Lemon
Lettuce
Lettuce Salad
Olive
Olive, Long
Oyster
Pastry
Pickle
Pie
Ramekin
Relish
Salad, Individual, Large
Salad, Individual, Small
Salad, Large
Salad, Small
Sardine
Serving
Table
Tea
Toast
Vegetable

Knives

Butter
Butter Spreader
Cake, Flat
Cheese
Crumb, Flat
Fish, Individual
Fish, Large
Fish, Small
Ice Cream Slicer, Large,
    Hollow Handle
Ice Cream Slicer, Small,
    Flat
Ice Cream Slicer, Steel
    Blade
Jelly, Large
Jelly, Small
Macaroni
Pickle
Pie
Waffle

Spoons

Berry, Large
Berry, Small
Bonbon
Bouillon
Chocolate
Coffee
Confection
Cracker
Dessert
Egg
Grapefruit
Gravy
Horseradish
Ice

Ice Cream
Iced Tea
Jelly
Lettuce Salad
Mustard
Nut
Olive
Olive, Long
Orange
Pap
Pea
Preserve
Relish
Salad, Large
Salad, Small
Salt, Individual
Salt, Master
Serving
Sorbet
Soup
Sugar
Table
Tea

Cutlery

Bird Forks
Bird Knives
Bone Holder
Dessert Knives, Hollow
    Handle
Dessert Knives, Hollow
    Handle, Unplated Blades
Duck Shears
Fruit, Hollow Handle
Game Carver
Game Fork
Joint Fork, Large

Knife Sharpener
Meat Carver
Meat Fork
Meat Steel
Medium Knives, Hollow
  Handle
Medium Knives, Hollow
  Handle, Unplated
  Blades
Orange, Hollow Handle
Steak Carver
Steak Fork
Steak Steel
Tea Knives, Hollow
  Handle

Ladles and Sifters

Bouillon Ladle
Cream Ladle, Large

Cream Ladle, Small
Gravy Ladle
Mayonnaise Ladle
Punch Ladle
Soup Ladle, Large
Soup Ladle, Small
Sugar Sifter, Large
Sugar Sifter, Small
Sugar Sifter, Tête-à-Tête

Servers

Asparagus
Cake
Cheese
Cucumber
Entree
Fried Oyster
Pie, Hollow Handle
Saratoga Chips

Sliced Tomato, Large
Sliced Tomato, Small

Miscellaneous

Asparagus Tongs
Asparagus Tongs,
  Individual
Butter Pick
Cheese Scoop, Large
Cheese Scoop, Small
Chocolate Muddler
Food Pusher
Ice Tongs
Lobster Pick
Nut Crack
Nut Picks
Sandwich Tongs
Sugar Tongs, Large
Sugar Tongs, Small

Butter Spreader, HH, paddled ST blade, 6 1/2″	30.00	
Carving Fork, ST tines, 9″	65.00	
Fork, 7 1/4″	50.00	
Fork, 8″	70.00	
Fork, cocktail, 5 5/8″	32.00	
Fork, ice cream, 5 1/2″	60.00	
Fork, salad, 6 1/2″	50.00	
Knife, HH, modern blade, 9″	40.00	
Knife, HH, modern blade, 9 5/8″	50.00	
Knife, steak, 8 3/4″	55.00	
Ladle, cream sauce, 5 3/8″	50.00	
Ladle, gravy, 6 3/8″	90.00	
Salad Set, two pieces	240.00	
Server, cheese, ST blade, 6 5/8″	45.00	
Server, pastry, ST bowl, 10″	60.00	
Spoon, bonbon, 4 7/8″	45.00	
Spoon, cream soup, round bowl, 6 3/8″	40.00	
Spoon, fruit, 5 7/8″	40.00	

Spoon, jelly, 6 1/4″	35.00
Spoon, soup, oval bowl, 7″	45.00
Spoon, sugar, 6″	40.00
Spoon, teaspoon, 5 7/8″	25.00

Gorham Corporation, Lyric, Sterling Silver
(Introduced in 1940)

Butter Spreader, FH, 5 3/4″	$25.00
Butter Spreader, HH, modern ST blade, 6 1/4″	25.00
Carving Set, two pieces, ST blade	110.00
Carving Set, three pieces, ST blade	175.00

Fork, 7 3/8″	40.00	Fork, 7 1/4″	55.00
Fork, 8″	55.00	Fork, 7 5/8″	65.00
Fork, baby, 4 3/8″	32.00	Fork, cocktail, 5 3/4″	35.00
Fork, cocktail, 5 5/8″	27.00	Fork, ice cream, 5 1/2″	55.00
Fork, ice cream, 5 5/8″	45.00	Fork, ice cream, 5 5/8″	55.00
Fork, lemon, 4 7/8″	30.00	Fork, lemon, 4 1/2″	32.00
Fork, pickle, short handle, 5 3/4″	32.00	Fork, pickle, short handle, 5 3/4″	35.00
Fork, salad, 6 1/2″	32.00	Fork, salad, 6 3/4″	55.00
Knife, HH, modern blade, 9 1/2″	50.00	Knife, cheese, ST blade, 7 1/8″	55.00
Knife, HH, New French blade, 8 7/8″	40.00	Knife, HH, modern blade, 8 7/8″	40.00
Knife, steak, 8 7/8″	50.00	Knife, HH, modern blade, 9 1/8″	40.00
Ladle, cream sauce, 5″	45.00	Knife, HH, modern blade, 9 5/8″	50.00
Ladle, gravy, 6 1/4″	80.00	Knife, HH, New French blade, 8 7/8″	40.00
Salad Set, two pieces	220.00	Knife, HH, New French blade, 9 1/2″	50.00
Server, cheese, ST blade, 6 5/8″	45.00	Ladle, gravy, 6 1/2″	100.00
Server, pie, ST blade, 10 1/8″	60.00	Salad Set, two pieces, wooden bowl	120.00
Serving Fork, cold meat, 8 1/8″	80.00	Server, cheese, ST blade, 6 5/8″	55.00
Serving Spoon, tablespoon, 8 1/2″	80.00	Server, pie/cake, ST blade, 10 3/4″	70.00
Spoon, baby, straight handle, 4 1/2″	32.00	Serving Fork, cold meat, 8 1/8″	100.00
Spoon, bonbon, 4 3/4″	45.00	Serving Spoon, tablespoon, 8 1/2″	90.00
Spoon, cream soup, round bowl, 6 1/4″	32.00	Spoon, bonbon, 4 7/8″	50.00
Spoon, demitasse, 4 3/8″	22.00	Spoon, cream soup, round bowl, 6 1/4″	55.00
Spoon, iced tea, 7 5/8″	35.00	Spoon, demitasse, 4 3/8″	30.00
Spoon, jelly, 6 1/4″	32.00	Spoon, fruit, 5 7/8″	50.00
Spoon, sugar, 6″	35.00	Spoon, iced tea, 7 5/8″	45.00
Spoon, teaspoon, 6″	25.00	Spoon, jelly, 6 1/8″	40.00
		Spoon, soup, oval bowl, 6 7/8″	55.00
		Spoon, sugar, 6 1/8″	45.00
		Spoon, teaspoon, 6″	30.00
		Sugar Tongs, 3 3/4″	70.00
		Sugar Tongs, 4″	70.00

Gorham Corporation, Melrose, Sterling Silver
(Introduced in 1948)

Butter Serving Knife, FH, 7″	$45.00
Butter Serving Knife, HH, 6 3/4″	45.00
Butter Spreader, FH, 5 3/4″	32.00
Butter Spreader, HH, modern ST blade, 6 1/4″	35.00
Butter Spreader, HH, paddled ST blade, 6 1/8″	35.00

Gorham Corporation, Newport Scroll, Sterling Silver

Butter Serving Knife, HH, 7″	$45.00
Cheese Cleaver, ST blade, 6 5/8″	40.00

Photo courtesy of Lenox, Inc.

Gorham Corporation, Old English Tipt, Sterling Silver
(Introduced in 1870)

Butter Serving Knife, HH, 6 ⁵⁄₈″	$45.00
Butter Spreader, HH, modern ST blade, 6 ¼″	30.00
Carving Set, two pieces, ST blade	160.00
Fork, 7 ¹⁄₈″	60.00
Fork, 7 ¹⁄₂″	75.00
Fork, lemon, 4 ¹⁄₂″	35.00
Fork, salad	50.00
Knife, HH, modern blade, 8 ³⁄₄″	40.00
Knife, HH, modern blade, 9 ¹⁄₂″	55.00
Knife, HH, New French blade, 8 ³⁄₄″	45.00
Serving Spoon, tablespoon, 9 ¼″	95.00
Spoon, bouillon, round bowl, 5 ³⁄₄″	55.00
Spoon, cream soup, round bowl, 6 ¹⁄₈″	65.00
Spoon, demitasse, 4 ¼″	30.00
Spoon, iced tea, 7 ¹⁄₂″	40.00
Spoon, soup, oval bowl, 6 ³⁄₄″	65.00
Spoon, sugar, 6 ¼″	45.00
Spoon, teaspoon, 6″	32.00
Sugar Tongs, 5″	75.00

Fork, 7 ⁵⁄₈″	65.00
Fork, cocktail, 5 ⁷⁄₈″	37.00
Fork, pickle, short handle, 5 ⁷⁄₈″	37.00
Fork, salad, 6 ³⁄₄″	50.00
Knife, HH, modern blade, 9 ¹⁄₈″	40.00
Knife, steak, 9 ¹⁄₂″	50.00
Ladle, soup, ST bowl, 11 ³⁄₄″	80.00
Salad Set, two pieces, ST bowl	90.00
Server, lasagna, ST blade, 12″	40.00
Server, pasta, ST bowl, 11 ³⁄₈″	40.00
Server, pastry, ST bowl, 11 ³⁄₈″	40.00
Server, pie/cake, ST blade, 10 ⁷⁄₈″	70.00
Serving Spoon, tablespoon, 8 ¹⁄₂″	95.00
Spoon, soup, oval bowl, 6 ³⁄₄″	50.00
Spoon, sugar, 6″	45.00
Spoon, teaspoon	30.00

Gorham Corporation, Old French, Sterling Silver

Butter Spreader, FH, 5 ³⁄₄″	$30.00
Butter Spreader, FH, 6 ¼″	30.00
Butter Spreader, HH, modern ST blade, 6 ¼″	32.00

Carving Fork, ST tines, 9″	75.00
Fork, 7 1/4″	55.00
Fork, 7 1/2″	70.00
Fork, 7 3/4″	70.00
Fork, cocktail, 5 1/4″	60.00
Fork, fish, ST tines, 7 7/8″	40.00
Fork, ice cream 5 1/4″	60.00
Fork, salad, 6″	50.00
Knife, cheese, ST blade, 7″	50.00
Knife, fruit, ST blade, 7″	35.00
Knife, HH, blunt blade, 8 1/2″	40.00
Knife, HH, blunt blade, 9 3/4″	55.00
Knife, HH, modern blade, 9″	40.00
Knife, HH, New French blade, 8 5/8″	40.00
Knife, HH, Old French blade, 8 1/2″	40.00
Knife, HH, Old French blade, 9 7/8″	55.00
Knife, steak, 8 1/2″	50.00
Ladle, cream sauce, 5 1/4″	50.00
Server, cheese, SP blade, 6 1/2″	60.00
Server, pie, ST blade, 9 3/8″	65.00
Server, pie/cake, ST blade, 10 1/2″	70.00
Serving Fork, cold meat, 7 1/4″	90.00
Serving Spoon, tablespoon, 8 1/2″	90.00
Spoon, bouillon, round bowl, 5 1/4″	45.00
Spoon, cream soup, round bowl, 6 3/8″	60.00
Spoon, demitasse, 4 1/8″	25.00
Spoon, fruit, 5 5/8″	40.00
Spoon, grapefruit, round bowl, 6 7/8″	60.00
Spoon, iced tea, 7 1/2″	45.00
Spoon, olive, long handle, 8 1/4″	170.00
Spoon, soup, oval bowl, 7 1/2″	65.00
Spoon, sugar, 5 7/8″	45.00
Spoon, teaspoon	30.00
Spoon, teaspoon, 5 o'clock, 5 1/2″	25.00
Spoon, teaspoon, 5 o'clock, 5 3/4″	25.00
Sugar Tongs, 4″	70.00

Gorham Corporation, Rondo, Sterling Silver
(Introduced in 1951)

Butter Serving Knife, FH, 6 7/8″	$40.00
Butter Spreader, FH, 5 7/8″	32.00
Butter Spreader, HH, modern ST blade, 6 1/4″	32.00
Butter Spreader, HH, paddled ST blade, 6 1/4″	32.00
Carving Set, two pieces, ST blade	150.00
Fork, 7 1/4″	55.00
Fork, 7 7/8″	75.00
Fork, ice cream, 5 1/2″	60.00
Fork, lemon, 4 1/2″	40.00
Fork, pickle, short handle, 5 7/8″	40.00
Knife, HH, modern blade, 9″	45.00
Knife, HH, modern blade, 9 5/8″	55.00
Ladle, cream sauce, 5 3/8″	50.00
Salt and Pepper Shakers, pair 4 3/8″	130.00
Server, cheese, ST blade, 6 3/4″	55.00
Server, pastry, ST bowl, 9 3/4″	70.00
Serving Spoon, tablespoon, 8 3/8″	100.00
Spoon, bonbon, 4 7/8″	50.00
Spoon, cream soup, round bowl, 6 1/2″	55.00
Spoon, iced tea, 7 1/2″	45.00
Spoon, jelly, 6 1/4″	40.00
Spoon, sugar, shell-shaped bowl, 6 1/8″	45.00
Spoon, teaspoon, 5 7/8″	30.00
Sugar Tongs, 3 3/4″	75.00

Gorham Corporation, Rose Tiara, Sterling Silver
(Introduced in 1962)

Butter Serving Knife, HH, 7″	$40.00
Butter Spreader, HH, modern ST blade, 6 1/2″	30.00
Carving Set, two pieces, large, ST blade	150.00
Carving Set, two pieces, small, ST blade	160.00
Fork, 7 1/2″	65.00
Fork, cocktail, 5 3/4″	30.00
Fork, salad, 6 7/8″	50.00
Knife, HH, modern blade, 9″	40.00
Ladle, gravy, 6 3/4″	90.00
Serving Fork, cold meat, 8 3/4″	90.00
Spoon, bonbon, 5″	45.00
Spoon, iced tea, 7 5/8″	40.00
Spoon, sugar, shell-shaped bowl, 6 1/4″	40.00
Spoon, teaspoon, 6″	30.00

Gorham Corporation, Sea Rose, Sterling Silver
(Introduced in 1958)

Butter Serving Knife, HH, 7″	$40.00
Butter Spreader, HH, modern ST blade, 6 1/2″	25.00
Fork, 7 1/2″	60.00
Fork, ice cream, 5 3/4″	50.00

Fork, pickle, short handle, 5 7/8″	30.00
Fork, salad	50.00
Gravy Boat, attached underplate, 6 1/8″	375.00
Knife, cheese, ST blade, 7 3/8″	45.00
Knife, HH, modern blade, 9 1/4″	35.00
Ladle, cream sauce, 5 1/4″	50.00
Ladle, gravy, 6 5/8″	85.00
Ladle, gravy, 7″	85.00
Server, pie/cake, ST blade, 10 5/8″	70.00
Serving Fork, salad, 9 3/8″	120.00
Serving Spoon, tablespoon, 8 5/8″	80.00
Spoon, demitasse, 4 3/8″	25.00
Spoon, jelly, 6 3/8″	35.00
Spoon, sugar, 6 1/4″	40.00
Spoon, teaspoon, 6″	25.00

Gorham Corporation, Southern Charm, Sterling Silver

Butter Serving Knife, FH, 7″	$35.00
Butter Spreader, FH, 5 3/4″	20.00
Butter Spreader, HH, paddled ST blade, 6 1/4″	22.00
Fork, 7 1/4″	40.00
Fork, 8″	60.00
Fork, cocktail, 5 5/8″	30.00
Fork, salad, 6 1/2″	35.00
Knife, HH, modern blade, 8 7/8″	35.00
Knife, HH, modern blade, 9 5/8″	45.00
Knife, HH, New French blade, 8 7/8″	35.00
Knife, HH, New French blade, 9 5/8″	45.00
Ladle, cream sauce, 5 1/4″	50.00
Ladle, gravy, 5 7/8″	80.00

Serving Fork, cold meat, 7 1/4″	70.00	Server, pie/cake, ST blade, 10 1/2″	50.00
Serving Spoon, tablespoon, 8 3/8″	70.00	Server, tomato, 7 1/2″	130.00
Serving Spoon, tablespoon, pierced, 8 3/8″	85.00	Serving Fork, cold meat, 8 1/2″	115.00
Spoon, cream soup, round bowl, 6 1/4″	32.00	Serving Spoon, casserole, shell-shaped bowl, 8 3/4″	150.00
Spoon, demitasse, 4 1/4″	20.00	Serving Spoon, casserole, 8 7/8″	150.00
Spoon, fruit, 6″	35.00	Serving Spoon, tablespoon, 8 1/2″	85.00
Spoon, iced tea, 7 1/2″	35.00	Serving Spoon, tablespoon, pierced, 8 1/2″	115.00
Spoon, jelly, 6 1/4″	32.00	Spoon, bonbon, 4 3/8″	45.00
Spoon, soup, oval bowl, 6 3/4″	35.00	Spoon, bouillon, round bowl, 5″	40.00
Spoon, sugar, 6″	40.00	Spoon, cream soup, round bowl, 6 1/4″	50.00
Spoon, teaspoon, 6″	25.00	Spoon, demitasse, 4″	30.00
		Spoon, iced tea, 7 5/8″	45.00
		Spoon, sugar, 6″	45.00
		Spoon, teaspoon, 5 7/8″	25.00
		Sugar Tongs, 4″	60.00
		Tea Set, three pieces	2,700.00

Gorham Corporation, Strasbourg, Sterling Silver
(Introduced in 1897)

Butter Serving Knife, HH, 6 5/8″	$40.00
Butter Spreader, HH, modern ST blade, 6 1/4″	30.00
Candelabra, five-light, 13 1/4″	1,300.00
Candlestick, 9″	230.00
Fork, 7″	45.00
Fork, 7 5/8″	60.00
Fork, cocktail, 5 5/8″	30.00
Fork, ice cream, 5 1/2″	55.00
Fork, lemon, 4 3/8″	30.00
Fork, salad, 6 3/8″	50.00
Knife, HH, blunt blade, 8 1/2″	40.00
Knife, HH, modern blade, 9″	40.00
Knife, HH, modern blade, 9 3/4″	50.00
Knife, steak, 8 5/8″	50.00
Knife, steak, 9 1/4″	50.00
Ladle, gravy, 6 5/8″	115.00
Ladle, gravy, 7″	115.00
Ladle, punch, ST bowl, 13 3/4″	70.00
Salt and Pepper Shakers, pair, 4 1/2″	250.00

Gorham Corporation, Versailles, Sterling Silver

Carving Set, two pieces, ST blade	$215.00
Fork, 6 3/4″	80.00
Fork, fish, 6 5/8″	90.00
Fork, ice cream 5 1/2″	85.00
Fork, salad	90.00
Knife	90.00
Server, pie, ST blade, 10″	130.00
Serving Spoon, tablespoon, 8 1/2″	130.00
Spoon, bouillon, round bowl, 5″	70.00
Spoon, cream soup, round bowl, 6 3/8″	90.00
Spoon, cream soup, round bowl, 6 3/4″	90.00
Spoon, demitasse, 4 1/4″	45.00
Spoon, fruit, 5 7/8″	80.00
Spoon, teaspoon	50.00
Spoon, teaspoon, 5 o'clock, 5″	35.00

STAINLESS

Gorham Corporation, Calais, Stainless

Butter Serving Knife, HH, 7″	$12.00
Fork, 8″	10.00
Fork, salad, 7″	10.00
Knife, HH, modern blade, 9 1/4″	15.00
Ladle, gravy, 7″	17.00
Ladle, gravy, 7 1/4″	17.00
Serving Fork, cold meat, 8 3/4″	17.00
Serving Spoon, tablespoon, 8 3/4″	15.00
Serving Spoon, tablespoon, pierced, 8 3/4″	15.00
Spoon, soup, oval bowl, 7″	10.00
Spoon, sugar, 6 1/8″	10.00
Spoon, teaspoon, 6 1/4″	7.00

Photo courtesy of Lenox, Inc.

Gorham Corporation, Colonial Tipt, Stainless

Butter Serving Knife, HH, 7″	$12.00
Fork, 8 1/8″	10.00
Fork, salad	10.00
Knife, pistol grip, modern blade, 9 1/4″	15.00
Ladle, gravy, 7″	17.00
Serving Fork, cold meat, 8 5/8″	17.00
Serving Spoon, tablespoon, 8 1/2″	15.00
Serving Spoon, tablespoon, pierced, 8 1/2″	15.00
Spoon, iced tea, 7 3/4″	10.00
Spoon, soup, oval bowl, 7″	10.00
Spoon, teaspoon, 6 1/8″	7.00

Gorham Corporation, Golden Melon Bud, Stainless, gold accent

Butter Serving Knife, HH, 7″	$20.00
Fork, 8 1/8″	15.00
Fork, salad, 7 1/8″	12.00
Knife, HH, modern blade, 9 1/4″	17.00
Ladle, gravy, 7 1/4″	22.00
Serving Fork, cold meat, 8 5/8″	22.00
Serving Spoon, tablespoon, 8 5/8″	20.00
Serving Spoon, tablespoon, pierced, 8 5/8″	20.00
Spoon, iced tea, 7 5/8″	12.00
Spoon, soup, oval bowl, 7″	12.00

Spoon, sugar, 6 1/8″	15.00
Spoon, teaspoon, 6 1/8″	10.00

Spoon, soup, oval bowl, 6 7/8″	12.00
Spoon, sugar, 6 1/8″	15.00
Spoon, teaspoon, 6 1/8″	10.00

Gorham Corporation, Golden Ribbon Edge, Stainless, gold accent

Butter Serving Knife, HH, 7″	$20.00
Fork, 8 1/8″	15.00
Fork, salad, 7 1/8″	12.00
Knife, HH, modern blade, 9 1/8″	17.00
Ladle, gravy, 7 1/8″	22.00
Serving Fork, cold meat, 8 3/4″	22.00
Serving Spoon, tablespoon, 8 3/4″	20.00
Serving Spoon, tablespoon, pierced, 8 3/4″	20.00
Spoon, iced tea, 7 3/4″	12.00

Gorham Corporation, Gorham Shell, Stainless

Butter Serving Knife, HH, 7″	$12.00
Fork, 7 7/8″	10.00
Fork, salad, 7″	10.00
Knife, HH, modern blade, 7 1/2″	15.00
Ladle, gravy, 7 1/4″	17.00
Serving Fork, cold meat, 8 1/2″	17.00
Serving Fork, cold meat, 8 7/8″	17.00
Serving Spoon, tablespoon, 8 5/8″	15.00
Serving Spoon, tablespoon, pierced, 8 5/8″	15.00
Spoon, iced tea, 7 3/4″	10.00
Spoon, soup, oval bowl, 6 7/8″	10.00
Spoon, sugar, 6″	10.00
Spoon, teaspoon, 6 1/8″	7.00

THE TOP FIVE PATTERNS

TRADITIONAL—

STAINLESS

GORHAM, COLONIAL TIPT

GORHAM, GORHAM SHELL

ONEIDA, CLASSIC SHELL

ONEIDA, PAUL REVERE

TOWLE, BEADED ANTIQUE

Gorham Corporation, Hacienda, Stainless

Butter Serving Knife, FH, 7 1/8″	$25.00
Butter Spreader, FH, 6 3/8″	25.00
Fork, 7 3/8″	25.00
Fork, cocktail, 5 7/8″	25.00
Fork, salad, 6 7/8″	25.00
Knife, HH, modern blade, 8 1/2″	32.00

Ladle, gravy, 6 3/4″	37.00		Ladle, gravy, 7 1/8″	45.00
Serving Fork, cold meat, 8 3/4″	37.00		Serving Fork, cold meat, 8 3/4″	45.00
Serving Spoon, tablespoon, 8 3/4″	37.00		Serving Spoon, tablespoon, pierced, 8 5/8″	45.00
Serving Spoon, tablespoon, pierced, 8 3/4″	37.00		Spoon, soup, oval bowl, 7″	22.00
Spoon, iced tea, 7 3/4″	25.00		Spoon, sugar, 6 1/8″	22.00
Spoon, soup, oval bowl, 7 1/8″	20.00		Spoon, teaspoon	25.00
Spoon, sugar, 6″	25.00			
Spoon, teaspoon, 6 1/8″	22.00			

Gorham Corporation, Melon Bud, Stainless

			Gorham Corporation, Ribbon Edge, Stainless	
Butter Serving Knife, HH, 7″	$12.00		Butter Serving Knife, HH, 7″	$12.00
Fork, 8″	10.00		Fork, 8″	10.00
Fork, salad, 7 1/8″	10.00		Fork, salad, 7 1/8″	10.00
Knife, HH, modern blade, 9 1/4″	15.00		Knife, HH, modern blade, 9 1/8″	15.00
Ladle, gravy, 7 1/8″	17.00		Ladle, gravy, 7 1/8″	17.00
Serving Fork, cold meat, 8 3/4″	17.00		Serving Fork, cold meat, 8 3/4″	17.00
Serving Spoon, tablespoon, 8 5/8″	15.00		Serving Spoon, tablespoon, 8 5/8″	15.00
Serving Spoon, tablespoon, pierced, 8 5/8″	15.00		Serving Spoon, tablespoon, pierced, 8 5/8″	15.00
Spoon, iced tea, 7 5/8″	10.00		Spoon, soup, oval bowl, 6 7/8″	10.00
Spoon, soup, oval bowl, 7″	10.00		Spoon, sugar, 6 1/8″	10.00
Spoon, sugar, 6 1/8″	10.00		Spoon, teaspoon	7.00
Spoon, teaspoon	7.00			

Gorham Corporation, Nouveau, Stainless

Butter Serving Knife, HH, 7″	$25.00
Fork, salad	25.00
Knife	30.00

The International Silver Company, an amalgamation of fourteen independent silverware manufacturers, was formed in November 1898. Many of these manufacturers were the result of previous consolidations and mergers. The member companies kept their identities and continued to mark silverware with their own touchmarks. In addition, an International Silver mark was used on products sold by the parent company.

International Silver traces its heritage back to Ashbil Griswold, who established a pewter shop in Meriden, Connecticut, in 1808. Under Griswold's leadership, Meriden soon became a leading center in the production of Britannia ware, pewter, and silverware.

In nearby Hartford, three brothers, Asa, Simeon, and William Rogers, opened a workshop to manufacture coin silver silverware. As the cost of coin silver rose, the brothers conducted electroplating experiments. By 1847, they had perfected the process and issued their first electroplated silverware under the name of Rogers Bros. The company introduced Olive, the first fancy electroplate flatware pattern made from start to finish in America.

Because of its more durable qualities, Britannia had replaced pewter in most American homes by the 1850s. H. C. Wilcox & Co., Meriden, was one of the leading manufacturers of this new ware. In 1852, The Meriden Britannia Company was organized. In 1862, it purchased Rogers Bros. and moved the company from Hartford to Meriden.

By the 1890s, Meriden Britannia had established branches in Canada and London and sales offices in Chicago, New York, and San Francisco. Assuming a leadership role, Meriden Britannia convinced other small independent silver shops in the Connecticut area that cooperation was more efficient. The International Silver Company was the result.

The Meriden-Wallingford, Connecticut, area became the American silverware manufacturing center by 1900. International Silver's Joan of Arc and Prelude flatware patterns proved to be popular in their introduction and are among the most desired of the company's products. Production reached its peak in the late 1940s.

International Silver has been marketed aggressively since its 1898 formation. In 1975, the company launched a "buy a three-piece setting and get one free" advertising sales campaign. A price war ensued. No one benefited.

In 1968, International Silver became part of Insilco, itself a large conglomerate. In 1972, International Silver spun off its hotel division as an independent subsidiary, World Tableware International. A group of private investors purchased World Tableware in 1983 and organized the American Silver Company.

International Silver ended its production of sterling hollowware in 1976. Oneida purchased International Silver's plated hollowware, the Webster-Wilcox division, in 1981. International Silver now focused entirely on flatware. Plated flatware accounted for approximately one-half of the production, and sterling accounted for about one-third.

Katy Industries, Inc., in Elgin, Illinois, owners of Wallace Silversmiths, bought International Silver in the mid-1980s and changed the name to Wallace International Silversmiths. The company marketed several brands of stainless steel flatware, plus sterling and silver-plated flatware trademarked Deepsilver, 1847 Rogers Bros., International Silverplate, Wallace Silversmiths. International Silver's archives include a dated sample spoon from every sterling flatware line it produced. Today, International Silver is part of the Syratech Corporation.

COMPANIES THAT BECAME PART OF THE INTERNATIONAL SILVER COMPANY

* indicates company involved in 1898 incorporation

American Silver Co., Bristol, Conn., est. 1901, bought 1935
*Barbour Silver Co., Hartford, Conn., est. 1892
*Derby Silver Co., Birmingham, Conn., est. 1873
*Forbes Silver Co., Meriden, Conn., est. 1894
*Hall & Elton Co., Wallingford, Conn., est. 1837
Holmes & Edwards Silver Co., Bridgeport, Conn., est. 1882, taken over in 1898
Holmes & Tuttle, Bristol, 1851, bought in 1935 as part of American Silver Co. purchase
International Silver Co. of Canada, Ltd., est. 1925, sold to Heritage Silversmiths in 1972
La Pierre Mfg. Co., Newark, N.J., est. 1895, bought in 1929
Maltby, Stevens & Curtiss, Shelton, Conn., est. 1879, purchased by Watrous Mfg. Co. in 1896
*Manhattan Silver Plate Co., Lyons, N.Y., est. 1877
*Meriden Britannia Co., Meriden, Conn., est. 1852
Meriden Britannia Co., Ltd, Hamilton, Ontario, est. 1879, merged with International Silver Co. of Canada around 1912
*Meriden Silver Plate Co., Meriden, Conn., est. 1869
Middletown Plate Co., Middletown, Conn., est. 1864, joined International Silver in 1899
*Norwich Cutlery Co., Norwich, Conn., est. 1890
Park & Casper, Meriden, Conn., est. 1867, sold to Wilcox Silver Plate Co. in 1869
C. Rogers & Bros., Meriden, Conn., est. 1866, bought in 1903
*Rogers Cutlery Co., Hartford, Conn., est. 1871

W. Rogers Mfg. Co., Ltd., Niagara Falls, Ontario, bought by Wm. Rogers Mfg. Co. in 1905

Rogers Bros., Hartford, Conn., est. 1847, became part of International Silver in 1898

*Rogers & Bro., Waterbury, Conn., est. 1858

*Rogers & Hamilton Co., Waterbury, Conn., est. 1886

Rogers, Smith & Co., Wallingford, Conn., est. 1856, only a trademark of Meriden Britannia at time of formation

*William Rogers Mfg. Co., Hartford, Conn., est. 1865

Simpson Nickel Silver Co., Wallingford, Conn., est.1871, became part of International Silver in 1898

Standard Silver Co. of Toronto, est. 1895, merged with International Silver Co. of Canada around 1912

*Watrous Mfg. Co., Wallingford, Conn., est. 1896

E. G. Webster & Sons, Brooklyn, N.Y., est. 1886, bought in 1928

Wilcox Britannia Co., Meriden, Conn., est. 1865, became Wilcox Silver Plate Co. in 1867

*Wilcox Silver Plate Co., Meriden, Conn., est. 1867

Wilcox & Evertsen, New York, N.Y., est. 1892, purchased by Meriden Britannia in 1896

STERLING

International Silver Company, 1810, Sterling Silver

Butter Serving Knife, FH, 7″	$40.00
Butter Serving Knife, HH, 6 5/8″	40.00
Butter Serving Knife, HH, 7″	40.00
Butter Spreader, FH, 6″	30.00
Butter Spreader, HH, paddled ST blade, 6″	35.00
Carving Set, two pieces, ST blade	100.00
Fork, 7 1/4″	45.00
Fork, 7 7/8″	55.00

Fork, baby, 4 1/8″	45.00
Fork, ice cream, 5 3/8″	45.00
Fork, lemon, 4 5/8″	40.00
Fork, pickle, short handle, 5 3/4″	40.00
Fork, salad, 6 3/8″	45.00
Knife, fruit, ST blade, 6 5/8″	40.00
Knife, HH, modern blade, 8 7/8″	35.00
Knife, HH, New French blade, 9 1/8″	35.00
Knife, steak, 8 3/4″	45.00
Ladle, cream sauce, 5 1/4″	50.00
Ladle, cream sauce, 5 1/2″	50.00
Ladle, gravy, 6 3/8″	100.00
Server, cheese, ST blade, 6 1/4″	40.00
Server, pie, ST blade, 9 1/2″	50.00
Server, pie, ST blade, 10 1/8″	50.00
Serving Fork, cold meat, 8 1/4″	100.00
Serving Spoon, casserole, 8 1/4″	130.00
Serving Spoon, tablespoon, 8″	90.00

Serving Spoon, tablespoon,
  pierced, 7 3/4″   100.00

Spoon, bonbon, 4 5/8″   50.00

Spoon, cream soup, round bowl, 6 1/4″   45.00

Spoon, demitasse, 4 1/4″   25.00

Spoon, iced tea, 7 1/4″   45.00

Spoon, jelly, 6 1/2″   50.00

Spoon, soup, oval bowl, 6 7/8″   50.00

Spoon, sugar, 5 3/4″   40.00

Spoon, teaspoon, 6 1/8″   30.00

Spoon, teaspoon, 5 o'clock, 5 5/8″   25.00

International Silver Company, Blossom Time, Sterling Silver

Butter Serving Knife, FH, 7 1/4″ $32.00

Butter Spreader, FH, 5 7/8″   25.00

Butter Spreader, HH,
  paddled ST blade, 5 7/8″   25.00

Carving Knife, ST blade, 10 1/2″   60.00

Fork, 7 1/4″   40.00

Fork, 7 3/4″   60.00

Fork, baby, 4 1/8″   35.00

Fork, ice cream, 5 3/4″   35.00

Fork, lemon, 4 5/8″   25.00

Fork, salad, 6 1/2″   35.00

Fork, youth, 6 3/8″   35.00

Knife, HH, modern blade, 9 1/4″   32.00

Knife, HH, modern blade, 9 5/8″   45.00

Knife, youth, 7″   35.00

Ladle, cream sauce, 5 1/2″   45.00

Ladle, gravy, 6 1/2″   80.00

Server, cheese, ST blade, 6 1/4″   45.00

Server, pie, ST blade, 10 5/8″   60.00

Server, tomato, 8″   90.00

Serving Fork, cold meat, 7 3/4″   70.00

Serving Fork, cold meat, 9″   85.00

Serving Spoon, tablespoon, 8 1/2″   70.00

Spoon, bonbon, 5″   40.00

Spoon, cream soup, round bowl, 6 5/8″   32.00

Spoon, demitasse, 4 1/4″   22.00

Spoon, iced tea, 7 3/8″   45.00

Spoon, jelly, 6 1/2″   30.00

Spoon, soup, oval bowl, 6 3/4″   37.00

Spoon, sugar, 6″   35.00

Spoon, teaspoon, 6″   22.00

International Silver Company, Angelique, Sterling Silver

Butter Serving Knife, HH, 7″ $32.00

Fork, 7 1/4″   40.00

Fork, ice cream, 5 3/4″   50.00

Fork, lemon, 5 3/8″   40.00

Fork, salad, 6 5/8″   40.00

Knife, HH, modern blade, 9 1/4″   32.00

Ladle, cream sauce, 5 3/8″   55.00

Ladle, gravy, 6 1/4″   90.00

Server, pie, ST blade, 10 5/8″   50.00

Spoon, demitasse, 4″   22.00

Spoon, iced tea, 7 3/8″   40.00

Spoon, jelly, 6 3/8″   40.00

Spoon, soup, oval bowl, 6 5/8″   45.00

Spoon, sugar, shell-shaped bowl, 6″   30.00

Spoon, teaspoon   25.00

Sugar Tongs, 5″   55.00

International Silver Company, Brocade, Sterling Silver

Butter Serving Knife, FH, 7 1/4″	$40.00
Butter Spreader, FH, 5 3/4″	30.00
Butter Spreader, HH, paddled ST blade, 5 7/8″	32.00
Fork, 7 3/8″	55.00
Fork, 7 3/4″	70.00
Fork, baby, 4 1/4″	40.00
Fork, cocktail, 5 1/2″	32.00
Fork, ice cream, 5 3/4″	55.00
Fork, salad, 6 1/2″	50.00
Knife, HH, modern blade, 9 1/4″	40.00
Knife, HH, modern blade, 9 5/8″	50.00
Ladle, gravy, 6 3/8″	100.00
Spoon, cream soup, round bowl, 6 1/2″	55.00
Spoon, demitasse, 4 1/4″	27.00
Spoon, iced tea, 7 3/8″	45.00
Spoon, jelly, 6 1/2″	40.00
Spoon, soup, oval bowl, 6 3/4″	60.00
Spoon, sugar, shell-shaped bowl, 6″	45.00
Spoon, teaspoon, 6″	27.00

International Silver Company, Courtship, Sterling Silver

Bowl, bonbon, 6 1/8″	$145.00
Bowl, mayonnaise, 6″	300.00
Bowl, vegetable, round, 10″	200.00
Butter Serving Knife, FH, 7 1/8″	40.00
Butter Spreader, FH, 5 5/8″	25.00
Butter Spreader, HH, paddled ST blade, 5 3/4″	25.00
Candleholder, 3 3/8″	95.00
Carving Fork, ST tines, 8 5/8″	70.00
Carving Set, two pieces, ST blade	140.00
Compote, 5 7/8″	95.00
Creamer and Sugar, open, mini, 3 1/2″	180.00
Fork, 7 1/4″	45.00
Fork, 7 7/8″	60.00
Fork, cocktail, 5 1/2″	30.00
Fork, ice cream 5″	50.00
Fork, ice cream, 5 3/4″	50.00
Fork, lemon, 4 5/8″	32.00
Fork, pickle, short handle, 5 7/8″	32.00
Fork, salad, 6 3/8″	45.00
Knife, HH, New French blade, 9 1/8″	35.00
Knife, HH, New French blade, 9 1/2″	45.00
Ladle, cream sauce, 5 1/2″	45.00
Ladle, gravy, 6 1/8″	85.00
Plate, sandwich, 10″	180.00
Salt and Pepper Shakers, pair, 5″	200.00
Server, cheese, ST blade, 6 1/8″	50.00
Server, pie, ST blade, 9 1/4″	70.00
Server, pie, ST blade, 9 7/8″	70.00
Server, tomato, 7 7/8″	95.00
Serving Fork, cold meat, 7 3/4″	85.00
Serving Fork, cold meat, 9″	90.00
Serving Spoon, casserole, 8 3/4″	120.00
Serving Spoon, tablespoon, 8 1/2″	80.00
Spoon, bonbon, 4 5/8″	45.00
Spoon, cream soup, round bowl, 6 3/8″	40.00
Spoon, demitasse, 4 1/8″	25.00
Spoon, fruit, 5 3/4″	40.00
Spoon, grapefruit, round bowl, 7 1/8″	40.00
Spoon, iced tea, 7 3/8″	35.00
Spoon, jelly, 6 1/2″	32.00
Spoon, soup, oval bowl, 6 3/4″	45.00
Spoon, sugar, 5 3/4″	40.00
Spoon, teaspoon, 6″	25.00
Sugar Tongs, 4 1/8″	60.00

International Silver Company, Du Barry, Sterling Silver

Butter Serving Knife, HH, 7 1/4″	$45.00
Butter Spreader, HH, modern ST blade, 6 1/2″	50.00
Fork, 7 1/2″	60.00
Fork, salad, 6 5/8″	50.00
Knife, cheese, ST blade, 7 3/8″	60.00
Knife, HH, modern blade, 9″	45.00
Ladle, gravy, 6 3/4″	115.00
Spoon, jelly, 6 1/2″	75.00
Spoon, soup, oval bowl, 7″	55.00
Spoon, teaspoon, 6″	40.00

International Silver Company, Enchantress, Sterling Silver

(The Enchantress pattern was designed by Alfred G. Kintz.)

Butter Serving Knife, FH, 7 1/8″	$40.00
Butter Spreader, FH, 5 3/4″	25.00
Butter Spreader, HH, modern ST blade, 6 1/2″	25.00
Butter Spreader, HH, paddled ST blade, 5 3/4″	25.00
Carving Set, two pieces, ST blade	130.00
Fork, 7 1/4″	45.00
Fork, 7 7/8″	60.00
Fork, cocktail, 5 1/2″	27.00

Fork, ice cream, 5″	45.00
Fork, ice cream, 5 1/2″	45.00
Fork, pickle, short handle, 6″	30.00
Fork, salad, 6 1/2″	45.00
Knife, HH, New French blade, 9 1/8″	32.00
Knife, HH, New French blade, 9 1/2″	45.00
Ladle, cream sauce, 5 3/8″	45.00
Ladle, gravy, 6 1/4″	85.00
Serving Fork, cold meat, 7 5/8″	80.00
Serving Spoon, casserole, 8 7/8″	100.00
Serving Spoon, casserole, 9 1/8″	100.00
Serving Spoon, tablespoon, 8 5/8″	75.00
Spoon, bouillon, round bowl, 5 5/8″	35.00
Spoon, cream soup, round bowl, 6 1/2″	37.00
Spoon, demitasse, 4 1/4″	22.00
Spoon, fruit, 5 7/8″	37.00
Spoon, grapefruit, round bowl, 7 1/4″	40.00
Spoon, iced tea, 7 3/8″	37.00
Spoon, jelly, 6 1/2″	35.00
Spoon, soup, oval bowl, 6 3/4″	40.00
Spoon, sugar, 5 7/8″	37.00
Spoon, teaspoon, 6″	25.00
Sugar Tongs, 4 1/8″	60.00

International Silver Company, Frontenac, Sterling Silver

Carving Knife, ST blade, 10″	$70.00
Cheese Plane, ST plane, 9 1/8″	50.00
Fork, 7 1/8″	55.00
Fork, dessert, 6 1/8″	50.00
Fork, ice cream, 5 3/4″	55.00
Fork, salad	70.00
Fork, strawberry, 5 1/8″	40.00
Knife	45.00
Knife, wedding cake, ST blade, 12 1/4″	60.00

Ladle, punch, ST bowl, 12 ¹/₂″	100.00	Knife, HH, New French blade, 9 ¹/₄″	32.00
Ladle, soup, ST bowl, 10 ³/₄″	100.00	Knife, HH, New French blade, 9 ⁵/₈″	40.00
Server, cranberry, ST bowl, 8 ¹/₄″	60.00	Ladle, cream sauce, 5 ¹/₂″	50.00
Spoon, baby, straight handle, 4 ¹/₄″	45.00	Ladle, gravy, 6 ¹/₂″	90.00
Spoon, demitasse, 4 ¹/₂″	25.00	Server, cheese, ST blade, 6 ¹/₄″	40.00
Spoon, grapefruit, round bowl, 6 ⁷/₈″	60.00	Server, lasagna, ST blade, 10 ¹/₄″	50.00
Spoon, rice, ST bowl, 9 ¹/₄″	60.00	Server, pie, ST blade, 10 ¹/₄″	50.00
Spoon, salt, 2 ¹/₂″	15.00	Serving Fork, cold meat, 7 ⁵/₈″	90.00
Spoon, teaspoon	30.00	Serving Fork, cold meat, 8 ³/₄″	95.00
Spoon, teaspoon, 5 o'clock, 5 ¹/₂″	25.00	Serving Spoon, casserole, shell-shaped bowl, 9 ³/₈″	160.00
Spoon, youth, 5 ¹/₈″	32.00	Serving Spoon, tablespoon, 8 ¹/₄″	80.00
Sugar Tongs, 3 ¹/₂″	60.00	Serving Spoon, tablespoon, pierced, 8 ¹/₄″	90.00
		Spoon, cream soup, round bowl, 6″	40.00
		Spoon, demitasse, 4 ¹/₈″	22.00
		Spoon, dessert, 6 ⁵/₈″	45.00
		Spoon, fruit, 5 ⁷/₈″	40.00
		Spoon, iced tea, 7 ¹/₂″	40.00
		Spoon, jelly, 6 ³/₈″	40.00
		Spoon, soup, oval bowl, 7 ¹/₄″	45.00

International Silver Company, Joan of Arc, Sterling Silver

(The Joan of Arc pattern was designed by Alfred G. Kintz.)

Butter Serving Knife, HH, 7″	$32.00
Butter Spreader, FH, 5 ³/₄″	25.00
Carving Fork, ST tines, 8 ¹/₂″	50.00
Carving Knife, ST blade, 10 ³/₄″	50.00
Carving Set, two pieces, ST blade	100.00
Fork, 7 ³/₈″	35.00
Fork, 7 ³/₄″	55.00
Fork, baby, 4 ¹/₄″	40.00
Fork, cocktail, 5 ¹/₂″	35.00
Fork, dessert, 6 ¹/₈″	40.00
Fork, fish, ST tines, 7 ⁵/₈″	40.00
Fork, lemon, 4 ¹/₂″	37.00
Fork, lemon, 6″	37.00
Fork, salad, 6 ¹/₈″	40.00
Fork, strawberry, 4 ⁷/₈″	40.00
Knife, fish, ST blade, 8 ³/₄″	40.00
Knife, HH, modern blade, 8 ⁵/₈″	32.00
Knife, HH, modern blade, 9 ¹/₄″	32.00

Photo courtesy of International Silver Company/Syratech Corporation.

Spoon, sugar, shell-shaped bowl, 6 1/8"	32.00	Spoon, demitasse, 4 1/8"	17.00
Spoon, teaspoon, 5 7/8"	22.00	Spoon, grapefruit, round bowl, 7 1/8"	40.00
Sugar Tongs, 4 1/8"	55.00	Spoon, jelly, 6 1/4"	30.00
		Spoon, relish, 6"	32.00
		Spoon, soup, oval bowl, 7 1/4"	32.00
		Spoon, sugar, 5 7/8"	32.00
		Spoon, teaspoon, 5 7/8"	20.00
		Spoon, teaspoon, 5 o'clock, 5 5/8"	15.00
		Sugar Tongs, 4 1/8"	50.00

International Silver Company, Minuet, Sterling Silver

Butter Serving Knife, FH, 7"	$32.00
Butter Spreader, FH, 5 5/8"	20.00
Carving Fork, ST tines, 8 3/4"	45.00
Carving Set, two pieces, ST blade	90.00
Fork, 7 1/4"	40.00
Fork, 7 3/4"	50.00
Fork, baby, 4 1/8"	30.00
Fork, cocktail, 5 3/8"	25.00
Fork, grille, 7 5/8"	32.00
Fork, ice cream, 5 3/8"	35.00
Fork, lemon, 5 7/8"	27.00
Fork, pickle, short handle, 5 3/4"	27.00
Fork, salad, 6"	32.00
Fork, youth, 6 1/8"	35.00
Knife, grille, HH, New French blade, 8 5/8"	27.00
Knife, HH, New French blade, 8 5/8"	30.00
Knife, HH, New French blade, 9"	30.00
Knife, HH, New French blade, 9 5/8"	37.00
Ladle, cream sauce, 5 1/2"	40.00
Ladle, gravy, 6 1/2"	70.00
Server, cheese, ST blade, 6 3/8"	40.00
Serving Fork, cold meat, 7 1/4"	60.00
Serving Spoon, tablespoon, 8 1/2"	60.00
Spoon, baby, straight handle, 4 1/4"	30.00
Spoon, bonbon, 5 7/8"	35.00
Spoon, bouillon, round bowl, 5 3/8"	30.00
Spoon, cream soup, round bowl, 5 7/8"	32.00

International Silver Company, Pine Spray, Sterling Silver

Butter Serving Knife, HH, 7"	$37.00
Butter Spreader, HH, modern ST blade, 6 3/8"	22.00
Fork, 7 1/4"	50.00
Fork, ice cream, 5 3/4"	40.00
Fork, lemon, 5 3/8"	30.00
Fork, salad, 6 5/8"	37.00
Knife, cheese, ST blade, 7 1/4"	45.00
Knife, HH, modern blade, 9 1/4"	35.00
Knife, youth, 7"	40.00
Ladle, cream sauce, 5 1/4"	50.00
Ladle, gravy, 6 1/4"	85.00
Salad Set, two pieces	195.00
Server, pie/cake, ST blade, 10 5/8"	60.00
Server, tomato, 7 7/8"	85.00
Serving Spoon, tablespoon, 8 1/2"	75.00
Serving Spoon, tablespoon, pierced, 8 1/2"	80.00
Spoon, iced tea, 7 3/8"	40.00
Spoon, soup, oval bowl, 6 3/4"	40.00
Spoon, sugar, 6"	40.00
Spoon, teaspoon, 6"	25.00

International Silver Company, Prelude, Sterling Silver

(The Prelude pattern was designed by Alfred G. Kintz.)

Bar Knife, 9 1/4"	$40.00
Bowl, bonbon, 5 7/8"	110.00
Bowl, Paul Revere, 4 3/4"	100.00
Bowl, vegetable, oval, 10 1/2"	300.00
Bowl, vegetable, round, 9 7/8"	400.00
Butter Serving Knife, HH, 7"	30.00
Butter Spreader, FH, 5 7/8"	25.00
Candleholder, 3 1/2"	95.00
Carving Fork, ST tines, 8 3/4"	50.00
Carving Knife, ST blade, 11 1/2"	50.00
Carving Set, two pieces, large, ST blade	110.00

Photo courtesy of International Silver Company/Syratech Corporation.

Carving Set, two pieces, small, ST blade	100.00
Compote, 3 3/4"	100.00
Compote, 6"	175.00
Creamer and Sugar, open, mini	220.00
Cup, demitasse	95.00
Fork, 7 1/4"	35.00
Fork, 8"	50.00
Fork, baby, 4 1/4"	35.00
Fork, cocktail, 5 5/8"	30.00
Fork, fish, ST tines, 8 3/8"	40.00
Fork, ice cream, 5 1/2"	45.00
Fork, lemon, 4 5/8"	35.00
Fork, pickle, short handle, 5 7/8"	35.00
Fork, salad, 6 5/8"	40.00
Fork, strawberry, 4 5/8"	35.00
Fork, strawberry, 4 7/8"	35.00
Fork, strawberry, 5 1/8"	35.00
Fork, youth, 6 3/8"	40.00
Knife, fruit, ST blade, 6 3/4"	30.00
Knife, HH, modern blade, 8 7/8"	30.00
Knife, HH, modern blade, 9 1/4"	30.00
Knife, HH, New French blade, 9 1/4"	30.00
Knife, HH, New French blade, 9 1/2"	45.00
Knife, steak, 9"	50.00
Knife, youth, 6 7/8"	30.00
Ladle, cream sauce, 5 1/2"	50.00
Ladle, gravy, 6 1/2"	90.00
Plate, sandwich, 10 3/8"	245.00
Salt and Pepper Shakers, pair, 5 1/8"	200.00
Server, cheese, ST blade, 6 1/4"	40.00
Server, pasta, ST bowl, 10 7/8"	40.00
Server, pie, ST blade, 10"	50.00
Server, tomato, 8"	95.00
Serving Fork, cold meat, 7 3/4"	90.00
Serving Spoon, casserole, 9 1/4"	140.00
Serving Spoon, tablespoon, 8 1/2"	85.00
Serving Spoon, tablespoon, pierced, 8 1/2"	100.00
Spoon, bonbon, 4 3/4"	40.00
Spoon, cream soup, round bowl, 6 1/2"	45.00
Spoon, demitasse, 4 1/8"	20.00

Spoon, fruit, 5 3/4"	40.00	Spoon, baby, straight handle, 4 3/8"	40.00
Spoon, fruit, 6"	40.00	Spoon, bonbon, 4 3/4"	45.00
Spoon, grapefruit, round bowl, 7 1/4"	50.00	Spoon, cream soup, round bowl, 6 1/2"	45.00
Spoon, iced tea, 7 3/8"	40.00	Spoon, iced tea, 7 3/8"	40.00
Spoon, infant feeding, 5 1/2"	40.00	Spoon, jelly, 5"	32.00
Spoon, jelly, 5 1/8"	40.00	Spoon, sugar, 6"	40.00
Spoon, jelly, 6 1/2"	40.00	Spoon, teaspoon	25.00
Spoon, soup, oval bowl, 6 3/4"	45.00		
Spoon, sugar, 5 7/8"	30.00		
Spoon, teaspoon, 6"	20.00		
Sugar, covered, no lid	300.00		
Sugar Tongs, 4 1/8"	50.00		
Tray, bread, 11 1/4"	300.00		

International Silver Company, Processional, Sterling Silver

Butter Serving Knife, FH, 7 1/4"	$25.00
Butter Spreader, FH, 5 3/4"	25.00
Butter Spreader, HH, paddled ST blade, 6 1/4"	30.00
Carving Knife, ST blade, 10 1/2"	65.00
Carving Set, two pieces, ST blade	140.00
Fork, 7 1/4"	45.00
Fork, baby, 4 1/4"	40.00
Fork, cocktail, 5 5/8"	32.00
Fork, ice cream, 5 5/8"	45.00
Fork, ice cream, 5 3/4"	45.00
Fork, lemon, 4 3/4"	32.00
Fork, salad, 6 1/2"	45.00
Knife, HH, modern blade, 9 1/4"	35.00
Knife, steak, 8 3/4"	50.00
Ladle, gravy, 6 1/2"	85.00
Serving Fork, cold meat, 9 1/8"	90.00
Serving Spoon, casserole, 9 1/4"	105.00
Serving Spoon, tablespoon, 8 1/2"	80.00

International Silver Company, Queen's Lace, Sterling Silver

Butter Serving Knife, FH, 7 1/8"	$32.00
Butter Spreader, FH, 5 7/8"	30.00
Butter Spreader, HH, paddled ST blade, 5 7/8"	30.00
Fork, 7 1/4"	40.00
Fork, cocktail, 5 5/8"	35.00
Fork, ice cream, 5 7/8"	50.00
Fork, lemon, 4 3/4"	40.00
Fork, salad, 6 1/2"	40.00
Fork, youth, 6 3/8"	40.00
Knife, HH, modern blade, 9 1/8"	32.00
Ladle, gravy, 6 1/2"	90.00
Serving Fork, cold meat, 9 1/8"	95.00
Serving Spoon, tablespoon, 8 1/2"	90.00
Spoon, cream soup, round bowl, 6 1/2"	40.00
Spoon, iced tea, 7 3/8"	40.00
Spoon, sugar, 5 7/8"	32.00
Spoon, teaspoon, 6"	27.00

International Silver Company, Rhapsody, new, Sterling Silver

Butter Serving Knife, HH, 7″	$32.00
Butter Spreader, HH, paddled ST blade, 6 3/8″	30.00
Butter Spreader, HH, paddled ST blade, 6 5/8″	30.00
Fork, 7 1/4″	40.00
Fork, baby, 4 1/8″	40.00
Fork, cocktail, 5 5/8″	35.00
Fork, ice cream, 5 7/8″	45.00
Fork, lemon, 5 3/8″	40.00
Fork, salad, 6 1/2″	40.00
Knife, cheese, ST blade, 7″	40.00
Knife, HH, modern blade, 9 1/4″	32.00
Knife, youth, 7″	32.00
Ladle, cream sauce, 5 1/2″	55.00
Salad Set, two pieces, 9 1/8″	240.00
Salad Set, two pieces, plastic bowl	80.00
Server, pie/cake, ST blade, 10 3/4″	55.00
Serving Fork, cold meat, 9″	110.00
Serving Fork, salad, 9 1/8″	125.00
Serving Spoon, tablespoon, 8″	85.00
Spoon, baby, straight handle, 4 1/4″	40.00
Spoon, bonbon, 4 7/8″	40.00
Spoon, demitasse, 4 1/8″	22.00
Spoon, iced tea, 7 1/4″	40.00
Spoon, jelly, 6 1/2″	40.00
Spoon, soup, oval bowl, 6 5/8″	40.00
Spoon, sugar, shell-shaped bowl, 6″	32.00
Spoon, teaspoon, 6 1/8″	25.00
Spoon, teaspoon, 5 o'clock, 5 1/2″	22.00
Sugar Sifter, 6″	30.00
Sugar Tongs, 5″	50.00

International Silver Company, Richelieu, Sterling Silver

(The Richelieu pattern was designed by Alfred G. Kintz.)

Butter Serving Knife, FH, 7 3/8″	$45.00
Butter Spreader, FH, 6″	30.00
Fork, 7 1/4″	50.00
Fork, 7 3/4″	75.00
Fork, cocktail, 5 1/2″	30.00
Fork, ice cream, 5 3/8″	55.00
Fork, salad, 6 5/8″	50.00
Knife, breakfast, 7 1/4″	40.00
Knife, HH, modern blade, 8 3/4″	40.00
Knife, HH, modern blade, 9 1/4″	40.00
Knife, HH, modern blade, 9 5/8″	55.00
Ladle, gravy, 6″	100.00
Server, cranberry, ST bowl, 8 1/2″	70.00
Spoon, cream soup, round bowl, 6 1/2″	50.00
Spoon, demitasse, 4 1/8″	30.00
Spoon, fruit, 5 3/4″	40.00
Spoon, iced tea, 7 1/4″	50.00
Spoon, soup, oval bowl, 6 3/4″	50.00
Spoon, sugar, 5 7/8″	40.00
Spoon, teaspoon, 6″	30.00

International Silver Company, Royal Danish, Sterling Silver

(The Royal Danish pattern was designed by Alfred G. Kintz.)

Butter Pick, 4 1/4″	$50.00

Photo courtesy of International Silver Company/Syratech Corporation.

Butter Serving Knife, FH, 7 1/8″	40.00
Butter Serving Knife, HH, 7″	40.00
Butter Spreader, HH, paddled blade, 6″	45.00
Carving Knife, ST blade, 10 1/2″	45.00
Carving Set, two pieces, ST blade	90.00
Coffeepot	900.00
Creamer	460.00
Fork, 7 1/4″	45.00
Fork, baby, 4 1/4″	45.00
Fork, cocktail, 5 5/8″	35.00
Fork, dessert, 6 1/8″	45.00
Fork, ice cream, 5 1/2″	50.00
Fork, lemon, 4 3/4″	40.00
Fork, pickle, short handle, 5 3/4″	40.00
Fork, salad, 6 3/8″	37.00
Fork, strawberry, 5″	45.00
Fork, youth, 6 1/4″	45.00
Gravy Boat, 8 3/8″	130.00
Knife, HH, modern blade, 8 7/8″	40.00
Knife, youth, 7″	40.00

Ladle, gravy, 6 1/2″	100.00
Ladle, gravy, HH, ST bowl, 8 3/4″	45.00
Pepper Shaker	110.00
Pitcher, water, 8 1/8″	1,000.00
Pitcher, water, 8 1/2″	1,000.00
Salad Set, two pieces	300.00
Server, cheese, ST blade, 6 1/4″	50.00
Server, pie, ST blade, 10″	50.00
Server, pie, ST blade, 10 1/4″	50.00
Server, pie, ST blade, 10 1/2″	50.00
Serving Fork, cold meat, 7 3/4″	95.00
Serving Fork, cold meat, 8 7/8″	100.00
Serving Fork, salad, 9″	140.00
Serving Spoon, casserole, 8 1/2″	140.00
Serving Spoon, casserole, 9 1/4″	140.00
Serving Spoon, salad, 9 1/4″	155.00
Serving Spoon, salad, plastic bowl, 11 3/4″	50.00
Serving Spoon, tablespoon, 8 1/2″	90.00
Serving Spoon, tablespoon, pierced, 8 1/2″	100.00
Spoon, bonbon, 4 7/8″	40.00
Spoon, cream soup, round bowl, 6 1/2″	45.00
Spoon, demitasse, 4 1/8″	30.00
Spoon, fruit, 6″	40.00
Spoon, iced tea, 7 3/8″	40.00
Spoon, jelly, 6 1/2″	45.00
Spoon, sherbet, 5 7/8″	45.00
Spoon, soup, oval bowl, 6 3/4″	50.00
Spoon, sugar, 6″	40.00
Spoon, teaspoon, 6″	25.00
Sugar, covered	500.00
Sugar Tongs, 4″	50.00
Tea Set, three pieces	1,500.00
Tea Set, four pieces, with tray, mini	1,500.00
Tray, bread, 13″	250.00

International Silver Company, Serenity, Sterling Silver

Butter Serving Knife, FH, 7 1/4"	$35.00
Butter Spreader, FH, 5 3/4"	25.00
Butter Spreader, HH, paddled ST blade, 6"	22.00
Fork, 7 1/4"	40.00
Fork, 7 3/4"	60.00
Fork, baby, 4 1/4"	35.00
Fork, ice cream, 5 3/4"	40.00
Fork, pickle, short handle, 6"	30.00
Fork, salad, 6 1/2"	35.00
Knife, HH, modern blade, 9 1/8"	35.00
Ladle, cream sauce, 4 1/4"	40.00
Ladle, cream sauce, 5 1/2"	40.00
Ladle, gravy, 6 3/8"	70.00
Salad Set, two pieces	200.00
Serving Fork, cold meat, 8"	80.00
Serving Fork, cold meat, 9 1/8"	90.00
Serving Spoon, tablespoon, 8 1/2"	65.00
Spoon, baby, straight handle, 4 1/4"	35.00
Spoon, bonbon, 4 3/4"	40.00
Spoon, cream soup, round bowl, 6 1/2"	35.00
Spoon, grapefruit, round bowl, 7 1/4"	40.00
Spoon, iced tea, 6 5/8"	30.00
Spoon, jelly, 5"	30.00
Spoon, jelly, 6 5/8"	30.00
Spoon, sugar, 5 7/8"	40.00
Spoon, teaspoon	25.00
Sugar Tongs, 4 1/8"	60.00

International Silver Company, Silver Rhythm, Sterling Silver

Butter Serving Knife, HH, 7"	$30.00
Butter Spreader, HH, modern ST blade, 6 1/4"	20.00
Fork, 7 1/4"	40.00
Fork, cocktail, 5 5/8"	27.00
Fork, joint, 9"	95.00
Fork, pickle, short handle, 5 7/8"	25.00
Fork, salad, 6 1/2"	40.00
Knife, HH, modern blade, 9 1/4"	32.00
Ladle, gravy, 5 3/4"	70.00
Salad Set, two pieces	165.00
Server, cheese, ST blade, 7 1/8"	40.00
Server, pie, ST blade, 10 5/8"	60.00
Serving Fork, cold meat, 9"	80.00
Serving Spoon, tablespoon, 8 1/2"	65.00
Spoon, demitasse, 4 1/4"	22.00
Spoon, jelly, 6 5/8"	30.00
Spoon, soup, oval bowl, 6 3/4"	35.00
Spoon, sugar, 5 3/4"	32.00
Spoon, teaspoon, 6"	20.00

International Silver Company, Southern Colonial, Sterling Silver

Butter Serving Knife, FH, 7"	$40.00
Butter Spreader, FH, 5 3/4"	25.00

Butter Spreader, HH, paddled ST blade, 6 1/8″	25.00
Carving Fork, ST tines, 8 3/4″	65.00
Carving Knife, ST blade, 10 5/8″	65.00
Carving Set, two pieces, ST blade	130.00
Fork, 7 3/8″	45.00
Fork, cocktail, 5 1/2″	30.00
Fork, lemon, 4 5/8″	30.00
Fork, salad, 6 1/2″	45.00
Knife, HH, modern blade, 9 1/4″	35.00
Knife, steak, 8 3/4″	45.00
Ladle, gravy, 6 1/2″	85.00
Serving Spoon, tablespoon, 8 1/4″	80.00
Spoon, bonbon, 4 3/4″	40.00
Spoon, cream soup, round bowl, 6 1/2″	40.00
Spoon, iced tea, 7 3/8″	37.00
Spoon, jelly, 5″	32.00
Spoon, jelly, 6 3/8″	32.00
Spoon, soup, oval bowl, 6 3/4″	40.00
Spoon, sugar, 6″	40.00
Spoon, teaspoon, 5 7/8″	25.00

Knife, HH, modern blade, 9 1/4″	35.00
Knife, HH, modern blade, 9 1/2″	50.00
Knife, HH, New French blade, 9 1/2″	50.00
Ladle, gravy, 6 3/8″	85.00
Server, pie, ST blade, 10 3/8″	60.00
Serving Spoon, tablespoon, 8 1/2″	70.00
Spoon, bonbon, 4 3/4″	40.00
Spoon, cream soup, round bowl, 6 1/2″	32.00
Spoon, grapefruit, round bowl, 7 1/4″	40.00
Spoon, iced tea, 7 3/8″	35.00
Spoon, soup, oval bowl, 6 3/4″	35.00
Spoon, sugar, 5 7/8″	35.00
Spoon, teaspoon, 6″	22.00
Sugar Tongs, 4 1/8″	60.00

International Silver Company, Valencia, Sterling Silver

Butter Serving Knife, HH, 7 3/8″	$40.00
Butter Spreader, HH, modern ST blade, 6 5/8″	32.00
Fork, 7 1/2″	65.00
Fork, ice cream 5 7/8″	60.00
Fork, pickle, short handle, 6″	37.00
Fork, salad, 6 7/8″	50.00
Knife, HH, modern blade, 9″	40.00
Ladle, gravy, 6 3/4″	100.00
Serving Spoon, tablespoon, 8 3/4″	90.00
Serving Spoon, tablespoon, pierced, 8 3/4″	95.00
Spoon, bonbon, 5 1/8″	55.00
Spoon, sugar, 6 1/4″	45.00
Spoon, teaspoon, 6 1/4″	30.00

International Silver Company, Spring Glory, Sterling Silver

Butter Serving Knife, FH, 7 1/8″	$35.00
Butter Spreader, HH, paddled ST blade, 5 7/8″	22.00
Carving Fork, ST tines, 9 3/8″	50.00
Fork, 7 1/4″	40.00
Fork, 7 3/4″	60.00
Fork, baby, 4 1/8″	35.00
Fork, cocktail, 5 5/8″	25.00
Fork, lemon, 4 3/4″	25.00
Fork, pickle, short handle, 6″	30.00
Fork, salad, 6 1/2″	32.00

International Silver Company, Wedgwood, Sterling Silver

Butter Serving Knife, FH, 7 ¼″	$40.00
Butter Spreader, FH, 5 ¾″	32.00
Butter Spreader, HH, paddled ST blade, 5 ¾″	35.00
Carving Knife, ST blade, 9 ⅞″	60.00
Carving Set, two pieces, ST blade	120.00
Fork, 7 ¼″	50.00
Fork, 7 ¾″	55.00
Fork, cocktail, 5 ½″	40.00
Fork, fish, ST tines, 7 ⅞″	45.00
Fork, ice cream, 5 ½″	45.00
Fork, salad, 6 ¼″	45.00
Knife, HH, modern blade, 9 ⅝″	50.00
Knife, HH, New French blade, 9″	40.00
Knife, HH, New French blade, 9 ½″	50.00
Knife, steak, 9″	50.00
Ladle, cream sauce, 5 ¾″	50.00
Ladle, cream sauce, 6″	50.00
Ladle, gravy, 6 ⅝″	100.00
Plate, sandwich, 8″	400.00
Salad Set, two pieces, ST bowl	90.00
Scoop, ice cream, ST bowl, 7 ¾″	45.00
Server, cranberry, ST bowl, 8 ½″	45.00
Server, fish, ST blade, 11 ¼″	45.00
Server, pasta, ST bowl, 10 ½″	45.00
Server, pastry, ST bowl, 8 ⅞″	45.00
Server, tomato, 7 ¾″	105.00
Serving Fork, cold meat, 7 ⅜″	105.00
Serving Spoon, casserole, pierced, ST bowl, 9 ⅜″	40.00
Serving Spoon, casserole, shell-shaped ST bowl, 10″	45.00
Serving Spoon, casserole, ST bowl, 9 ½″	40.00

Serving Spoon, dressing, ST bowl, 11″	45.00
Serving Spoon, tablespoon, 8 ⅝″	90.00
Spoon, bouillon, round bowl, 5 ½″	40.00
Spoon, cream soup, round bowl, 6″	50.00
Spoon, demitasse, 4″	25.00
Spoon, fruit, 5 ⅞″	40.00
Spoon, grapefruit, round bowl, 7 ¼″	55.00
Spoon, iced tea, 7 ⅜″	40.00
Spoon, jelly, 6 ⅜″	50.00
Spoon, sugar, 6 ¼″	40.00
Spoon, teaspoon, 6″	27.00

International Silver Company, Wild Rose, Sterling Silver

(The Wild Rose pattern was designed by Alfred G. Kintz.)

Bar Knife, 9 ⅜″	$40.00
Bowl, bonbon, 6 ⅝″	90.00
Bowl, vegetable, round, 10″	250.00
Butter Serving Knife, FH, 7 ⅛″	30.00
Butter Spreader, FH, 7 ⅛″	30.00
Butter Spreader, HH, paddled ST blade, 5 ¾″	30.00
Candleholder, 3 ½″	80.00
Carving Fork, ST tines, 8 ¾″	50.00
Carving Knife, ST blade, 10 ¼″	55.00
Creamer and Sugar, open, mini	200.00
Fork, 7 ⅜″	40.00
Fork, 7 ¾″	50.00
Fork, baby, 4 ¼″	40.00
Fork, cocktail, 5 ½″	35.00
Fork, fish, ST tines, 8 ½″	40.00
Fork, ice cream, 5 ¼″	45.00
Fork, ice cream, 5 ⅝″	45.00
Fork, lemon, 4 ½″	40.00
Fork, lemon, 4 ¾″	40.00

Fork, pickle, short handle, 5 $\frac{7}{8}$″	40.00
Fork, salad, 6 $\frac{1}{8}$″	40.00
Fork, youth, 6 $\frac{1}{8}$″	40.00
Knife, HH, modern blade, 8 $\frac{7}{8}$″	32.00
Knife, HH, modern blade, 9 $\frac{3}{8}$″	32.00
Knife, HH, New French blade, 9 $\frac{1}{4}$″	32.00
Knife, HH, New French blade, 9 $\frac{5}{8}$″	40.00
Knife, steak, 9 $\frac{1}{2}$″	40.00
Ladle, cream, 5 $\frac{3}{8}$″	55.00
Ladle, gravy, 6 $\frac{1}{4}$″	90.00
Ladle, gravy, 6 $\frac{1}{2}$″	90.00
Pizza Cutter, ST blade, 8 $\frac{1}{4}$″	40.00
Salt and Pepper Shakers, pair	200.00
Scoop, ice cream, ST bowl, 8 $\frac{1}{2}$″	40.00
Server, pie, ST blade, 10 $\frac{1}{4}$″	50.00
Serving Fork, cold meat, 7 $\frac{3}{4}$″	90.00
Serving Fork, cold meat, 8 $\frac{7}{8}$″	90.00
Serving Fork, fish, 8″	135.00
Serving Spoon, casserole, shell-shaped bowl, 9 $\frac{1}{4}$″	160.00
Serving Spoon, tablespoon, 8 $\frac{1}{4}$″	80.00
Serving Spoon, tablespoon, pierced, 8 $\frac{1}{4}$″	100.00
Spoon, bonbon, 4 $\frac{5}{8}$″	40.00
Spoon, bouillon, round bowl, 5 $\frac{3}{4}$″	35.00
Spoon, cream soup, round bowl, 6″	40.00
Spoon, demitasse, 4 $\frac{1}{8}$″	22.00
Spoon, dessert, 6 $\frac{3}{4}$″	40.00
Spoon, grapefruit, round, bowl, 7 $\frac{1}{4}$″	40.00
Spoon, iced tea, 7 $\frac{3}{8}$″	35.00
Spoon, infant feeding, 5 $\frac{1}{2}$″	40.00
Spoon, jelly, 6 $\frac{1}{2}$″	40.00
Spoon, soup, oval bowl, 7 $\frac{1}{4}$″	40.00
Spoon, sugar, 6″	32.00
Spoon, sugar, shell-shaped bowl, 6 $\frac{1}{8}$″	30.00
Spoon, teaspoon, 5 $\frac{7}{8}$″	25.00
Sugar Bowl, open, mini	120.00
Sugar Tongs, 4″	55.00
Toothpick Holder, 3″	50.00

SILVER PLATE

International Silver Company, Adoration, Silver Plate

Butter Serving Knife, FH, 6 $\frac{3}{4}$″	$20.00
Butter Spreader, FH, 6 $\frac{1}{4}$″	15.00
Carving Set, two pieces, ST blade	145.00
Fork, 7 $\frac{3}{4}$″	17.00
Fork, cocktail, 5 $\frac{1}{2}$″	15.00
Fork, grille, 7 $\frac{3}{4}$″	15.00
Fork, salad, 6 $\frac{3}{4}$″	15.00
Knife, grille, HH, modern blade, 8 $\frac{1}{2}$″	15.00
Knife, HH, modern blade, 9 $\frac{3}{8}$″	17.00
Knife, HH, New French blade, 9 $\frac{3}{4}$″	17.00
Server, pie, ST blade, 10 $\frac{1}{2}$″	55.00
Serving Fork, cold meat, 8 $\frac{7}{8}$″	40.00
Serving Spoon, casserole, 9″	40.00
Serving Spoon, tablespoon, 8 $\frac{1}{2}$″	27.00
Serving Spoon, tablespoon, pierced, 8 $\frac{1}{2}$″	55.00
Spoon, cream soup, round bowl, 6 $\frac{5}{8}$″	17.00
Spoon, grapefruit, round bowl, 7 $\frac{1}{8}$″	15.00
Spoon, iced tea, 7 $\frac{7}{8}$″	17.00
Spoon, soup, oval bowl, 7 $\frac{1}{4}$″	17.00
Spoon, sugar, 6″	20.00
Spoon, teaspoon, 6 $\frac{1}{8}$″	12.00

International Silver Company, Ambassador, Silver Plate

Butter Serving Knife, FH, 7 1/8″	$20.00
Butter Spreader, FH, 5 3/4″	15.00
Carving Fork, ST tines, 8 1/2″	60.00
Carving Knife, ST blade, 10 1/4″	60.00
Carving Knife, ST blade, 11 1/4″	60.00
Carving Set, two pieces, large, ST blade	145.00
Carving Set, two pieces, small, ST blade	120.00
Coffeepot, 10 1/2″	100.00
Creamer, 5 1/4″	50.00
Fork, 7″	15.00
Fork, 7 3/8″	15.00
Fork, 7 5/8″	15.00
Fork, 7 3/4″	15.00
Fork, cocktail, 6″	12.00
Fork, dessert, 6 5/8″	17.00
Fork, grille, 7 3/4″	15.00
Fork, salad, 6 1/8″	15.00
Knife, blunt blade, 8″	15.00
Knife, blunt blade, 9 1/4″	15.00
Knife, grille, HH, New French blade, 8 5/8″	15.00
Knife, HH, blunt blade, 8 3/4″	15.00
Knife, HH, New French blade, 9 1/4″	15.00
Knife, HH, New French blade, 9 1/2″	15.00
Knife, HH, Old French blade, 8 1/2″	15.00
Knife, HH, Old French blade, 9″	15.00
Knife, HH, Old French blade, 9 3/4″	15.00
Knife, New French blade, 9 1/4″	15.00
Ladle, cream sauce, 5 3/4″	32.00
Ladle, gravy, 6 5/8″	35.00
Ladle, gravy, 6 7/8″	35.00
Server, pie, 10″	70.00

THE TOP FIVE PATTERNS
MODERN—SILVER PLATE
INTERNATIONAL, AMBASSADOR
INTERNATIONAL, FLAIR
ONEIDA, CAPRICE
ONEIDA, MORNING STAR
ONEIDA, SOUTH SEAS

Server, pie, 10 1/2″	70.00
Serving Fork, cold meat, 8 1/2″	40.00
Serving Spoon, tablespoon, 8 1/4″	25.00
Spoon, bouillon, round bowl, 5 3/8″	15.00
Spoon, demitasse, 4 3/8″	12.00
Spoon, dessert, 6 1/2″	20.00
Spoon, fruit, 5 3/4″	15.00
Spoon, grapefruit, round bowl, 7 1/8″	15.00
Spoon, iced tea, 7 5/8″	17.00
Spoon, relish, 5 7/8″	25.00
Spoon, sugar, 6″	20.00
Spoon, teaspoon, 6″	10.00
Spoon, teaspoon, 5 o'clock, 5 3/8″	7.00

International Silver Company, Daffodil, Silver Plate

Butter Serving Knife, FH, 6 3/4″	$20.00
Fork, 7″	17.00

Fork, cocktail, 5 ½"	15.00	Fork, cocktail, 5 ½"	12.00
Fork, grille, 7 ¾"	15.00	Fork, grille, 7 ¾"	15.00
Fork, pickle, short handle, 6 ⅛"	17.00	Fork, pickle, short handle, 6 ¼"	15.00
Fork, salad, 6 ¾"	15.00	Fork, salad, 6 ¾"	15.00
Fork, youth, 6 ¼"	17.00	Fork, youth, 6 ¼"	17.00
Knife, grille, HH, modern blade, 8 ½"	15.00	Knife, grille, HH, modern blade, 8 ½"	15.00
Knife, HH, modern blade, 9 ¼"	17.00	Knife, HH, modern blade, 9"	15.00
Knife, HH, modern blade, 9 ½"	17.00	Knife, HH, modern blade, 9 ½"	15.00
Server, pie, 10 ¾"	70.00	Knife, steak, 8 ¼"	25.00
Server, pie, ST blade, 10 ½"	70.00	Knife, youth, 7 ¼"	20.00
Server, tomato, 7 ⅝"	45.00	Ladle, gravy, 6"	35.00
Serving Fork, cold meat, 8 ⅞"	40.00	Ladle, gravy, 6 ½"	35.00
Serving Spoon, casserole, 9"	45.00	Server, pie, 10 ¾"	55.00
Serving Spoon, tablespoon, 8 ½"	27.00	Server, pie, ST blade, 10 ¼"	55.00
Serving Spoon, tablespoon,		Serving Fork, cold meat, 9"	40.00
pierced, 8 ½"	35.00	Serving Spoon, casserole, 9"	35.00
Spoon, cream soup, round bowl, 6 ⅝"	17.00	Serving Spoon, tablespoon, 8 ½"	25.00
Spoon, grapefruit, round bowl, 7"	15.00	Serving Spoon, tablespoon,	
Spoon, iced tea, 7 ¾"	22.00	pierced, 8 ½"	30.00
Spoon, soup, oval bowl, 7 ⅜"	15.00	Spoon, demitasse, 4 ½"	12.00
Spoon, sugar, 6"	17.00	Spoon, dessert, 7 ½"	15.00
Spoon, teaspoon, 6 ⅛"	10.00	Spoon, grapefruit, round bowl, 7"	15.00
Spoon, teaspoon, 5 o'clock, 5 ⅝"	15.00	Spoon, iced tea, 7 ¾"	15.00
		Spoon, jelly, 6 ¼"	15.00
		Spoon, jelly, 6 ½"	15.00
		Spoon, soup, oval bowl, 6 ⅞"	15.00
		Spoon, sugar, 6"	15.00
		Spoon, teaspoon, 6 ¼"	10.00
		Spoon, teaspoon, 5 o'clock, 5 ½"	10.00
		Sugar Tongs, 4 ⅛"	50.00

International Silver Company, Danish Princess, Silver Plate

Butter Serving Knife, FH, 6 ¾"	$15.00
Butter Spreader, FH, 6 ⅛"	12.00
Carving Fork, ST tines, 8 ⅝"	60.00
Carving Knife, ST blade, 11 ½"	60.00
Carving Knife, ST blade, 13"	70.00
Carving Knife, ST blade, 13 ½"	70.00
Fork, 7 ½"	15.00
Fork, baby, 4 ¼"	20.00

International Silver Company, Eternally Yours, Silver Plate

Butter Serving Knife, FH, 6 ¾"	$20.00
Butter Spreader, FH, 6 ⅜"	15.00

Fork, 7″	17.00
Fork, cocktail, 5 ½″	15.00
Fork, grille, 7 ⅝″	15.00
Fork, salad, 6 ¾″	17.00
Knife, grille, HH, modern blade, 8 ½″	15.00
Knife, HH, modern blade, 9 ½″	17.00
Ladle, gravy, 6″	40.00
Server, pie, 10 ¼″	70.00
Serving Fork, cold meat, 8 ¾″	45.00
Serving Spoon, casserole, 9″	45.00
Serving Spoon, tablespoon, 8 ⅝″	25.00
Spoon, cream soup, round bowl, 6 ⅜″	15.00
Spoon, fruit, 6″	17.00
Spoon, grapefruit, round bowl, 7″	15.00
Spoon, iced tea, 7 ½″	17.00
Spoon, soup, oval bowl, 7 ¼″	15.00
Spoon, sugar, 5 ¾″	20.00
Spoon, teaspoon, 6 ⅛″	10.00
Spoon, teaspoon, 5 o'clock, 5 ½″	15.00

Spoon, soup, oval bowl, 7 ⅜″	12.00
Spoon, sugar, 5 ⅞″	15.00
Spoon, teaspoon, 6 ⅛″	7.00
Spoon, teaspoon, 5 o'clock, 5 ⅝″	7.00

International Silver Company, First Love, Silver Plate

Butter Serving Knife, FH, 6 ¾″	$17.00
Carving Set, two pieces, ST blade	160.00
Fork, 7″	17.00
Fork, 7 ¾″	17.00
Fork, baby, 4 ⅜″	17.00
Fork, cocktail, 5 ½″	15.00
Fork, dessert, 6 ¼″	17.00
Fork, grille, 7 ¾″	15.00
Fork, salad, 6 ¾″	17.00
Knife, grille, HH, modern blade, 8 ½″	15.00
Knife, HH, modern blade, 9 ¼″	17.00
Knife, HH, modern blade, 9 ½″	17.00
Knife, HH, New French blade, 9 ¾″	17.00
Ladle, gravy, 6 ⅛″	40.00
Server, pie, 10 ½″	65.00
Serving Fork, cold meat, 9″	50.00
Serving Spoon, casserole, 9″	50.00
Serving Spoon, tablespoon, 8 ½″	25.00
Spoon, demitasse, 4 ½″	15.00
Spoon, dessert, 6 ¾″	20.00
Spoon, grapefruit, round bowl, 7″	15.00
Spoon, iced tea, 7 ¾″	17.00
Spoon, soup, oval bowl, 7 ⅜″	15.00
Spoon, sugar, 6″	20.00
Spoon, teaspoon, 6 ⅛″	7.00
Sugar Tongs, 4″	50.00

International Silver Company, Exquisite, Silver Plate

Butter Serving Knife, FH, 6 ⅞″	$12.00
Butter Spreader, FH, 6 ¼″	10.00
Fork, 7 ⅝″	12.00
Fork, salad, 6 ¾″	10.00
Fork, youth, 6 ¼″	15.00
Knife, grille, HH, modern blade, 8 ½″	12.00
Knife, HH, modern blade, 9″	12.00
Knife, HH, New French blade, 9 ⅜″	12.00
Serving Spoon, tablespoon, 8 ⅜″	17.00
Spoon, cream soup, round bowl, 6 ⅝″	12.00
Spoon, demitasse, 4 ⅜″	10.00
Spoon, grapefruit, round bowl, 7″	12.00
Spoon, iced tea, 7 ¾″	12.00
Spoon, soup, oval bowl, 6 ⅜″	12.00

International Silver Company, Flair, Silver Plate

Bowl, bonbon, 7″	$20.00
Butter Serving Knife, FH, 7 1/4″	20.00
Butter Spreader, FH, 6 1/4″	15.00
Carving Fork, ST tines, 11 1/4″	75.00
Carving Set, two pieces, ST blade	145.00
Fork, 7 1/2″	17.00
Fork, cocktail, 5 1/2″	15.00
Fork, pickle, short handle, 5 7/8″	17.00
Fork, salad, 6 7/8″	15.00
Knife, cheese, ST blade, 7 1/8″	35.00
Knife, HH, modern blade, 9 1/8″	17.00
Knife, wedding cake, ST blade, 13 1/4″	70.00
Knife, youth, 7″	17.00
Ladle, gravy, 6 3/8″	35.00
Salad Set, two pieces	80.00
Server, pie, 10 5/8″	70.00
Server, pie/cake, ST blade, 10 5/8″	70.00
Server, tomato, 7 3/4″	45.00
Serving Fork, cold meat, 9″	45.00
Serving Spoon, casserole, 9 1/8″	40.00
Serving Spoon, tablespoon, 8 1/2″	27.00
Serving Spoon, tablespoon, pierced, 8 3/8″	30.00
Spoon, baby, straight handle, 4 1/8″	17.00
Spoon, bonbon, 6 1/8″	17.00
Spoon, demitasse, 4 3/8″	15.00
Spoon, fruit, 6″	17.00
Spoon, iced tea, 7 5/8″	17.00
Spoon, infant feeding, 5 5/8″	17.00
Spoon, jelly, 6 1/4″	20.00
Spoon, soup, oval bowl, 6 3/4″	17.00
Spoon, sugar, 6″	20.00
Spoon, teaspoon, 6″	12.00
Spoon, teaspoon, 5 o'clock, 5 1/2″	15.00
Sugar Sifter, 6 1/8″	20.00
Sugar Tongs, 4 7/8″	45.00

International Silver Company, Heritage, Silver Plate

Butter Serving Knife, FH, 6 3/4″	$17.00
Butter Spreader, FH, 6 1/8″	15.00
Carving Knife, ST blade, 10 1/2″	55.00
Fork, 7″	17.00
Fork, cocktail, 5 1/2″	15.00
Fork, grille, 7 5/8″	17.00
Fork, salad, 6 3/4″	17.00
Knife, grille, HH, modern blade, 8 1/2″	17.00
Knife, HH, modern blade, 8 5/8″	17.00
Knife, HH, modern blade, 9 1/2″	17.00
Knife, youth, 7 1/4″	25.00
Knife, youth, 7 1/2″	25.00

Ladle, gravy, 6″	35.00
Server, pie, 8 ½″	50.00
Server, pie, 10 ⅝″	50.00
Server, pie, ST blade, 10 ⅝″	55.00
Server, tomato, 7 ½″	45.00
Serving Fork, cold meat, 8 ⅞″	35.00
Serving Spoon, casserole, shell-shaped bowl, 9″	45.00
Serving Spoon, dressing, 12 ¾″	90.00
Serving Spoon, tablespoon, 8 ½″	25.00
Serving Spoon, tablespoon, pierced, 8 ½″	30.00
Spoon, bonbon, 6″	15.00
Spoon, demitasse, 4 ½″	15.00
Spoon, fruit, 6″	17.00
Spoon, grapefruit, round bowl, 7 ⅛″	17.00
Spoon, iced tea, 7 ¾″	17.00
Spoon, infant feeding, 5 ⅛″	17.00
Spoon, jelly, 6 ⅜″	20.00
Spoon, soup, oval bowl, 7 ¼″	15.00
Spoon, sugar, shell-shaped bowl, 5 ¾″	17.00
Spoon, teaspoon, 6 ⅛″	10.00
Spoon, teaspoon, 5 o'clock, 5 ½″	10.00

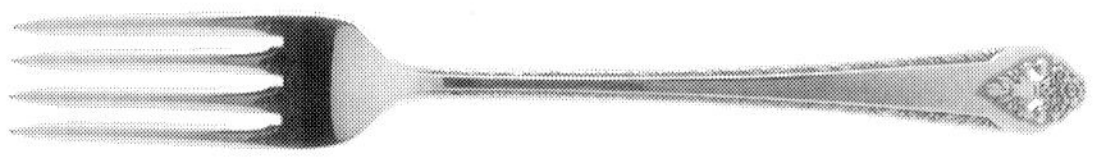

International Silver Company, Lovely Lady, Silver Plate

Butter Serving Knife, FH, 6 ¾″	$17.00
Butter Spreader, FH, 6 ¼″	12.00
Fork, 7 ¾″	15.00
Fork, salad	12.00
Knife, grille, HH, modern blade, 8 ½″	12.00
Knife, HH, modern blade, 8 ¼″	15.00
Knife, HH, modern blade, 9″	15.00
Spoon, grapefruit, round bowl, 7 ⅛″	12.00
Spoon, soup, oval bowl, 7 ½″	12.00

Spoon, sugar, 6″	15.00
Spoon, teaspoon, 6 ⅛″	7.00

International Silver Company, Old Colony, Silver Plate

Butter Serving Knife, FH, 7 ⅛″	$15.00
Butter Spreader, FH, 5 ⅞″	12.00
Carving Fork, ST tines, 8 ⅝″	55.00
Carving Fork, ST tines, 11″	65.00
Fork, 7 ⅛″	15.00
Fork, 7 ⅜″	15.00
Fork, 7 ⅝″	15.00
Fork, cocktail, 5 ¾″	15.00
Fork, pickle, long handle, 8″	22.00
Fork, pickle, short handle, 6 ¼″	15.00
Fork, salad, 6″	15.00
Knife, blunt blade, 8 ⅛″	15.00
Knife, blunt blade, 8 ⅜″	15.00
Knife, blunt blade, 9 ⅜″	15.00
Knife, fruit, 6 ⅝″	15.00
Knife, HH, Old French blade, 8 ¾″	22.00
Knife, HH, Old French blade, 10 ⅛″	22.00
Ladle, gravy, 7 ⅛″	32.00
Ladle, soup, 11 ¾″	125.00
Server, pie, 10″	60.00
Serving Fork, cold meat, 9 ½″	40.00
Serving Spoon, casserole, 9″	40.00
Serving Spoon, tablespoon, 8 ¼″	22.00
Spoon, bouillon, 5 ⅛″	15.00
Spoon, demitasse, 4 ⅜″	12.00
Spoon, fruit, 5 ⅞″	17.00
Spoon, grapefruit, round bowl, 7″	15.00
Spoon, soup, oval bowl, 7 ⅛″	15.00
Spoon, sugar, 6″	15.00
Spoon, teaspoon, 5 ⅞″	10.00
Spoon, teaspoon, 5 o'clock, 5 ¼″	15.00

International Silver Company, Orleans, Silver Plate

Bowl, bonbon, 8 5/8″	$20.00
Butter Serving Knife, FH, 6 3/4″	17.00
Butter Spreader, FH, 6 1/8″	15.00
Fork, 7 3/8″	15.00
Fork, baby, 4 1/4″	10.00
Fork, cocktail, 5 1/2″	15.00
Fork, salad, 6 5/8″	15.00
Knife, HH, modern blade, 9 1/4″	17.00
Ladle, gravy, 6 1/8″	30.00
Ladle, gravy, 6 3/8″	30.00
Ladle, gravy, 7″	30.00
Server, pie, 10 3/8″	45.00
Server, pie, 10 5/8″	45.00
Serving Fork, cold meat, 8 3/4″	30.00
Serving Spoon, casserole, shell-shaped bowl, 9″	40.00
Serving Spoon, tablespoon, 8 3/8″	20.00
Serving Spoon, tablespoon, pierced, 8 3/8″	25.00
Spoon, demitasse, 4 3/8″	10.00
Spoon, iced tea, 7 1/2″	15.00
Spoon, infant feeding, 5 1/8″	15.00
Spoon, soup, oval bowl, 6 3/4″	15.00
Spoon, sugar, shell-shaped bowl, 5 1/2″	15.00
Spoon, teaspoon, 5 7/8″	10.00

International Silver Company, Reflection, Silver Plate

Butter Serving Knife, FH, 6 7/8″	$15.00
Butter Spreader, FH, 6 1/8″	12.00
Fork, 7 3/8″	15.00
Fork, baby, 4 1/4″	10.00
Fork, cocktail, 5 1/2″	12.00
Fork, pickle, short handle, 6 1/4″	15.00
Knife, HH, modern blade, 9 1/4″	17.00
Knife, youth, 7 3/8″	15.00
Ladle, gravy, 6 1/8″	30.00
Server, pie, 10 3/8″	50.00
Server, pie, 10 5/8″	50.00
Serving Fork, cold meat, 8 7/8″	35.00
Serving Spoon, casserole, shell-shaped bowl, 9″	40.00
Serving Spoon, tablespoon, 8 1/2″	20.00
Serving Spoon, tablespoon, pierced, 8 1/2″	20.00
Spoon, baby, straight handle, 4 1/4″	10.00
Spoon, demitasse, 4 1/4″	7.00
Spoon, fruit, 6″	15.00
Spoon, iced tea, 7 3/8″	15.00
Spoon, infant feeding, 5 5/8″	15.00
Spoon, soup, oval bowl, 6 3/4″	15.00
Spoon, sugar, shell-shaped bowl, 6″	12.00
Spoon, teaspoon, 6 1/8″	10.00
Spoon, teaspoon, 5 o'clock, 5 1/2″	7.00
Spoon, youth, 5 1/2″	12.00
Sugar Sifter, 6″	15.00
Tea Set, four pieces	700.00
Tea Set, five pieces, with tray	1,000.00
Youth Set, three pieces	40.00

International Silver Company, Remembrance, Silver Plate

Butter Serving Knife, FH, 6 ¾″	$15.00
Butter Spreader, FH, 6 ⅛″	10.00
Fork, 7 ½″	15.00
Fork, cocktail, 5 ½″	10.00
Fork, grille, 7 ⅝″	12.00
Fork, salad, 6 ¾″	15.00
Knife, grille, HH, modern blade, 8 ½″	12.00
Knife, HH, modern blade, 9 ⅜″	15.00
Ladle, gravy, 6 ⅛″	30.00
Serving Spoon, tablespoon, 8 ½″	20.00
Spoon, cream soup, round bowl, 6 ⅜″	15.00
Spoon, demitasse, 4 ½″	12.00
Spoon, fruit, 6″	12.00
Spoon, grapefruit, round bowl, 7″	12.00
Spoon, iced tea, 7 ¾″	12.00
Spoon, soup, oval bowl, 7 ⅜″	15.00
Spoon, sugar, 5 ¾″	15.00
Spoon, teaspoon, 6 ⅛″	10.00
Sugar Sifter, 5 ¾″	20.00
Sugar Tongs, 4″	45.00

International Silver Company, Springtime, Silver Plate

Butter Serving Knife, FH, 7 ¼″	$17.00
Butter Spreader, FH, 5 ⅞″	12.00
Cheese Pick, 6 ⅛″	30.00
Fork	15.00

Fork, cocktail, 5 ¾″	12.00
Fork, salad, 6 ¾″	15.00
Fork, youth, 6 ⅛″	20.00
Knife	15.00
Server, pie, 10 ½″	60.00
Server, tomato, 7 ⅞″	40.00
Serving Fork, cold meat, 9″	40.00
Serving Spoon, casserole, 9 ⅛″	45.00
Serving Spoon, tablespoon, pierced, 8 ½″	25.00
Spoon, fruit, 6″	15.00
Spoon, iced tea, 7 ⅜″	15.00
Spoon, soup, oval bowl, 6 ¾″	15.00
Spoon, sugar, 5 ¾″	17.00
Spoon, teaspoon, 6″	10.00
Spoon, teaspoon, 5 o'clock, 5 ¾″	7.00
Sugar Sifter, 5 ¾″	20.00

International Silver Company, Vintage, Silver Plate

Butter Serving Knife, FH, 7 ⅛″	$35.00
Carving Fork, ST tines, 11″	125.00
Fork, 7 ⅛″	35.00
Fork, 7 ½″	30.00
Fork, 7 ¾″	30.00
Fork, cocktail, 6″	22.00
Fork, salad	60.00
Knife, blunt blade, 9 ⅜″	40.00
Knife, HH, Old French blade, 9″	50.00
Knife, HH, Old French blade, 9 ¾″	50.00
Knife, youth, 7 ½″	40.00
Ladle, cream sauce, 5 ½″	50.00
Ladle, cream sauce, 5 ⅝″	50.00
Ladle, gravy, 7 ⅛″	75.00
Serving Fork, cold meat, 8 ¼″	65.00
Serving Fork, cold meat, 8 ½″	65.00

Serving Spoon, casserole, 8 ⅞"	75.00	Spoon, soup, oval bowl, 7 ¼"	35.00
Serving Spoon, tablespoon, 8 ¼"	40.00	Spoon, sugar, 6"	30.00
Spoon, fruit, 5 ¾"	30.00	Spoon, teaspoon, 6"	20.00

FORMS AVAILABLE IN INTERNATIONAL SILVER'S VINTAGE PATTERN

Samuel Stohr received Design Patent #37,059 for the Vintage pattern on August 2, 1904. It was assigned to the International Silver Company and introduced that same year. This is one of International's most popular silver-plated patterns.

Manufacturers did not always use the same terms to advertise and list pieces. The same piece also had multiple uses.

a.k.a. indicates also known as

Forks, Individual

Cocktail Fork, a.k.a., Oyster Cocktail Fork, Oyster Fork, Seafood Fork, Shrimp Fork
Dinner Fork, three styles, a.k.a., Medium Fork, Notch Handle Fork, Place Fork, Table Fork
Fish Fork, a.k.a., Individual Fish Fork
Ice Cream Fork
Luncheon Fork, two styles, a.k.a., Dessert Fork, Lunch Fork, Notch Handle Fork
Pastry Fork, a.k.a., Individual Pastry Fork, Pie Fork
Salad Fork, a.k.a., Individual Salad Fork

Knives, Individual

Butter Spreader, Individual
Dinner Knife, two styles, a.k.a., Medium Knife, Place Knife, Table Knife
Fish Knife, a.k.a., Individual Fish Knife
Fruit Knife, three styles, a.k.a., No. 1 Fruit Knife, No. 2 Fruit Knife, No. 45 Fruit Knife, Orange Knife
Luncheon Knife., two styles, a.k.a., Dessert Knife

Spoons, Individual

Baby Spoon, bent handle, a.k.a., Infant Spoon
Bouillon Spoon, a.k.a., Cream Soup Spoon, Small Cream Soup Spoon, Small Round Bowl Soup Spoon
Chocolate Spoon

Demitasse Spoon, a.k.a., Coffee Spoon
Dessert Place Spoon, a.k.a., Dessert Cereal Spoon, Dessert Spoon, Oval Bowl Soup
   Spoon, Oval Soup Spoon, Place Spoon
Egg Spoon, a.k.a., Youth Spoon
5 o'clock Teaspoon, a.k.a., Coffee Spoon, Youth Spoon
Fruit Spoon, a.k.a., Citrus Spoon, Grapefruit Spoon, Orange Spoon
Gumbo Spoon, a.k.a., Cream Soup Spoon, Large Cream Soup Spoon, Round Bowl
   Soup Spoon, Round Soup Spoon, Soup Spoon
Ice Cream Spoon, a.k.a., Sherbet Spoon, Sundae Spoon
Iced Tea Spoon, a.k.a., Iced Beverage Spoon, Soda Spoon
Teaspoon

Miscellaneous, Individual

Food Pusher, a.k.a., Pusher
Lobster Pick
Napkin Ring
Nut Pick, a.k.a., Pick
Youth Set—Child's/Youth Fork, Child's/Youth Knife, Child's/Youth Spoon

Serving Pieces

Asparagus Tongs
Berry Spoon, a.k.a., Casserole Spoon, Nut Spoon, Serving Spoon
Bottle Opener
Butter Pick
Butter Knife
Butter Knife, Twist Handle, a.k.a., Twist Handle Butter Server, Twisted Butter
   Knife
Cake Fork, a.k.a., Cake Server
Cake Knife
Cake Saw, a.k.a., Saw Tooth Cake Knife
Carving Set, a.k.a., Beef Carving Set, Roast Carving Set, Three-Piece Carving
   Set—Carving Knife, Carving Fork, Carving Steel
Cheese Knife
Cheese Scoop
Cheese Server
Chipped Beef Fork, a.k.a., Beef Fork, Small Cold Meat Fork, Small Serving Fork
Chocolate Muddler
Cold Meat Fork, a.k.a., Buffet Fork, Serving Fork

Cream Ladle, a.k.a., Dressing Ladle, Mayonnaise Ladle, Sauce Ladle

Crumber—Crumber and Crumber Knife

Fish Set—Fish Knife, Fish Serving Fork, Fish Slice

Game Set, a.k.a., Two-Piece Carving Set—Game Fork, Game Knife

Gravy Ladle

Ice Cream Knife, a.k.a., Ice Cream Ladle, Ice Cream Server

Ice Spoon

Jelly Trowel, a.k.a., Aspic Slice, Jelly Knife, Jelly Server

Knife Sharpener

Nut Cracker, a.k.a., Nut Crack

Olive Spoon-Fork, a.k.a., Ideal Olive Spoon, Olive Fork, Olive Spoon, Open Bowl Olive Spoon

Oyster Ladle

Pastry Server, a.k.a., Cake Server, Pie Server

Pickle Fork, a.k.a., Pickle Fork, Short

Pickle Fork, Long, a.k.a., Long Handle Pickle Fork, Long Pickle Fork

Pie Knife, a.k.a., Cake Server, Pie Server

Platter Spoon, a.k.a., Dressing Spoon, Gravy Spoon, Ragout Spoon, Stuffing Spoon

Poultry Shears, a.k.a., Duck Shears, Game Shears

Punch Ladle, two styles

Roast Holder, a.k.a., Bone Holder, Carver's Assistant

Salad Serving Set, two styles—Salad Serving Fork, Salad Serving Spoon

Soup Ladle, a.k.a., Medium Ladle

Steak Set, a.k.a., Bird Set, Breakfast Set, Steak Carving Set—Steak Carving Fork, Steak Carving Hone, Steak Carving Knife

Sugar Sifter

Sugar Spoon, a.k.a., Sugar Shell

Sugar Tongs

Tablespoons, a.k.a., Serving Spoon, Table Serving Spoon

Tomato Server, a.k.a. Entree Server, Flat Server

STAINLESS

International Silver Company, Americana, Stainless

Butter Serving Knife, HH, 7 1/8″	$15.00
Butter Spreader, FH, 6 3/8″	15.00
Butter Spreader, HH, modern blade, 6 3/8″	20.00
Fork, 7 1/2″	17.00
Fork, salad, 6 7/8″	15.00
Knife, HH, modern blade, 9 3/8″	15.00
Ladle, gravy, 6 3/4″	25.00
Serving Fork, cold meat, 9″	27.00
Serving Spoon, tablespoon, pierced, 8 5/8″	25.00
Spoon, iced tea, 7 1/4″	15.00
Spoon, soup, oval bowl, 6 7/8″	15.00
Spoon, sugar, shell-shaped bowl, 6 1/8″	15.00
Spoon, teaspoon, 6 1/8″	15.00

Spoon, soup, oval bowl, 7″	7.00
Spoon, sugar, 6″	7.00
Spoon, teaspoon, 5 7/8″	5.00

International Silver Company, Norse, Stainless

Butter Spreader, FH, 6 3/4″	$22.00
Fork	25.00
Fork, salad, 7″	22.00
Knife	27.00
Ladle, gravy, 7″	30.00
Serving Fork, cold meat, 9″	35.00
Serving Spoon, tablespoon, 8 7/8″	30.00
Spoon, iced tea, 7 1/2″	22.00
Spoon, soup, oval bowl, 7 1/4″	20.00
Spoon, sugar, 6 1/8″	22.00
Spoon, teaspoon, 6 1/4″	20.00

International Silver Company, New Charm, Stainless

Butter Serving Knife, HH, 7″	$7.00
Fork, 7 1/2″	7.00
Fork, salad, 7 1/8″	5.00
Knife, HH, modern blade, 9 1/8″	10.00
Ladle, gravy, 6 1/2″	12.00
Serving Fork, cold meat, 8 5/8″	12.00
Serving Spoon, tablespoon, 8 1/2″	12.00
Serving Spoon, tablespoon, pierced, 8 1/2″	12.00

International Silver Company, Queen's Fancy, Stainless

Butter Serving Knife, HH, 7″	$25.00
Fork, salad	22.00
Knife, youth, 7″	25.00
Ladle, gravy, 6 5/8″	35.00
Server, pie/cake, 10 1/4″	35.00
Serving Fork, cold meat, 9″	32.00
Serving Spoon, tablespoon, 8 5/8″	30.00
Serving Spoon, tablespoon, pierced, 8 5/8″	30.00

Spoon, soup, oval bowl, 7″	20.00	Fork	25.00
Spoon, sugar, 6″	20.00	Fork, salad, 6 ¾″	25.00
Spoon, teaspoon	25.00	Knife	32.00
		Knife, youth, 7″	30.00
		Ladle, gravy, 6 ⅜″	45.00
		Serving Spoon, tablespoon, 8 ⅝″	40.00
		Spoon, dessert, 6 ⅞″	25.00
		Spoon, iced tea, 7 ¾″	30.00
		Spoon, infant feeding, 5 ¾″	25.00
International Silver Company, Today, Stainless		Spoon, soup, oval bowl, 7 ⅜″	25.00
		Spoon, sugar, 6″	30.00
Butter Serving Knife, FH, 7″	$30.00	Spoon, teaspoon	25.00
Butter Spreader, FH, 6 ⅛″	30.00	Spoon, teaspoon, 5 o'clock, 5 ½″	25.00

Georg Arthur Jensen (1866–1935) was a Danish metalworker. He apprenticed as a goldsmith under Holm in Copenhagen, becoming a journeyman in 1884. Working with Christian Joachim, he made ceramics in the 1890s, utilizing the workshop of Mogens Ballin, a Copenhagen painter and designer. In addition, he worked in the potteries of Aluminia and Bing & Grondahl Porcelaensfabrik and studied sculpture at Det Kongelige Danske Kunstakademi in Copenhagen.

In 1904, Jensen, with one assistant, opened a small silversmith shop at 36 Bregade, Copenhagen, to sell the jewelry and silverware he designed. Jensen broke with classical design, preferring a more naturalistic, modern approach.

The ability to attract the leaders of twentieth-century modern design to his studio was key to Jensen's success. Gundorph Albertus, Sigvard Bernadotte, Harald Nielsen, and Johan Rohde were just a few of the individuals who contributed their talents to the Jensen studio. By 1930, Jensen had employed over 250 workers.

William Randolph Hearst bought Jensen's entire exhibit from the 1915 San Francisco Panama-Pacific Exposition. Jensen opened a Fifth Avenue showroom in New York in 1920. International made direct copies of two Jensen flatware patterns—Johan Rhode's 1915 Acorn pattern and Georg Jensen's Blossom pattern

When Georg Jensen died in 1935, Jørgen Jensen (1895–1966), Georg's son, assumed management of the company. Jørgen contributed actively to the design of jewelry, silver flatware, and larger silver pieces such as bowls, jugs, and tea sets.

When precious metals became scarce during World War II, Jensen began designing and producing products in stainless steel. Henning Koppe and Tias Eckhoff were two of the company's post–World War II designers.

Georg Jensen, Acorn, Sterling Silver

Bottle Opener, 4 ½″	$120.00	Carving Fork, ST tines, 10 ¾″	450.00
Butter Spreader, HH,		Carving Set, two pieces,	
paddled blade, 5 ⅞″	130.00	ST blade, 11 ½″	600.00
		Cheese Plane, ST blade, 8 ¼″	115.00
		Fork, 6 ⅝″	115.00
		Fork, 7 ½″	135.00
		Fork, cocktail, 5 ¾″	90.00
		Fork, salad	115.00
		Fork, youth, 5 ⅝″	130.00

Knife	110.00	Salad Set	750.00
Knife, cake, ST blade, 10 $\frac{3}{8}''$	150.00	Server, cheese, ST blade, 6 $\frac{3}{8}''$	115.00
Knife, cheese, ST blade, 7 $\frac{3}{4}''$	115.00	Serving Spoon, salad, 8 $\frac{7}{8}''$	375.00
Knife, dinner, long handle, modern blade, 9 $\frac{1}{8}''$	165.00	Spoon, demitasse, 3 $\frac{7}{8}''$	50.00
		Spoon, dessert, 6 $\frac{3}{4}''$	120.00
Knife, fruit, ST blade, 6 $\frac{3}{4}''$	85.00	Spoon, fruit, 5 $\frac{7}{8}''$	140.00
Lobster Pick, 7 $\frac{3}{8}''$	145.00	Spoon, teaspoon, 5 $\frac{3}{4}''$	80.00

Samuel Kirk & Sons, Inc., traces its origin to Samuel Kirk, who began his career as a Baltimore silversmith in partnership with John Smith. Kirk & Smith lasted only five years, from 1815 to 1820. Committed to the Baltimore area, Kirk struck out on his own in 1820.

He quickly attracted a large following because of his emphasis on quality and detailed workmanship. Kirk's revival of the highly ornamental Repoussé style in the late 1820s ensured his firm's long-term success.

Kirk responded quickly to the public's changing tastes. The company's earliest pieces reflect the chaste, simple lines of America's Federal era. As trade with China grew, pieces in Oriental shapes and motifs were made. The Victorian era saw the manufacture of highly elaborate and ornate pieces. Kirk also successfully captured the geometric influence of the Art Deco period and the sleek, trim lines of the Modern period.

Kirk's son, Henry Child Kirk, and his descendants managed the firm for approximately 160 years. The firm has served both royalty and American presidents. When President Monroe's 550-piece gold flatware dinnerware service needed renovation, Kirk was commissioned to restore it.

The Stieff Company arrived on the Baltimore scene over seventy years after Samuel Kirk opened his first shop. Charles C. Stieff established a silver factory in 1892 to manufacture sterling silver flatware and accessories. A high-quality product and strict adherence to the 925/1000 sterling standard were the two goals that motivated Charles Stieff.

Following World War I, the company expanded its manufacturing capabilities and launched a national advertising campaign under the leadership of Gideon Stieff, Charles's son. Stieff expanded its line of sterling flatware and hollowware. Its Rose pattern is so identified with Baltimore that it is frequently referred to as "Baltimore Rose."

Colonial Williamsburg's selection of Stieff as the manufacturer of its silver reproductions greatly enhanced Stieff's reputation and directed the company into a totally new area of business. Today, it supplies reproductions to over ten American historic sites and museums.

In 1979, The Stieff Company acquired Samuel Kirk & Sons, Inc. Kirk Stieff, a new company, was created. Today, Kirk Stieff is part of Lenox Brands.

Kirk Stieff, Corsage, Sterling Silver

Butter Serving Knife, HH, 7 1/8″	$40.00
Butter Spreader, HH, modern ST blade, 5 7/8″	30.00
Fork, 7 1/8″	45.00
Fork, baby, 4 1/2″	45.00
Fork, salad, 6″	45.00
Knife, HH, New French blade, 8 7/8″	35.00
Knife, HH, New French blade, 9 1/2″	50.00
Serving Fork, bacon, 8 1/4″	120.00
Serving Fork, cold meat, 7 5/8″	85.00
Serving Fork, cold meat, 7 7/8″	85.00
Serving Spoon, tablespoon, 7 3/4″	80.00
Spoon, bouillon, round bowl, 5 1/2″	45.00
Spoon, cream soup, round bowl, 6 1/2″	50.00
Spoon, egg, 6 1/8″	40.00
Spoon, iced tea, 7 1/2″	40.00
Spoon, soup, oval bowl, 6 1/2″	55.00
Spoon, sugar, 6 1/8″	40.00
Spoon, teaspoon	27.00
Spoon, teaspoon, 5 o'clock, 5 1/2″	20.00

Kirk Stieff, Golden Winslow, Sterling Silver, gold accent

Fork, 7 1/4″	$60.00
Fork, 7 3/4″	75.00
Fork, baby, 3 3/4″	45.00
Fork, salad	65.00
Knife	45.00

Knife, wedding cake, ST blade, 11 7/8″	80.00
Spoon, baby, straight handle, 3 3/4″	45.00
Spoon, soup, oval bowl, 6 1/8″	70.00
Spoon, soup, oval bowl, 7 3/8″	70.00
Spoon, teaspoon, 6″	35.00

Kirk Stieff, Lady Claire, Sterling Silver, hand engraved

Bar Knife, 9″	$40.00
Butter Serving Knife, HH, 7 5/8″	45.00
Butter Spreader, HH, modern ST blade, 6 1/4″	35.00
Carving Fork, ST tines, 8 5/8″	75.00
Fork, 7 1/2″	70.00
Fork, cocktail, 5 3/4″	32.00
Fork, salad, 6″	50.00
Knife, HH, modern blade, 9″	40.00
Server, cheese, ST blade, 6 1/4″	55.00

Photo courtesy of Lenox, Inc.

Server, pie, ST blade, 10″	75.00
Serving Spoon, tablespoon, 7 3/4″	100.00
Spoon, cream soup, round bowl, 6 1/8″	60.00
Spoon, demitasse, 4 3/8″	27.00
Spoon, iced tea, 7 1/2″	45.00
Spoon, soup, oval bowl, 6 1/2″	60.00
Spoon, sugar, 6″	45.00
Spoon, teaspoon	27.00

Kirk Stieff, Old Maryland Engraved, Sterling Silver

Butter Serving Knife, HH, 6 7/8″	$50.00
Carving Knife, ST blade, 10 3/8″	80.00
Food Pusher, 3 1/4″	60.00
Fork, 7 1/4″	60.00
Fork, baby, 4 3/8″	45.00
Fork, salad, 6 1/4″	60.00
Fork, youth, 6 1/4″	55.00
Ice Cream Slicer, ST blade, 10 1/4″	80.00
Knife, cheese, ST blade, 7 1/8″	55.00
Knife, HH, modern blade, 9″	50.00
Knife, steak, 8 5/8″	55.00
Knife, wedding cake, ST blade, 11 3/4″	90.00
Knife, youth, 7 3/8″	50.00
Ladle, mayonnaise, 5 1/2″	55.00
Server, pastry, 10 3/8″	140.00
Server, pie, ST blade, 9 1/2″	80.00
Server, pie/cake, ST blade, 10 3/8″	80.00
Serving Fork, cold meat, 8 1/2″	140.00
Serving Spoon, casserole, 8 3/8″	130.00
Serving Spoon, tablespoon, 8 1/2″	100.00
Serving Spoon, tablespoon, pierced, 8 1/2″	105.00
Spoon, bonbon, 5 1/4″	50.00
Spoon, infant feeding, 5 5/8″	47.00
Spoon, soup, oval bowl, 6 3/4″	55.00
Spoon, sugar, shell-shaped bowl, 6 1/4″	50.00
Spoon, teaspoon, 6″	35.00

Kirk Stieff, Old Maryland Plain, Sterling Silver

Butter Spreader, FH, 5 3/8″	$22.00
Butter Spreader, HH, modern ST blade, 6 1/4″	22.00
Fork, 7 1/4″	50.00
Fork, baby, 4 3/8″	35.00
Fork, cocktail, 5 3/4″	30.00
Fork, salad	40.00
Knife	40.00
Knife, cheese, ST blade, 7″	40.00
Knife, youth, 7 1/4″	35.00
Ladle, cream soup, 5 1/2″	45.00
Ladle, gravy, 7″	80.00
Server, fish, ST blade, 10 3/8″	60.00
Server, pie, ST blade, 9 3/4″	60.00
Server, pie, ST blade, 10 1/8″	60.00
Spoon, bouillon, round bowl, 5 1/2″	32.00
Spoon, fruit, 5 7/8″	35.00
Spoon, salt, 2 1/2″	15.00
Spoon, teaspoon	25.00
Spoon, teaspoon, 5 o'clock, 5 5/8″	20.00

Kirk Stieff, Repoussé, Sterling Silver

Ashtray, 2 5/8″	$70.00
Ashtray, 3 1/4″	70.00
Bowl, bonbon, 6 1/4″	200.00
Bowl, vegetable, round, 9 1/2″	1,000.00
Butter Spreader, HH, modern ST blade, 6 1/4″	30.00

Carving Set, two pieces, ST blade 130.00
Creamer 1,300.00
Creamer and Sugar, covered, mini 2,200.00
Fork, 7 1/4″ 60.00
Fork, baby, 3 3/4″ 40.00
Fork, baby, 4 1/4″ 40.00
Fork, ice cream, 6″ 50.00
Fork, pickle, short handle, 5 3/4″ 30.00
Fork, salad, 6 1/4″ 50.00
Fork, youth, 6 1/4″ 50.00
Gravy Boat and Underplate 1,500.00
Knife, fruit, SP blade, 7 1/2″ 55.00
Knife, HH, modern blade, 9″ 40.00
Knife, HH, modern blade, 9 3/4″ 50.00
Knife, HH, Old French blade, 8 5/8″ 40.00
Knife, youth, 7 1/8″ 45.00
Ladle, gravy, 7″ 100.00
Letter Opener, ST blade, 5 7/8″ 45.00
Mayonnaise Bowl, 2 5/8″ 1,200.00
Pepper and Open Salt,
  stacking, 3 7/8″ 400.00
Plate, bread and butter, 6 1/4″ 100.00

Repoussé
Kirk Rose

America's first flower and foliage design, introduced by Samuel Kirk in 1828. The detailed artistry in design makes Repousse an incomparable pattern that will harmonize with any home decorative treatment. Kirk Rose combines the richness of ornate Repousse with an impressive monogram shield. The deep relief of chased roses in the heavy silver handles are perfect examples of the silver artisan's craftsmanship.

THE TOP FIVE PATTERNS
BAROQUE/RENAISSANCE—
STERLING

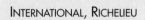

INTERNATIONAL, RICHELIEU

KIRK STIEFF, REPOUSSÉ

REED & BARTON, FRANCIS I

WALLACE, GRANDE BAROQUE

WHITING, LILY

Server, cheese, ST blade, 6 1/2″ 50.00
Server, pie, ST blade, 10″ 70.00
Serving Fork, cold meat, 7 1/2″ 80.00
Serving Fork, cold meat, 8 5/8″ 100.00
Serving Fork, cold meat, 9 1/4″ 130.00
Serving Spoon, 8 1/2″ 100.00
Serving Spoon, casserole, 7 1/2″ 160.00
Serving Spoon, casserole, 9 1/4″ 160.00
Serving Spoon, salad, 9 1/8″ 150.00
Serving Spoon, tablespoon, 8 3/8″ 85.00
Serving Spoon, tablespoon,
  pierced, 8 3/8″ 95.00
Spoon, fruit, 6 1/8″ 40.00
Spoon, iced tea, 7 5/8″ 40.00
Spoon, sugar, 6″ 45.00
Spoon, sugar, shell-shaped bowl, 6″ 45.00

Kirk Stieff, Rose, Sterling Silver

Butter Serving Knife, FH, 7 ³/₈″	$50.00
Butter Serving Knife, HH, 6 ⁷/₈″	50.00
Butter Spreader, FH, 5 ³/₈″	35.00
Butter Spreader, HH, modern ST blade, 6 ¹/₄″	35.00
Fork, 7 ³/₈″	60.00
Fork, salad, 6 ³/₈″	60.00
Knife, HH, New French blade, 9 ¹/₈″	45.00
Ladle, gravy, 7 ¹/₄″	115.00
Serving Spoon, tablespoon, 8 ³/₈″	100.00
Spoon, cream soup, round bowl, 6″	70.00
Spoon, demitasse, 4 ¹/₈″	32.00
Spoon, dessert, 6 ¹/₂″	60.00
Spoon, iced tea, 7 ⁵/₈″	45.00
Spoon, sugar, shell-shaped bowl, 6 ¹/₄″	50.00
Spoon, teaspoon, 6″	35.00

Ladle, cream sauce, 5 ¹/₄″	45.00
Ladle, gravy, 5 ³/₄″	80.00
Server, cheese, ST blade, 6 ¹/₄″	45.00
Server, pie, ST blade, 10 ¹/₈″	60.00
Server, pie/cake, ST blade, 10 ¹/₈″	60.00
Serving Fork, cold meat, 7 ¹/₂″	70.00
Serving Fork, salad, 8″	90.00
Serving Spoon, casserole, 8″	90.00
Serving Spoon, tablespoon, 7 ³/₄″	70.00
Spoon, baby, straight handle, 4 ¹/₂″	40.00
Spoon, bonbon, 5 ³/₈″	40.00
Spoon, chocolate, short handle, 4 ¹/₈″	32.00
Spoon, demitasse, 4 ³/₈″	25.00
Spoon, egg, 6″	40.00
Spoon, fruit, 6″	40.00
Spoon, grapefruit, round bowl, 7″	45.00
Spoon, iced tea, 7 ¹/₂″	35.00
Spoon, olive, 5 ³/₄″	80.00
Spoon, sugar, 6 ¹/₄″	40.00
Spoon, teaspoon, 5 ⁷/₈″	25.00
Spoon, teaspoon, 5 o'clock, 5 ⁵/₈″	15.00

Kirk Stieff, Stieff Rose, Sterling Silver

Ashtray, 3 ¹/₄″	$45.00
Butter Serving Knife, FH, 7 ¹/₈″	40.00
Carving Fork, ST tines, 9 ¹/₂″	65.00
Carving Set, two pieces, ST blade	110.00
Fork, 6 ⁷/₈″	45.00
Fork, baby, 4 ¹/₂″	40.00
Fork, bacon, 8 ¹/₄″	110.00
Fork, lemon, 4 ⁷/₈″	27.00
Fork, salad	35.00
Fork, youth, 6 ¹/₈″	45.00
Knife, HH, New French blade, 8 ⁷/₈″	35.00

Kirk Stieff, Williamsburg Queen Anne, Sterling Silver

Fork	$60.00
Fork, 7 ³/₄″	80.00
Fork, baby, 4 ⁵/₈″	45.00
Fork, salad	60.00
Knife	50.00
Knife, steak, 8 ¹/₄″	60.00
Serving Spoon, tablespoon, 7 ⁷/₈″	120.00
Spoon, sugar, 5 ⁵/₈″	50.00
Spoon, teaspoon	40.00

Kirk Stieff, Williamsburg Shell, Sterling Silver

Fork, 7 5/8″	$75.00
Fork, baby, 5″	50.00
Fork, salad, 6 5/8″	55.00
Fork, youth, 6 1/2″	55.00
Knife, fish, ST blade, 8″	50.00
Knife, pistol grip, modern blade, 9 3/4″	55.00
Spoon, teaspoon	35.00

LUNT SILVERSMITHS
(ROGERS, LUNT & BOWLEN)

Lunt Silversmiths traces its origin to William Moulton II, a seventeenth-century silversmith, and his descendants. Anthony Towle, born in 1814, apprenticed under Joseph Moulton. Anthony Towle and his son established A. F. Towle & Son Manufacturing Company in Newburyport, Massachusetts, in 1880. Three years later, the Towles left and created a completely different firm, A. F. Towle & Son Company, also located in Newburyport. New management assumed control of the old firm and retained its name, thus causing confusion relative to the Towles' role.

A. F. Towle & Son Company continued to manufacture silverware in Newburyport until 1890, at which time they transferred their operations to a new factory in Greenfield, Massachusetts. In an attempt to diversify, the company turned to the manufacture of automobiles. The company failed in November 1900, due in part to the lack of financing and interest in the firm's Hertle Horseless Carriages.

George C. Lunt, apprenticed to Anthony Towle to learn the engraving trade, obtained outside financing, purchased what remained of A. F. Towle, and established Rogers, Lunt & Bowlen Company in 1902. Rogers was a local Greenfield resident, not a member of the famous Rogers silversmith dynasty. William C. Bowlen, like Lunt, was a former A. F. Towle employee who supervised the manufacturing operations while Lunt managed the office. The company acquired the Franklin Silver Plate Company in Greenfield, Massachusetts, in the early 1920s.

George Lunt is responsible for the sculptured quality of many Lunt flatware patterns. He studied modeling and design under Max Bachman, a Boston sculptor. Nord Lunt, George's son, succeeded his father as head designer.

Rogers, Lunt & Bowlen first used the Lunt Silversmiths trade name in 1935. Pieces are trademarked "LUNT STERLING." Lunt favored jewelry stores as outlets for its products. In fact, he developed "LUNT EXCLUSIVES," a line of products sold only through fine jewelry and silverware stores. Much of the company's advertising emphasized monogramming, that is, personalizing silver flatware. The company included engraving among its services.

Rogers, Lunt & Bowlen acquired the King Silver Company of Boston around 1957. The trademarks and assets of the Richard Dimes Co. came with the purchase. Lunt introduced a line of stainless steel flatware in 1979 and a line of silver-plated flatware in 1980.

ROGERS, LUNT & BOWLEN COMPANY MARKS

The earliest pieces are marked with the letters "R / L / BCo.," each in a block attached to a triangle with "&" in its center and flanked to the left by "TRADEMARK" and to the right by "STERLING." The company registered and used the trademark "Treasure" between 1921 and 1954. Today, only LUNT is used as a trademark.

The company's baby goods are trademarked "Little Men and Little Women." Some silver-plated baby ware is marked "Wee Folks."

Lunt Silversmiths, American Victorian, Sterling Silver

Butter Serving Knife, FH, 6 7/8"	$35.00
Butter Spreader, FH, 5 7/8"	25.00
Butter Spreader, HH, paddled ST blade, 6 1/8"	25.00
Fork, 7 1/4"	45.00
Fork, 7 5/8"	65.00
Fork, lemon, 4 7/8"	32.00
Fork, pickle, short handle, 5 5/8"	32.00
Fork, salad, 6 3/8"	35.00
Knife, HH, modern blade, 9 3/4"	45.00
Knife, HH, New French blade, 8 3/4"	32.00
Ladle, gravy, 5 7/8"	80.00
Server, cheese, ST blade, 6 1/2"	45.00
Server, pie, ST blade, 10"	65.00
Serving Spoon, casserole, 7 1/2"	110.00
Serving Spoon, tablespoon, 8 3/8"	70.00
Spoon, cream soup, round bowl, 6 1/4"	32.00
Spoon, demitasse, 4 3/8"	22.00
Spoon, iced tea, 7 3/8"	35.00
Spoon, sugar, 5 7/8"	40.00
Spoon, teaspoon, 5 3/4"	22.00

Lunt Silversmiths, Bel Chateau, Sterling Silver

Carving Knife, ST blade, 10 3/4"	$80.00
Carving Set, two pieces, ST blade	160.00
Fork, 7 3/8"	55.00
Fork, salad, 6 1/2"	60.00
Knife, HH, modern blade, 9"	45.00
Knife, steak, 9"	55.00
Ladle, soup, 12 1/2"	250.00
Ladle, soup, ST bowl, 12 1/2"	100.00
Salad Set, two pieces	230.00
Server, asparagus, 9 3/4"	200.00
Server, pastry, 9 3/4"	125.00
Server, pie/cake, ST blade, 10 1/2"	80.00
Server, pie/cake, ST blade, 10 3/4"	80.00
Server, tomato, 9 1/2"	100.00
Serving Fork, cold meat, 8"	95.00
Serving Spoon, ice, 9 3/8"	150.00
Serving Spoon, tablespoon, pierced, 8 1/2"	105.00
Spoon, infant feeding, 5 3/8"	45.00
Spoon, soup, oval bowl, 6 5/8"	60.00
Spoon, teaspoon	35.00

Lunt Silversmiths, Eloquence, Sterling Silver

Butter Spreader, FH, 6″	$35.00
Fork, 7 3/8″	50.00
Fork, 7 7/8″	70.00
Fork, ice cream, 5 7/8″	55.00
Fork, pickle, short handle, 5 7/8″	35.00
Fork, salad	50.00

Fork, strawberry, 4 3/4″	35.00
Knife, HH, modern blade, 9″	40.00
Knife, HH, modern blade, 9 3/4″	50.00
Knife, steak, 9 1/4″	45.00
Ladle, gravy, 6 1/4″	95.00
Ladle, soup, 12 1/2″	275.00
Salad Set, two pieces, plastic bowl, 11 1/8″	90.00
Salad Set, two pieces, 9 1/4″	200.00
Server, asparagus, 9 3/4″	100.00
Server, egg, 9 3/8″	110.00
Server, pastry, 9 3/4″	120.00
Serving Fork, buffet, 11 1/8″	200.00
Serving Fork, fish, 9 1/4″	110.00
Serving Fork, salad, 9 1/4″	100.00
Serving Set, fish, two pieces	200.00
Serving Spoon, ice, 9 3/8″	110.00
Spoon, cracker, 7 3/4″	130.00
Spoon, cream soup, round bowl, 6 1/4″	50.00
Spoon, sugar, 6 1/4″	45.00
Spoon, teaspoon	30.00

Lunt Silversmiths, Lace Point, Sterling Silver

Butter Serving Knife, HH, 6 3/4″	$35.00
Fork, 7 1/2″	50.00
Fork, baby, 3 7/8″	40.00
Fork, salad	45.00
Knife, HH, modern blade, 9″	35.00
Ladle, gravy, 6 1/4″	90.00
Spoon, bonbon, 4 7/8″	45.00
Spoon, jelly, 6 1/8″	35.00
Spoon, sugar spoon, 6 1/8″	35.00
Spoon, teaspoon	25.00

Lunt Silversmiths, Madrigal, Sterling Silver

Butter Serving Knife, HH, 6 ¾″	$35.00
Carving Fork, ST tines, 9 ¼″	55.00
Fork, 7 ½″	55.00
Fork, pickle, short handle, 5 ¾″	30.00
Fork, salad	37.00
Knife, HH, modern blade, 9″	32.00
Knife, steak, 9 ⅛″	45.00
Salad Set, two pieces, plastic bowl	80.00
Server, pie/cake, ST blade, 10 ½″	60.00
Serving Fork, cold meat, 8 ⅛″	80.00
Serving Spoon, tablespoon, 8 ¼″	75.00
Serving Spoon, tablespoon, pierced, 8 ¼″	80.00
Spoon, sugar, 6″	37.00
Spoon, teaspoon, 6″	25.00

Lunt Silversmiths, Mignonette, Sterling Silver

Butter Serving Knife, 6 ¾″	$45.00
Butter Spreader, HH, modern ST blade, 6 ¼″	32.00
Carving Knife, ST blade, 12″	80.00
Fork, 7 ½″	70.00
Fork, pickle, short handle, 5 ¾″	40.00
Fork, salad, 6 ⅝″	60.00
Knife, HH, modern blade, 9 ⅛″	50.00
Knife, steak, 9 ⅛″	60.00
Ladle, cream sauce, 5 ½″	65.00

Ladle, gravy, 6 ½″	110.00
Server, pie/cake, ST blade, 10 ⅝″	85.00
Serving Fork, cold meat, 7 ⅞″	100.00
Serving Spoon, tablespoon, 8 ¼″	95.00
Spoon, baby, straight handle, 4 ¼″	50.00
Spoon, bonbon, 6″	55.00
Spoon, iced tea, 7 ⅜″	45.00
Spoon, jelly, 6 ¼″	50.00
Spoon, sugar, 6 ¼″	50.00
Spoon, teaspoon, 6 ⅛″	35.00

Lunt Silversmiths, Modern Victorian, Sterling Silver

Butter Serving Knife, FH, 6 ¾″	$35.00
Butter Serving Knife, HH, 6 ⅞″	35.00
Butter Spreader, FH, 5 ⅞″	25.00
Butter Spreader, HH, modern ST blade, 6 ¼″	25.00
Butter Spreader, HH, paddled ST blade, 6 ⅛″	25.00
Fork, 7 ¼″	40.00
Fork, 7 ⅝″	60.00
Fork, baby, 4 ⅛″	35.00
Fork, cocktail, 5 ⅞″	30.00
Fork, lemon, 5″	30.00
Fork, salad, 6 ⅜″	40.00
Fork, strawberry, 4 ⅞″	35.00
Knife, HH, modern blade, 9″	35.00
Knife, HH, modern blade, 9 ¾″	45.00
Knife, HH, New French blade, 8 ⅝″	35.00
Knife, HH, New French blade, 9 ½″	45.00
Knife, youth, 7″	40.00
Ladle, cream sauce, 5 ⅛″	45.00
Ladle, gravy, 6″	80.00
Server, asparagus, 9 ½″	140.00
Server, cheese, ST blade, 6 ⅝″	45.00

Server, pie, ST blade, 9 3/4″	60.00	Fork, pickle, short handle, 5 7/8″	30.00
Serving Fork, cold meat, 7 1/2″	80.00	Fork, youth, 6 1/4″	50.00
Serving Fork, salad, 9″	85.00	Knife, cheese, ST blade, 7 1/8″	45.00
Serving Set, fish, two pieces	240.00	Knife, HH, modern blade, 8 7/8″	37.00
Serving Spoon, casserole, 8 7/8″	110.00	Knife, youth, 7 5/8″	40.00
Serving Spoon, casserole, 9 1/8″	110.00	Ladle, cream sauce, 5″	45.00
Serving Spoon, dressing, 10 3/4″	170.00	Server, pie, ST blade, 9 3/4″	70.00
Serving Spoon, ice, 9 1/4″	130.00	Server, pie/cake, ST blade, 10 1/2″	70.00
Serving Spoon, tablespoon, 8 3/8″	70.00	Serving Fork, cold meat, 7 5/8″	85.00
Spoon, bonbon, 5″	40.00	Spoon, bonbon, 5″	45.00
Spoon, cracker, 7 1/2″	140.00	Spoon, cream soup, round bowl, 6 1/4″	50.00
Spoon, cream soup, round bowl, 6 1/4″	40.00	Spoon, soup, oval bowl, 6 3/4″	60.00
Spoon, demitasse, 4 1/2″	22.00	Spoon, sugar, 6″	40.00
Spoon, fruit, 5 3/4″	40.00	Spoon, teaspoon, 6″	25.00
Spoon, iced tea, 7 3/8″	40.00	Spoon, teaspoon, 5 o'clock, 5 3/8″	20.00
Spoon, infant feeding, 5 3/8″	35.00		
Spoon, jelly, 6 1/8″	30.00		
Spoon, salt, 2 5/8″	15.00		
Spoon, soup, oval bowl, 6 5/8″	445.00		
Spoon, sugar, 5 7/8″	40.00		
Spoon, teaspoon, 6″	25.00		
Spoon, teaspoon, 5 o'clock, 5 3/4″	20.00		

Lunt Silversmiths, William & Mary, Sterling Silver

Butter Serving Knife, FH, 7″	$35.00
Butter Serving Knife, HH, 6 3/4″	35.00
Butter Spreader, FH, 5 3/4″	22.00
Butter Spreader, HH, modern ST blade, 6 1/4″	22.00
Butter Spreader, HH, paddled ST blade, 6 1/8″	22.00
Carving Knife, ST blade, 14 1/8″	55.00
Carving Set, two pieces, ST blade	110.00
Fork, 7 1/8″	35.00
Fork, 7 3/4″	55.00
Fork, cocktail, 5 5/8″	27.00
Fork, lemon, 4 7/8″	32.00
Fork, pickle, short handle, 5 5/8″	32.00
Fork, salad, 6″	35.00
Fork, strawberry, 4 7/8″	35.00
Knife, cheese, ST blade, 7 1/8″	45.00
Knife, HH, blunt blade, 8 7/8″	35.00
Knife, HH, New French blade, 9″	35.00

Lunt Silversmiths, Sweetheart Rose, Sterling Silver

Butter Serving Knife, HH, 6 3/4″	$40.00
Butter Spreader, FH, 5 3/4″	27.00
Butter Spreader, HH, modern ST blade, 6 1/4″	27.00
Butter Spreader, HH, paddled ST blade, 6 1/8″	27.00
Fork, 7 1/4″	50.00
Fork, 7 3/4″	65.00
Fork, baby, 4″	40.00
Fork, cocktail, 5 7/8″	30.00
Fork, lemon, 5″	30.00

THE TOP FIVE PATTERNS

TRADITIONAL—

STERLING

GORHAM, CHANTILLY

KIRK STIEFF, WILLIAMSBURG SHELL

LUNT, WILLIAM AND MARY

WALLACE, GRAND COLONIAL

WESTMORLAND, GEORGE AND MARTHA WASHINGTON

Knife, HH, Old French blade, 9 ½″	45.00
Knife, steak, 8 ⅞″	45.00
Knife, steak, 9 ¼″	45.00
Knife Sharpener, steel sharpener, 10 ¼″	55.00
Ladle, cream sauce, 5″	45.00
Ladle, gravy, 5 ⅞″	80.00
Ladle, mayonnaise, 4 ¾″	45.00

Ladle, soup, 12″	220.00
Server, asparagus, 9 ¾″	140.00
Server, cheese, ST blade, 6 ⅝″	45.00
Server, pastry, 9″	95.00
Server, pie, SP blade, 10 ⅜″	60.00
Server, pie, ST blade, 9 ¾″	60.00
Server, pie, ST blade, 10 ⅜″	60.00
Server, tomato, 7 ⅝″	100.00
Server, tomato, 9 ⅜″	100.00
Serving Fork, buffet, 11 ¼″	140.00
Serving Fork, cold meat, 7 ½″	80.00
Serving Spoon, dressing, 11 ⅛″	150.00
Serving Spoon, ice, 9 ¼″	130.00
Serving Spoon, tablespoon, 8 ⅝″	65.00
Spoon, baby, straight handle, 4 ¼″	35.00
Spoon, bonbon, 4 ¾″	40.00
Spoon, bouillon, round bowl, 5 ½″	35.00
Spoon, cracker, 7 ⅝″	120.00
Spoon, demitasse, 4 ⅜″	20.00
Spoon, fruit, 5 ¾″	40.00
Spoon, ice cream, 5 ⅝″	37.00
Spoon, iced tea, 7 ¾″	37.00
Spoon, jelly, 6″	32.00
Spoon, sugar, 5 ¾″	37.00
Spoon, teaspoon, 6″	25.00
Spoon, teaspoon, 5 o'clock, 5 ¾″	17.00
Spoon, youth, 5 ½″	35.00
Sugar Tongs, 3 ½″	50.00

In March 1848, John Humphrey Noyes and his followers, largely New Englanders, created the Oneida Community, a Utopian religious and social society, in Oneida, New York.

Two years earlier, Noyes and a small group of followers had gathered at his homestead in Putney, Vermont. Noyes developed the concept of Perfectionism, a form of Christianity based on the values of self-perfection and communalism. These ideals were translated into everyday life through shared property, work, and "complex marriage," that is, monogamous marriage was abandoned and children were communally raised. The religious leaders of Putney found Noyes's views distasteful, and he and his followers were asked to leave.

Fortunately, the Ackley, Burt, and Nash families, followers of Noyes, had established residences on the banks of the Oneida Creek in New York. They invited Noyes and the other Vermont exiles to New York.

Realizing that farming would not sustain its members, the Oneida Community, driven by a strong work ethic, began a number of business ventures. By the 1860s, the community offered a line of canned fruits and vegetables, chains, mop sticks, silk thread, straw hats, traps, and traveling bags. Oneida's Newhouse trap achieved worldwide recognition.

The Oneida Community's Wallingford factory manufactured Lily and Oval, two patterns of ungraded, tinned iron spoons in 1877. Within a year, the factory was selling large quantities of steel spoon blanks to the Meriden Britannia Company, which plated and sold them under their own brand name. In 1880, Oneida moved its flatware operations to a factory in Niagara Falls, New York.

In 1880, the Oneida Community abandoned its communal society. The Oneida Community, Ltd., a joint stock company designed to continue the many businesses conducted by the Oneida Community, was created. The initial stock was divided among the 226 men, women, and children who comprised the Community. The fifteen years following the reorganization were troubling ones, due to internal management strife. The situation changed dramatically after Pierrepont Burt Noyes, John's son, led an 1894 proxy fight against the directors who clung to the old ways. Noyes began his reign at Oneida by becoming superintendent at Oneida's Niagara Falls plant.

The last decades of the nineteenth century were devoted to improving the quality of Oneida's flatware. A new design, Avalon, was introduced at the 1901 Buffalo Exposition. In January 1902, Oneida began marketing its Community Plate line.

Pierrepont Burt Noyes became general manager, with the authority to oversee all of the company's divisions—canning, and the manufacture of chains, silk thread, tableware, and traps. Noyes introduced new production methods, competitive strategies, and large-scale distribution methods and pursued an ambitious marketing campaign. Print advertising was aggressively promoted in women's magazines. Rather than picturing an entire line of silverware, Oneida illustrated one or two silver plate patterns. Oneida was one of the first companies to employ celebrity spokespersons to promote its products. Irene Castle, a famous dancer and fashion plate, was one of the first celebrities to promote Oneida's Community ware.

Oneida gradually moved its flatware manufacturing from Niagara Falls to Sherrill, New York, between 1912 and 1914. It sold its chain business in 1912, its silk business in 1913, and its canning operations in 1915. In 1916, a factory was opened in Niagara Falls, Ontario, Canada. The Kenwood Silver Company (Sheffield, England), an Oneida marketing and distribution group, was established in 1926. In 1929, Oneida bought Wm. A. Rogers, Ltd. The sales included the brand names of *1881 Rogers, Heirloom,* and *Simeon L. & George H. Rogers Company.*

Oneida began producing silver-plated hollowware in 1926. It entered the sterling silver flatware market in 1933, introducing thirty-one different patterns between 1933 and 1982. In 1935, the company's name was changed to Oneida, Ltd., more commonly known as Oneida Silversmith.

Following World War II, the company once again faced difficult financial circumstances. The workforce declined from 3,800 in 1949 to 2,000 in 1960. Oneida's commitment to stainless steel flatware reversed the situation. Chateau, one of the first stainless patterns to emulate sterlinglike designs successfully, was introduced in the early 1960s. In 1965, Oneida adopted the Roman cube "tessera hospitalis" as the company's symbol of excellence. The solid silver cube is engraved with the company's name on all of its surfaces. By the late 1960s, technological advances enabled Oneida to introduce the first ornate traditional pierced pattern in stainless.

In 1977, Oneida acquired Camden Wire Company, a leading producer of industrial wire products. Rena-Ware, a cookware manufacturer with operations in thirty-four countries, was added in 1978. International sold Oneida Webster-Wilcox, a manufacturer of plated hollowware, in 1981. Buffalo China, a major manufacturer of restaurant and institutional dinnerware, joined the Oneida family in 1983. One year later, Oneida purchased D. J. Tableware, a marketer of high-quality flatware, hollowware, and china for the food service industry. Oneida also entered the cut crystal stemware and giftware markets.

John Marcellus, the first chief executive officer who was not a descendent of one of the founding Noyes families, became president in 1978. William Matthews succeeded him in 1986. Oneida responded to shifting market conditions with a renewed emphasis on its high-volume, less-expensive flatware lines to complement its sterling flatware line.

Oneida invested more than $100 million into plant improvements, including computer design and manufacturing systems, plant consolidation, and machinery upgrades between the late 1980s and early 1990s. The company sold its Rena-Ware holdings in the early 1980s. A few years later, Oneida, Ltd., became a majority owner of Oneida International, Inc., a joint venture formed to market Italian-designed tabletop products. The products are sold in the international food service market through an Italian subsidiary, Sant'Andrea. The Kenwood Silver subsidiary, now headquartered in the United States, expanded its network of retail stores in resort and destination shopping areas. An employee stock ownership plan was begun in 1987. Oneida sold its Northern Ireland manufacturing facilities in 1989 and the Camden Wire Company in 1997.

By the early 1990s, Oneida's dominance of the American flatware market was reflected in a 52 percent market share. A 1992 independent national consumer study found that 87 percent of consumers named Oneida as the first company they think of when asked about stainless steel flatware.

ONEIDA'S WARTIME CONTRIBUTIONS

Although exempt from Civil War duty because of their religious beliefs, the Oneida Community and its adherents played an active role in World War I, World War II, and the Korean War.

Over 250 members enlisted for service in World War I. The company turned its efforts to producing much-needed wartime supplies—ammunition clips, combat knives, and lead-plated gas shells. Surgical instruments were their best-known products.

Pierrepont Burt Noyes served with the U.S. government's Fuel Administration. Later, he served in Europe on the World War I Peace Conference and the Rhineland Commission to decide the particulars of the Allied occupation of Germany.

An additional 900 members served in World War II and Korea. Oneida made flatware for the army and navy. The company resumed its surgical instrument business. Other wartime products from the company included aircraft fuel tanks, aircraft elevators, bayonets, bomb shackle releases, carbine slides, chemical bombs, engine bearing plating, hand grenades, parachute hardware, parachute quick-release devices, rifle sights, shells, and survival guns. Oneida even purchased a separate factory in Canastoga, New York, where the company made aircraft survival kits, various army trucks, and photographic trailers.

For a brief period of time following the wars, Oneida made compressor rotor and stator blades for jet engines.

STERLING

Oneida Silversmiths, Damask Rose, Sterling Silver, Heirloom Sterling
(Introduced in 1946)

Butter Serving Knife, FH, 6 ⅞″	$30.00
Butter Serving Knife, HH, 6 ⅜″	30.00
Butter Spreader, FH, 5 ⅞″	22.00
Butter Spreader, HH, paddled ST blade, 6 ¼″	22.00
Carving Set, two pieces, ST blade	100.00
Fork, 7 ¼″	40.00
Fork, 7 ⅝″	50.00

Fork, baby, 4 ⅜″	35.00
Fork, cocktail, 5 ½″	25.00
Fork, lemon, 5 ⅜″	25.00
Fork, pickle, short handle, 5 ¾″	25.00
Fork, salad, 6 ½″	30.00
Fork, youth, 5 ⅞″	35.00
Knife, HH, modern blade, 8 ⅞″	30.00
Knife, HH, modern blade, 9 ½″	35.00
Ladle, cream sauce, 5 ½″	40.00
Ladle, gravy, 6 ½″	70.00
Server, pie, ST blade, 10″	55.00
Server, pie/cake, ST blade, 10 ½″	55.00
Serving Fork, cold meat, 8 ¼″	70.00
Spoon, cream soup, round bowl, 6 ½″	30.00
Spoon, dessert, 6 ⅝″	35.00
Spoon, fruit, 6″	32.00
Spoon, iced tea, 7 ½″	35.00
Spoon, infant feeding, 5 ⅝″	35.00
Spoon, jelly, 6 ⅜″	30.00
Spoon, soup, oval soup, 7″	35.00
Spoon, sugar, 6 ⅛″	35.00
Spoon, teaspoon	25.00

Photo courtesy of Oneida, Ltd.

Oneida Silversmiths, Heiress, Sterling Silver

Butter Serving Knife, FH, 6 ⅞″	$30.00
Butter Spreader, FH, 5 ¾″	20.00
Carving Set, two pieces, ST blade	110.00
Fork, 7 ⅛″	40.00
Fork, cocktail, 5 ½″	20.00
Fork, grille, 7 ⅝″	35.00
Fork, salad, 6 ¼″	30.00
Knife, grille, HH, modern blade, 8 ⅜″	27.00
Knife, HH, modern blade, 9 ⅛″	27.00
Ladle, gravy, 6 ⅜″	70.00

Serving Fork, cold meat, 8 ⅛″	70.00
Serving Spoon, tablespoon, 8 ½″	60.00
Spoon, cream soup, round bowl, 6″	32.00
Spoon, demitasse, 4 ⅛″	20.00
Spoon, fruit, 5 ⅞″	30.00
Spoon, iced tea, 7 ½″	30.00
Spoon, sugar, 6″	30.00
Spoon, teaspoon, 6″	20.00

Spoon, sugar, 6 ⅛″	30.00
Spoon, teaspoon, 6 ⅛″	20.00
Spoon, teaspoon, 5 o'clock, 5 ¼″	17.00

Oneida Silversmiths, Michelangelo, Sterling Silver, Heirloom Sterling
(Introduced in 1970)

Butter Serving Knife, HH, 6 ¾″	$40.00
Butter Spreader, HH, paddled ST blade, 6 ½″	25.00
Fork, 7 ⅜″	45.00
Fork, cocktail, 6″	32.00
Fork, salad, 6 ½″	40.00
Knife, HH, modern blade, 9″	32.00
Server, pie/cake, ST blade, 10 ¾″	70.00
Serving Spoon, tablespoon, pierced, 8 ¼″	90.00
Spoon, iced tea, 7 ⅜″	40.00
Spoon, soup, oval bowl, 6 ⅝″	45.00
Spoon, sugar, shell-shaped bowl, 6″	40.00
Spoon, teaspoon, 6″	20.00

Oneida Silversmiths, Lasting Spring, Sterling Silver, Heirloom Sterling
(Introduced in 1949)

Butter Serving knife, FH, 6 ⅞″	$30.00
Butter Spreader, FH, 6 ⅛″	22.00
Butter Spreader, HH, paddled ST blade, 6 ¼″	22.00
Carving Set, two pieces, ST blade	100.00
Fork, 7 ¼″	37.00
Fork, 7 ⅞″	50.00
Fork, baby, 4 ¼″	32.00
Fork, cocktail, 5 ⅜″	22.00
Fork, dessert, 6 ⅝″	40.00
Fork, lemon, 5 ⅜″	25.00
Fork, pickle, short handle, 5 ⅞″	25.00
Fork, salad, 6 ⅝″	32.00
Fork, youth, 5 ⅞″	35.00
Knife, HH, modern blade, 8 ⅞″	27.00
Knife Sharpener, steel sharpener, 11 ¼″	45.00
Ladle, cream sauce, 5 ⅜″	40.00
Ladle, gravy, 6 ⅜″	65.00
Serving Fork, cold meat, 8 ⅛″	60.00
Serving Spoon, casserole, 8 ½″	85.00
Serving Spoon, tablespoon, 8 ¼″	60.00
Spoon, cream soup, round bowl, 6 ½″	35.00
Spoon, iced tea, 7 ½″	30.00
Spoon, jelly, 6 ¼″	27.00

Oneida Silversmiths, Virginian, Sterling Silver

Butter Serving Knife, FH, 6 ⅞″	$35.00
Butter Spreader, FH, 5 ¾″	25.00
Carving Set, two pieces, ST blade	120.00
Fork, 7 ¼″	45.00

Fork, grille, 7 1/2″	40.00
Fork, salad, 6 3/8″	35.00
Knife, grille, HH, modern blade, 8 1/2″	30.00
Knife, HH, modern blade, 9 1/4″	32.00
Ladle, gravy, 6 3/8″	80.00
Server, pie, ST blade, 9 7/8″	60.00
Serving Fork, cold meat, 8 1/8″	80.00
Serving Spoon, casserole, 8 5/8″	90.00
Spoon, cream soup, round bowl, 6 1/4″	35.00
Spoon, iced tea, 7 1/2″	35.00
Spoon, sugar, 6 1/8″	40.00
Spoon, teaspoon, 6″	25.00

Serving Fork, cold meat, 8 1/2″	30.00
Serving Spoon, tablespoon, 8 1/4″	20.00
Spoon, cream soup, round bowl, 6 1/8″	12.00
Spoon, demitasse, 4 1/2″	12.00
Spoon, iced tea, 7 1/2″	12.00
Spoon, soup, oval bowl, 7 3/8″	12.00
Spoon, sugar, 6 1/8″	15.00
Spoon, teaspoon, 6 1/8″	10.00

SILVER PLATE

Oneida Silversmiths, Bordeaux, Silver Plate

Butter Serving Knife, FH, 6 3/4″	$15.00
Butter Spreader, FH, 6 3/8″	12.00
Carving Fork, ST tines, 8 1/4″	40.00
Carving Fork, ST tines, 8 3/4″	40.00
Carving Set, two pieces, ST blade	80.00
Carving Set, three pieces, ST blade	115.00
Fork, 7 5/8″	15.00
Fork, cocktail, 6 1/8″	12.00
Fork, grille, 7 5/8″	12.00
Fork, salad, 6 3/8″	12.00
Knife, grille, HH, modern blade, 8 1/2″	12.00
Knife, HH, modern blade, 9 1/4″	15.00
Knife Sharpener, steel sharpener, 10 7/8″	40.00
Ladle, gravy, 7 1/8″	25.00
Salad Set, two pieces, wooden bowl	50.00
Server, pie, 10 7/8″	45.00
Server, pie, ST blade, 10″	45.00
Server, tomato, 7 7/8″	30.00

Oneida Silversmiths, Caprice, Silver Plate

Butter Serving Knife, FH, 7″	$15.00
Butter Spreader, FH, 6 3/8″	10.00
Butter Spreader, HH, paddled ST blade, 6 3/8″	12.00
Carving Fork, ST tines, 8 3/4″	40.00

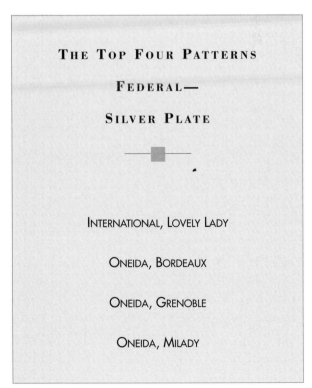

THE TOP FOUR PATTERNS

FEDERAL—

SILVER PLATE

INTERNATIONAL, LOVELY LADY

ONEIDA, BORDEAUX

ONEIDA, GRENOBLE

ONEIDA, MILADY

Carving Set, two pieces, ST blade	80.00		Fork, baby, 5 1/8″	15.00
Carving Set, three pieces, ST blade	115.00		Fork, cocktail, 6″	10.00
Fork	15.00		Fork, grille, 7 1/2″	12.00
Fork, cocktail, 6″	10.00		Fork, pie, 5 1/2″	15.00
Fork, grille, 7 1/2″	12.00		Fork, salad, 6 3/8″	12.00
Fork, salad, 6 1/2″	12.00		Fork, salad, 6 3/4″	12.00
Knife, grille, HH, New French blade, 8 3/8″	12.00		Knife, grille, HH, modern blade, 8 1/2″	12.00
Knife, HH, New French blade, 9 1/2″	15.00		Knife, grille, HH, New French blade, 8 1/2″	12.00
Knife Sharpener, steel sharpener, 11″	40.00		Knife, HH, modern blade, 8 3/4″	15.00
Ladle, gravy, 7 1/8″	25.00		Knife, HH, modern blade, 9″	15.00
Server, pie, ST blade, 9 7/8″	50.00		Knife, HH, modern blade, 9 1/2″	15.00
Server, tomato, 7 3/4″	30.00		Knife, HH, New French blade, 8 5/8″	15.00
Serving Fork, cold meat, 8 1/2″	30.00		Knife, HH, New French blade, 9 1/2″	15.00
Serving Spoon, tablespoon, 8 3/8″	20.00		Knife, steak, 9 1/8″	15.00
Spoon, cream soup, round bowl, 6 1/8″	12.00		Ladle, gravy, 7 1/8″	27.00
Spoon, fruit, 6 1/8″	12.00		Server, pie, 9 3/4 ″	45.00
Spoon, grapefruit, round bowl, 6 7/8″	12.00		Server, pie, 10 1/4″	45.00
Spoon, iced tea, 7 1/2″	12.00		Server, pie, 10 3/4″	45.00
Spoon, soup, oval bowl, 7 1/4″	12.00		Server, pie, ST blade, 10″	45.00
Spoon, sugar, 6 1/8″	15.00		Server, pie, ST blade, 10 1/2″	45.00
Spoon, teaspoon, 6 1/8″	7.00		Server, pie/cake, ST blade, 10 3/4″	55.00
Spoon, teaspoon, 5 o'clock, 5 3/8″	7.00		Serving Fork, cold meat, 8 3/8″	30.00
			Serving Spoon, tablespoon, 8 1/4″	20.00
			Serving Spoon, tablespoon, 8 1/2″	20.00
			Spoon, bonbon, 4 1/2″	15.00
			Spoon, cream soup, round bowl, 6 1/8″	12.00
			Spoon, demitasse, 4 3/8″	12.00
			Spoon, dessert, 6 7/8″	15.00
			Spoon, grapefruit, round bowl, 6 7/8″	12.00
			Spoon, iced tea, 7 1/2″	12.00
			Spoon, infant feeding, 5 5/8″	15.00
			Spoon, jelly, 6 1/4″	20.00
			Spoon, soup, oval bowl, 7 1/4″	12.00
			Spoon, sugar, 6″	15.00
			Spoon, teaspoon, 6 1/8″	7.00
			Spoon, teaspoon, 5 o'clock, 5 1/4″	7.00

Oneida Silversmiths, Coronation, Silver Plate

Butter Serving Knife, FH, 6 7/8″	$15.00
Butter Spreader, FH, 5 1/2″	12.00
Butter Spreader, FH, 6 1/4″	12.00
Carving Fork, ST tines, 8 5/8″	45.00
Carving Fork, ST tines, 9″	45.00
Carving Knife, ST blade, 11 3/8″	60.00
Carving Set, two pieces, ST blade	90.00
Fork, 7 1/4″	15.00
Fork, 7 1/2″	15.00
Fork, baby, 4 3/4″	15.00

Carving Fork, ST tines, 8 ⅝″	50.00
Carving Set, two pieces, ST blade	100.00
Carving Set, three pieces, ST blade	145.00
Fork, 7 ⅛″	17.00
Fork, 7 ⅝″	17.00
Fork, cocktail, 6″	12.00
Fork, grille, 7 ½″	15.00
Fork, pickle, short handle, 6 ⅜″	17.00
Fork, salad, 6 ½″	15.00
Knife, grille, HH, modern blade, 8 ⅜″	15.00
Knife, grille, HH, New French blade, 8 ⅜″	15.00
Knife, HH, New French blade, 8 ⅝″	17.00
Knife Sharpener, steel sharpener, 10 ⅞″	50.00
Ladle, gravy, 7 ⅛″	30.00
Salad Set, two pieces, plastic bowl	50.00
Server, pie, ST blade, 9 ⅞″	60.00
Server, tomato, 7 ¾″	37.00
Serving Fork, cold meat, 8 ½″	35.00
Serving Spoon, casserole, 9″	35.00
Serving Spoon, tablespoon, 8 ½″	20.00
Spoon, bouillon, round bowl, 5″	12.00
Spoon, cream soup, round bowl, 6 ⅛″	15.00
Spoon, demitasse, 4 ½″	12.00
Spoon, fruit, 6″	15.00
Spoon, grapefruit, round bowl, 6 ⅞″	12.00
Spoon, iced tea, 7 ½″	15.00
Spoon, soup, oval bowl, 7 ⅜″	15.00
Spoon, sugar, 6″	17.00
Spoon, teaspoon, 6 ¼″	10.00
Sugar Tongs, 3 ½″	45.00

Oneida Silversmiths, Evening Star, Silver Plate

Butter Serving Knife, FH, 7″	$17.00
Butter Spreader, FH, 6 ¼″	12.00
Fork, 7 ⅝″	15.00
Fork, cocktail, 6 ⅛″	12.00
Fork, grille, 7 ¾″	12.00
Fork, salad, 6 ⅝″	12.00
Knife, grille, HH, modern blade, 8 ½″	12.00
Knife, HH, modern blade, 9 ¼″	15.00
Ladle, gravy, 7 ⅛″	30.00
Server, pie, 10 ¼″	50.00
Server, pie, ST blade, 10″	50.00
Server, tomato, 8″	40.00
Serving Fork, cold meat, 8 ½″	30.00
Serving Spoon, tablespoon, 8 ⅜″	20.00
Spoon, cream soup, round bowl, 6 ¼″	15.00
Spoon, demitasse, 4 ½″	12.00
Spoon, grapefruit, round bowl, 7″	10.00
Spoon, iced tea, 7 ½″	15.00
Spoon, jelly, 6 ¼″	17.00
Spoon, soup, oval bowl, 7 ½″	12.00
Spoon, sugar, 6 ¼″	17.00
Spoon, teaspoon, 6 ⅛″	8.00

Oneida Silversmiths, Grenoble, Silver Plate

Butter Serving Knife, FH, 6 ⅞″	$17.00
Butter Serving Knife, FH, 7 ¼″	17.00
Butter Spreader, FH, 6 ⅜″	12.00

Oneida Silversmiths, Grosvenor, Silver Plate

Butter Serving Knife, FH, 7 ¼″	$15.00
Butter Spreader, FH, 6 ¼″	7.00

Butter Spreader, FH, 6 3/8″	7.00	Serving Spoon, tablespoon,		
Carving Fork, ST tines, 9″	40.00	pierced, 8 1/4″	22.00	
Carving Fork, ST tines, 11 1/4″	55.00	Spoon, bouillon, round bowl, 5″	12.00	
Carving Set, two pieces, ST blade	85.00	Spoon, cream soup, round bowl, 6 1/8″	15.00	
Fork, 7 1/8″	15.00	Spoon, demitasse, 4 3/8″	12.00	
Fork, 7 3/4″	15.00	Spoon, fruit, 5 1/2″	12.00	
Fork, cocktail, 6 1/8″	10.00	Spoon, grapefruit, round bowl, 7 1/4″	12.00	
Fork, grille, 7 1/2″	12.00	Spoon, iced tea, 7 1/2″	15.00	
Fork, pickle, short handle, 6 3/8″	15.00	Spoon, jelly, 6 1/4″	17.00	
Fork, salad, 6 1/4″	12.00	Spoon, soup, oval bowl, 7 3/8″	12.00	
Knife, fruit, ST blade, 6 1/2″	15.00	Spoon, sugar, 6″	15.00	
Knife, grille, HH, New French		Spoon, teaspoon, 6 1/8″	7.00	
blade, 8 1/2″	12.00	Spoon, teaspoon, 5 o'clock, 5″	7.00	
Knife, HH, New French blade, 8 3/4″	15.00	Sugar Tongs, 3 1/2″	40.00	
Knife, HH, New French blade, 9 3/4″	15.00			
Knife, New French blade, 9 1/2″	15.00			
Knife Sharpener, steel sharpener, 6″	35.00			
Server, pie, 10 3/4″	50.00			
Serving Fork, cold meat, 8 1/2″	30.00			
Serving Spoon, casserole, 9 1/4″	35.00			
Serving Spoon, tablespoon, 8 1/4″	20.00			

Photo courtesy of Oneida, Ltd.

Oneida Silversmiths, Lady Hamilton, Silver Plate, Community Silver Plate

Butter Serving Knife, FH, 7 1/8″	$15.00
Butter Spreader, FH, 6 1/2″	12.00
Carving Fork, ST tines, 9 7/8″	45.00
Carving Set, two pieces, large, ST blade	120.00
Carving Set, two pieces, small, ST blade	90.00
Fork, 7 1/4″	15.00
Fork, 7 3/4″	15.00
Fork, cocktail, 6 1/8″	12.00
Fork, grille, 7 1/2″	12.00
Fork, pickle, short handle, 6″	17.00
Fork, salad, 6 1/8″	15.00
Fork, salad, 6 3/8″	15.00
Fork, salad, 6 3/4″	15.00
Knife, grille, HH, modern blade, 8 1/2″	12.00

Knife, grille, HH, New French blade, 8 ½″	12.00
Knife, HH, modern blade, 9 ⅜″	15.00
Knife, HH, New French blade, 9 ⅝″	15.00
Knife, New French blade, 9 ⅛″	15.00
Server, pie, 10 ¾″	55.00
Server, pie, ST blade, 10″	55.00
Server, pie, ST blade, 10 ¼″	55.00
Serving Fork, cold meat, 8 ½″	40.00
Serving Spoon, casserole, 9 ⅜″	35.00
Serving Spoon, tablespoon, 8 ½″	22.00
Spoon, bouillon, round bowl, 5 ⅛″	12.00
Spoon, cream soup, round bowl, 6 ¼″	17.00
Spoon, demitasse, 4 ½″	12.00
Spoon, fruit, 6″	17.00
Spoon, grapefruit, round bowl, 7″	12.00
Spoon, iced tea, 7 ⅝″	15.00
Spoon, jelly, 6 ⅛″	17.00
Spoon, soup, oval bowl, 7 ½″	17.00
Spoon, sugar, 6″	15.00
Spoon, teaspoon, 6 ⅛″	10.00
Spoon, teaspoon, 5 o'clock, 5 ¼″	7.00

Knife, HH, modern blade, 9 ¼″	12.00
Knife, HH, modern blade, 9 ½″	12.00
Serving Fork, cake, 9 ⅜″	30.00
Serving Fork, cold meat, 8 ½″	30.00
Serving Spoon, tablespoon, 8 ¼″	20.00
Serving Spoon, tablespoon, pierced, 8 ½″	20.00
Spoon, bonbon, 4 ½″	15.00
Spoon, bouillon, round bowl, 5 ⅛″	12.00
Spoon, cream soup, round bowl, 6 ¼″	12.00
Spoon, demitasse, 4 ⅜″	12.00
Spoon, grapefruit, round bowl, 7″	12.00
Spoon, iced tea, 7 ½″	12.00
Spoon, jelly, 6 ¼″	17.00
Spoon, soup, oval bowl, 7 ⅜″	12.00
Spoon, sugar, 6 ⅛″	15.00
Spoon, teaspoon, 6″	7.00
Spoon, teaspoon, 5 o'clock, 5 ¼″	7.00

Oneida Silversmiths, Milady, Silver Plate

Butter Serving Knife, FH, 6 ¾″	$15.00
Butter Spreader, FH, 6 ⅜″	10.00
Butter Spreader, FH, 6 ¾″	10.00
Fork, 7″	12.00
Fork, 7 ⅝″	12.00
Fork, cocktail, 6″	10.00
Fork, grille, 7 ½″	12.00
Fork, salad, 6 ½″	10.00
Knife, grille, HH, modern blade, 8 ½″	12.00
Knife, HH, modern blade, 8 ¾″	12.00

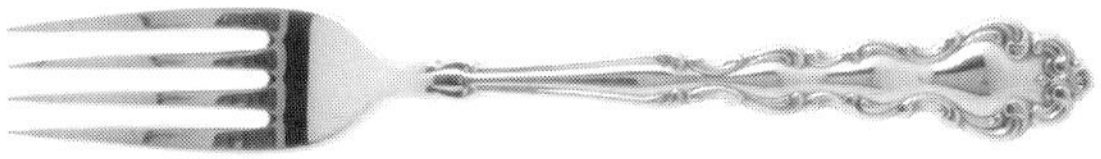

Oneida Silversmiths, Modern Baroque, Silver Plate

Butter Serving Knife, HH, 7″	$20.00
Butter Spreader, HH, paddled ST blade, 6 ¾″	$17.00
Fork	12.00
Fork, baby, 4 ¾″	12.00
Fork, salad, 6 ¾″	17.00
Fork, youth, 6 ¼″	15.00
Knife, HH, modern blade, 8 ⅝″	17.00
Knife, youth, 6 ¾″	15.00
Ladle, gravy, 7 ½″	27.00
Ladle, gravy, 7 ¾″	27.00
Server, pie, 9 ¾″	45.00
Serving Fork, cold meat, 8 ⅝″	30.00
Serving Spoon, casserole, shell-shaped bowl, 8 ⅞″	40.00

Serving Spoon, tablespoon, 8 ½″	22.00
Serving Spoon, tablespoon, pierced, 8 ½″	25.00
Spoon, baby, straight handle, 4 ⅝″	12.00
Spoon, dessert, 6 ⅞″	15.00
Spoon, fruit, 6″	15.00
Spoon, infant feeding, 5 ½″	15.00
Spoon, sugar, shell-shaped bowl, 5 ¾″	15.00
Spoon, teaspoon, 6 ⅛″	12.00
Spoon, teaspoon, 5 o'clock, 5 ½″	7.00
Spoon, youth, 5 ⅜″	15.00
Youth Set, three pieces	35.00

Spoon, dessert, 6 ¾″	15.00
Spoon, grapefruit, round bowl, 7″	15.00
Spoon, iced tea, 7 ½″	15.00
Spoon, infant feeding, 5 ⅝″	17.00
Spoon, jelly, 6 ¼″	17.00
Spoon, soup, oval bowl, 7 ⅜″	15.00
Spoon, sugar, 6 ⅛″	15.00
Spoon, teaspoon, 6 ⅛″	10.00

Oneida Silversmiths, Queen Bess II, Silver Plate

Butter Serving Knife, FH, 6 ⅞″	$12.00
Butter Spreader, FH, 6 ¼″	7.00
Fork, 7 ½″	12.00
Fork, baby, 4 ⅞″	15.00
Fork, cocktail, 6″	10.00
Fork, salad, 6 ½″	12.00
Fork, youth, 6 ½″	15.00
Knife, HH, modern blade, 9 ½″	12.00
Knife, modern blade, 9″	12.00
Ladle, gravy, 7″	12.00
Server, pie, 9 ⅝″	40.00
Serving Fork, cold meat, 8 ¼″	25.00
Serving Spoon, casserole, 8 ⅝″	25.00
Serving Spoon, tablespoon, 8 ¼″	17.00
Spoon, grapefruit, round bowl, 7″	12.00
Spoon, iced tea, 7 ⅝″	12.00
Spoon, jelly, 6 ¼″	15.00
Spoon, soup, oval bowl, 7 ¼″	12.00
Spoon, sugar, 6″	12.00
Spoon, teaspoon, 6″	7.00

Oneida Silversmiths, Morning Star, Silver Plate

Butter Serving Knife, FH, 7″	$15.00
Butter Spreader, FH, 6 ¼″	12.00
Carving Set, two pieces, ST blade	95.00
Fork, 7 ⅛″	15.00
Fork, 7 ⅜″	15.00
Fork, 7 ⅝″	15.00
Fork, cocktail, 6″	12.00
Fork, dessert, 6 ⅜″	15.00
Fork, grille, 7 ½″	12.00
Fork, salad, 6 ¾″	15.00
Knife, grille, HH, modern blade, 8 ½″	12.00
Knife, HH, modern blade, 8 ½″	15.00
Knife, HH, modern blade, 8 ¾″	15.00
Knife, HH, modern blade, 9 ⅛″	15.00
Knife, HH, modern blade, 9 ⅜″	15.00
Ladle, gravy, 7″	32.00
Server, pie, 10 ¼″	60.00
Server, pie, ST blade, 9 ⅞″	60.00
Serving Fork, cold meat, 8 ⅜″	35.00
Serving Spoon, tablespoon, 8 ⅜″	20.00
Spoon, baby, straight handle, 4 ¾″	17.00
Spoon, cream soup, round bowl, 6 ⅛″	15.00

Oneida Silversmiths, Royal Rose, Silver Plate

Butter Serving Knife, FH, 7 1/8″	$15.00
Butter Spreader, FH, 6 3/8″	12.00
Carving Set, two pieces, ST blade	80.00
Carving Set, three pieces, ST blade	115.00
Fork, 7 3/4″	15.00
Fork, cocktail, 6 1/4″	12.00
Fork, grille, 7 5/8″	12.00
Fork, salad, 6 1/4″	12.00
Knife, grille, HH, New French blade, 8 1/2″	12.00
Knife, HH, modern blade, 9 3/8″	15.00
Knife, HH, New French blade, 9 5/8″	15.00
Knife Sharpener, steel sharpener, 11″	40.00
Ladle, gravy, 7 1/4″	25.00

Photo courtesy of Oneida, Ltd.

Salad Set, two pieces, plastic bowl	50.00
Server, pie, 10 3/4″	50.00
Server, tomato, 8″	32.00
Serving Fork, cold meat, 8 5/8″	30.00
Serving Spoon, tablespoon, 8 3/8″	20.00
Spoon, cream soup, round bowl, 6″	12.00
Spoon, cream soup, round bowl, 6 1/4″	12.00
Spoon, demitasse, 4 1/2″	12.00
Spoon, grapefruit, round bowl, 7″	12.00
Spoon, iced tea, 7 3/8″	12.00
Spoon, iced tea, 7 5/8″	12.00
Spoon, soup, oval bowl, 7 3/8″	12.00
Spoon, sugar, 6 1/8″	15.00
Spoon, teaspoon, 6 1/4″	10.00

Oneida Silversmiths, Silver Artistry, Silver Plate, Community Silver Plate

Butter Serving Knife, FH, 6 5/8″	$15.00
Fork, 7 1/2″	15.00
Fork, baby, 4 3/4″	15.00
Fork, salad, 6 7/8″	12.00
Knife, HH, modern blade, 9 1/4″	15.00
Knife, steak, 9 1/8″	17.00
Ladle, gravy, 7 3/4″	25.00
Server, pie, 8 1/2″	45.00
Server, pie, 9 3/4″	45.00
Server, pie/cake, ST blade, 10 3/4″	45.00
Serving Fork, cold meat, 8 3/4″	30.00
Serving Spoon, casserole, shell-shaped bowl, 9″	32.00
Serving Spoon, tablespoon, 8 1/2″	20.00
Serving Spoon, tablespoon, pierced, 8 1/2″	22.00
Spoon, baby, straight handle, 4 3/4″	15.00
Spoon, demitasse, 4 1/2″	10.00
Spoon, iced tea, 7 1/2″	15.00

Spoon, infant feeding, 5 5/8"	17.00
Spoon, soup, oval bowl, 7"	12.00
Spoon, sugar, shell-shaped bowl, 5 3/4"	15.00
Spoon, teaspoon, 6 1/8"	10.00
Spoon, teaspoon, 5 o'clock, 5 1/2"	7.00

Fork, baby, 4 3/4"	17.00
Fork, grille, 7 3/4"	15.00
Fork, salad, 6 3/4"	17.00
Fork, youth, 6 3/8"	17.00
Knife, grille, HH, modern blade, 8 1/2"	15.00
Knife, HH, modern blade, 8 5/8"	20.00
Knife, HH, modern blade, 9 1/8"	20.00
Knife, HH, modern blade, 9 1/2"	20.00
Knife, youth, 7 1/4"	20.00
Ladle, gravy, 7 1/4"	40.00
Server, pie, 10 1/4"	60.00
Server, pie, ST blade, 9 7/8"	60.00
Serving Fork, cold meat, 8 3/8"	40.00
Serving Spoon, casserole, 8 3/4"	40.00
Serving Spoon, tablespoon, 8 1/4"	25.00
Spoon, baby, straight handle, 4 3/4"	17.00
Spoon, bonbon, 6 1/8"	22.00
Spoon, cream soup, round bowl, 6 1/4"	15.00
Spoon, demitasse, 4 1/2"	12.00
Spoon, grapefruit, round bowl, 7"	15.00
Spoon, iced tea, 7 1/2"	15.00
Spoon, soup, oval bowl, 6 7/8"	15.00
Spoon, soup, oval bowl, 7 1/2"	15.00
Spoon, sugar, 6 1/8"	20.00
Spoon, teaspoon, 6 1/8"	12.00
Spoon, teaspoon, 5 o'clock, 5 3/8"	12.00

Oneida Silversmiths, South Seas, Silver Plate

Butter Serving Knife, FH, 6 1/2"	$15.00
Fork, baby, 4 7/8"	17.00
Fork, cocktail, 6"	15.00
Fork, pickle, short handle, 6 1/8"	17.00
Fork, salad, 6 7/8"	15.00
Knife, HH, modern blade, 8 5/8"	17.00
Server, pie, 9 1/2"	50.00
Serving Fork, cold meat, 8 5/8"	40.00
Serving Spoon, casserole, 8 3/4"	40.00
Spoon, bonbon, 5 1/2"	20.00
Spoon, cream soup, round bowl, 6 3/4"	15.00
Spoon, demitasse, 4 1/2"	15.00
Spoon, iced tea, 7 5/8"	17.00
Spoon, soup, oval bowl, 7 1/2"	15.00
Spoon, sugar, 5 1/2"	15.00
Spoon, teaspoon, 6 1/4"	10.00

S T A I N L E S S

Oneida Silversmiths, White Orchid, Silver Plate

Butter Serving Knife, FH, 6 7/8"	$20.00
Butter Spreader, FH, 6 1/4"	15.00
Carving Fork, ST tines, 8 7/8"	60.00
Fork, 7 3/8"	20.00
Fork, 7 3/4"	20.00

Oneida Silversmiths, Act II, Stainless, Heirloom Ltd. Stainless

Butter Serving Knife, HH, 6 3/4"	$22.00
Butter Spreader, HH, paddled blade, 6 3/8"	22.00
Fork, 8"	22.00

Fork, cocktail, 6 1/8"	20.00
Fork, salad, 7"	20.00
Knife, HH, modern blade, 9 1/4"	25.00
Knife, steak, 9 1/4"	25.00
Ladle, gravy, 6 7/8"	32.00
Ladle, gravy, 7 3/8"	32.00
Serving Fork, cold meat, 8 5/8"	35.00
Serving Spoon, casserole, 8 7/8"	35.00
Serving Spoon, tablespoon, 8 5/8"	32.00
Serving Spoon, tablespoon, pierced, 8 5/8"	35.00
Spoon, iced tea, 7 3/8"	22.00
Spoon, soup, oval bowl, 7 1/8"	20.00
Spoon, sugar, 6 1/2"	22.00
Spoon, teaspoon, 6 1/2"	20.00

Photo courtesy of Oneida, Ltd.

Oneida Silversmiths, Alexis, Stainless, Deluxe Stainless

Butter Serving Knife, FH, 6 3/4"	$12.00
Fork, 7 1/4"	15.00
Fork, cocktail, 6"	10.00
Fork, salad, 6 3/4"	12.00
Knife, HH, modern blade, 9"	15.00
Ladle, gravy, 7 3/4"	17.00
Server, pie, 8 3/8"	20.00
Serving Fork, cold meat, 8 1/2"	17.00
Serving Spoon, tablespoon, 8 3/8"	15.00
Serving Spoon, tablespoon, pierced, 8 3/8"	15.00
Spoon, cream soup, round bowl, 5 7/8"	12.00
Spoon, fruit, 6"	12.00
Spoon, iced tea, 7 5/8"	12.00
Spoon, soup, oval bowl, 6 3/4"	12.00
Spoon, sugar, 6"	12.00
Spoon, teaspoon, 6"	10.00

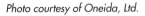

Oneida Silversmiths, American Colonial, Stainless, Heirloom Stainless

Butter Serving Knife, HH, 6 3/4"	$15.00
Butter Spreader, HH, paddled blade, 6 1/2"	15.00
Carving Fork, 9"	37.00
Fork, 7 1/4"	12.00
Fork, 7 3/4"	15.00
Fork, cocktail, 6"	12.00
Fork, salad, 6 1/2"	12.00
Knife, HH, modern blade, 9"	15.00
Knife, pistol grip, Old French blade, 9 1/8"	15.00

Serving Fork, cold meat, 8 3/8"   30.00
Serving Spoon, casserole, 8 3/4"   30.00
Serving Spoon, tablespoon, 8 1/4"   20.00
Spoon, cream soup, round bowl, 5 7/8"   12.00
Spoon, demitasse, 4 1/4"   10.00
Spoon, iced tea, 7 3/8"   12.00
Spoon, soup, oval bowl, 6 5/8"   12.00
Spoon, sugar, 6"   15.00
Spoon, teaspoon, 6"   12.00
Spoon, teaspoon, 5 o'clock, 5 1/4"   12.00

Oneida Silversmiths, Capistrano, Stainless, Profile Stainless

Butter Serving Knife, FH, 6 5/8" $17.00
Butter Spreader, FH, 6 1/4"   17.00
Fork, cocktail, 6"   17.00
Fork, fish, 6 7/8"   15.00
Fork, pastry, 5 3/8"   15.00
Fork, salad, 6 1/4"   15.00
Knife, fish, 7 7/8"   20.00
Knife, HH, modern blade, 8 3/4"   17.00
Knife, HH, modern blade, 9 1/4"   17.00
Ladle, gravy, 7"   25.00
Ladle, gravy, 7 1/2"   25.00
Server, pie, 8 3/8"   30.00
Serving Fork, cold meat, 8 3/8"   25.00
Serving Spoon, tablespoon, 8 1/4"   25.00
Serving Spoon, tablespoon,
   pierced, 8 1/4"   27.00
Spoon, iced tea, 7 5/8"   15.00
Spoon, soup, oval bowl, 6 7/8"   15.00
Spoon, sugar, 6"   15.00
Spoon, teaspoon, 6 1/8"   15.00
Spoon, teaspoon, 5 o'clock, 5 1/4"   12.00

Oneida Silversmiths, Chandelier, Stainless

Butter Serving Knife, FH, 6 3/8" $22.00
Carving Set, two pieces   90.00
Fork, 7 3/8"   20.00
Fork, cocktail, 6"   20.00
Fork, salad, 6 7/8"   20.00
Knife, HH, modern blade, 9 1/8"   25.00
Knife, steak, 9"   25.00
Knife, steak, 9 1/4"   25.00
Ladle, gravy, 7 3/4"   30.00
Salad Set, two pieces   90.00
Server, pie, 9 5/8"   45.00
Serving Fork, cold meat, 8 1/2"   30.00
Serving Spoon, casserole, 8 7/8"   30.00
Serving Spoon, tablespoon, 8 3/8"   30.00
Serving Spoon, tablespoon,
   pierced, 8 3/8"   30.00
Spoon, demitasse, 4 1/2"   20.00
Spoon, fruit, 5 7/8"   20.00
Spoon, grapefruit, round bowl, 6 7/8"   20.00
Spoon, ice cream, 6"   20.00
Spoon, iced tea, 7 1/2"   20.00
Spoon, jelly, 6"   20.00
Spoon, soup, oval bowl, 6 7/8"   20.00
Spoon, sugar, shell-shaped bowl, 6"   22.00
Spoon, teaspoon, 6"   22.00

Oneida Silversmiths, Chateau, Stainless, Deluxe Stainless

Butter Serving Knife, FH, 6 3/4"	$7.00
Butter Spreader, 6 1/2"	7.00
Fork, 7 1/4"	5.00
Fork, baby, 4 3/8"	5.00
Fork, cocktail, 6 1/8"	5.00
Fork, salad, 6 1/8"	5.00
Fork, youth, 5 7/8"	10.00
Knife, HH, modern blade, 8 1/2"	7.00
Knife, modern blade, 8 1/4"	7.00
Knife, youth, 6 3/4"	10.00
Ladle, gravy, 7 1/8"	10.00
Ladle, gravy, 7 1/2"	10.00
Server, pie, 8 3/8"	12.00
Serving Fork, cold meat, 8 3/8"	10.00
Serving Spoon, casserole, 8 1/2"	12.00
Serving Spoon, tablespoon, 8 1/4"	10.00
Serving Spoon, tablespoon, pierced, 8 1/4"	10.00
Spoon, baby, straight handle, 4 3/8"	7.00
Spoon, fruit, 5 7/8"	5.00
Spoon, iced tea, 7 1/2"	5.00
Spoon, infant feeding, 5 1/2"	5.00
Spoon, soup, oval bowl, 6 7/8"	5.00
Spoon, sugar, 5 7/8"	7.00
Spoon, teaspoon, 6"	5.00
Spoon, youth, 5 1/8"	7.00

Oneida Silversmiths, Cherbourg, Stainless, Community Stainless

Butter Serving Knife, HH, 6 1/2"	$20.00
Butter Spreader, HH, paddled blade, 6 1/4"	17.00
Fork, 7 1/4"	17.00
Fork, cocktail, 6"	17.00
Fork, salad, 6 3/4"	15.00
Knife, HH, modern blade, 9"	17.00
Knife, steak, 9 1/8"	17.00
Ladle, gravy, 7 3/4"	25.00
Server, pie, 9 3/4"	35.00
Serving Fork, cold meat, 8 1/2"	32.00
Serving Spoon, tablespoon, 8 1/2"	25.00
Serving Spoon, tablespoon, pierced, 8 1/2"	27.00
Spoon, fruit, 6"	15.00
Spoon, iced tea, 7 1/2"	17.00
Spoon, soup, oval bowl, 6 7/8"	15.00
Spoon, sugar, 6"	17.00
Spoon, sugar, shell-shaped bowl, 6"	17.00
Spoon, teaspoon, 6"	15.00

Oneida Silversmiths, Classic Shell, Stainless, Heirloom Stainless

Butter Serving Knife, HH, 7"	$12.00
Butter Spreader, HH, paddled blade, 6 3/4"	12.00
Fork, 7 5/8"	10.00

Fork, cocktail, 5 ⅞″ 10.00
Fork, salad, 6 ¾″ 10.00
Knife, HH, modern blade, 9 ½″ 12.00
Ladle, gravy, 7 ¾″ 17.00
Server, pie, 9 ½″ 20.00
Serving Fork, cold meat, 8 ½″ 17.00
Serving Spoon, casserole, 8 ⅞″ 20.00
Serving Spoon, tablespoon, 8 ⅜″ 17.00
Serving Spoon, tablespoon,
   pierced, 8 ⅜″ 17.00
Spoon, cream soup, round bowl, 6″ 12.00
Spoon, demitasse, 4 ½″ 10.00
Spoon, iced tea, 7 ⅝″ 10.00
Spoon, soup, oval bowl, 6 ⅞″ 10.00
Spoon, sugar, shell-shaped bowl, 6″ ... 12.00
Spoon, teaspoon, 6″ 10.00

Oneida Silversmiths, Da Vinci, Stainless, Heirloom Ltd. Stainless

Butter Serving Knife, HH, 6 ¾″ $27.00
Fork, 8 ¼″ 25.00
Fork, salad 25.00
Knife, HH, modern blade, 9 ¾″ 32.00
Knife, HH, New French blade, 9 ¾″ ... 32.00
Serving Fork, cold meat, 9″ 45.00
Serving Spoon, casserole, 8 ¼″ 37.00
Serving Spoon, casserole, 9″ 37.00
Serving Spoon, tablespoon,
   pierced, 8 ¾″ 40.00
Spoon, demitasse, 4 ¼″ 25.00
Spoon, soup, oval bowl, 7″ 25.00
Spoon, sugar, 6″ 27.00
Spoon, teaspoon, 6 ¼″ 25.00

Oneida Silversmiths, Dover, Stainless, Heirloom Stainless

Butter Serving Knife, HH, 6 ¾″ $12.00
Butter Spreader, HH,
   paddled blade, 6 ½″ 12.00
Carving Knife, 11 ½″ 20.00
Fork, 7 ¼″ 10.00
Fork, cocktail, 6″ 10.00
Fork, salad, 6 ½″ 10.00
Knife, HH, modern blade, 9″ 10.00
Ladle, gravy, 6 ½″ 17.00
Ladle, gravy, 6 ⅞″ 17.00
Server, pie, 9 ½″ 20.00
Serving Fork, cold meat, 8 ½″ 17.00
Serving Spoon, casserole,
   shell-shaped bowl, 8 ¾″ 12.00
Serving Spoon, tablespoon, 8 ⅜″ 17.00
Serving Spoon, tablespoon,
   pierced, 8 ⅜″ 17.00
Spoon, fruit, 6″ 7.00
Spoon, iced tea, 7 ⅜″ 10.00
Spoon, soup, oval bowl, 6 ⅝″ 10.00
Spoon, sugar, shell-shaped bowl, 6″ ... 12.00
Spoon, teaspoon, 6″ 10.00

Oneida Silversmiths, Easton, Stainless, Heirloom Stainless

Butter Serving Knife, FH, 7 ½″ $12.00
Butter Spreader, FH, 6 ¾″ 10.00

Fork, 8 ⅛″	10.00
Fork, cocktail, 5 ⅞″	10.00
Fork, salad, 7 ⅛″	10.00
Knife, fish, 8 ⅛″	12.00
Knife, HH, modern blade, 9 ¼″	10.00
Ladle, gravy, 7 ¼″	17.00
Server, pie, 9 ⅝″	20.00
Serving Fork, cold meat, 8 ½″	17.00
Serving Spoon, casserole, 8 ¾″	20.00
Serving Spoon, tablespoon, 8 ⅜″	17.00
Serving Spoon, tablespoon, pierced, 8 ⅜″	17.00
Spoon, demitasse, 4 ½″	10.00
Spoon, iced tea, 7 ½″	10.00
Spoon, soup, oval bowl, 7 ⅜″	10.00
Spoon, sugar, 6 ¼″	10.00
Spoon, teaspoon, 5 o'clock, 5 ⅜″	7.00
Spoon, teaspoon, 6 ⅜″	10.00

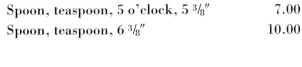

Oneida Silversmiths, Frostfire, Stainless, Community Stainless

Butter Serving Knife, FH, 6 ½″	$15.00
Butter Serving Knife, HH, 6 ½″	15.00
Butter Spreader, FH, 6 ⅜″	12.00
Fork, cocktail, 6″	10.00
Fork, salad, 6 ½″	12.00
Knife, fish, 7 ⅞″	15.00
Knife, HH, modern blade, 9 ⅛″	15.00
Ladle, gravy, 7 ¼″	20.00
Server, pie, 9 ¾″	27.00
Serving Fork, cold meat, 8 ⅝″	20.00
Spoon, demitasse, 4 ½″	8.00
Spoon, grapefruit, round bowl, 6 ⅞″	12.00
Spoon, iced tea, 7 ½″	12.00

Spoon, soup, oval bowl, 6 ¾″	10.00
Spoon, sugar, 6″	15.00
Spoon, teaspoon, 6 ⅛″	12.00

Oneida Silversmiths, Golden Juilliard, Stainless, gold accent, Heirloom Stainless

Butter Serving Knife, HH, 6 ⅞″	$15.00
Butter Spreader, HH, paddled blade, 6 ½″	15.00
Fork, 8 ⅛″	10.00
Fork, cocktail, 6″	10.00
Fork, salad, 6 ⅞″	10.00
Knife, HH, New French blade, 9 ½″	15.00
Ladle, gravy, 7 ⅜″	20.00
Ladle, gravy, 7 ⅞″	20.00
Serving Fork, cold meat, 8 ¾″	20.00
Serving Spoon, casserole, shell-shaped bowl, 8 ⅞″	25.00
Serving Spoon, tablespoon, 8 ½″	20.00
Serving Spoon, tablespoon, pierced, 8 ½″	20.00
Spoon, iced tea, 7 ⅜″	10.00
Spoon, iced tea, 7 ⅝″	10.00
Spoon, soup, oval bowl, 7 ¼″	10.00
Spoon, sugar, shell-shaped bowl, 6 ¼″	15.00
Spoon, teaspoon, 6 ⅛″	10.00

Oneida Silversmiths, Independence, Stainless, Deluxe Stainless

Butter Serving Knife, FH, 6 ½″	$15.00
Butter Serving Knife, HH, 6 ¾″	15.00

Oneida Silversmiths, Juilliard, Stainless, Heirloom Stainless

Butter Serving Knife, HH, 6 ⅞″	$12.00
Butter Spreader, HH, paddled blade, 6 ⅝″	12.00
Fork, 7 ¼″	10.00
Fork, 8″	10.00
Fork, cocktail, 6 ⅛″	10.00
Fork, pie, 5 ½″	10.00
Fork, salad, 7″	10.00
Knife, HH, New French blade, 9 ½″	10.00
Knife, New French blade, 9″	10.00
Ladle, gravy, 7 ⅞″	17.00
Ladle, soup, 11″	27.00
Server, pie, 9 ¾″	20.00
Serving Fork, cold meat, 8 ⅝″	17.00
Serving Spoon, casserole, shell-shaped bowl, 8 ⅞″	12.00
Serving Spoon, tablespoon, 8 ½″	17.00
Serving Spoon, tablespoon, pierced, 8 ½″	17.00
Spoon, cream soup, round bowl, 6″	12.00
Spoon, demitasse, 4 ⅜″	10.00
Spoon, iced tea, 7 ½″	10.00
Spoon, soup, oval bowl, 7 ¼″	10.00
Spoon, sugar, shell-shaped bowl, 6 ⅛″	12.00
Spoon, teaspoon, 6″	10.00

Photo courtesy of Oneida, Ltd.

Fork, 7 ¼″	12.00
Fork, 7 ½″	12.00
Fork, cocktail, 6 ⅛″	10.00
Fork, salad, 6 ¾″	12.00
Knife, HH, modern blade, 9″	15.00
Knife, pistol grip, modern blade, 9″	15.00
Knife, steak, pistol grip, 9 ⅛″	15.00
Ladle, gravy, 6 ¾″	17.00
Ladle, gravy, 7 ⅜″	17.00
Ladle, gravy, 7 ¾″	17.00
Serving Fork, cold meat, 8 ⅜″	15.00
Serving Spoon, casserole, 8 ½″	20.00
Serving Spoon, tablespoon, 8 ⅜″	15.00
Spoon, demitasse, 4 ⅜″	10.00
Spoon, iced tea, 7 ½″	10.00
Spoon, soup, oval bowl, 6 ¾″	12.00
Spoon, sugar, 6″	12.00
Spoon, teaspoon, 6″	10.00

Oneida Silversmiths, Lasting Rose, Stainless

Butter Serving Knife, FH, 6 ¾″	$17.00
Butter Spreader, FH, 6 ⅜″	17.00

Fork, 7 ¼″	17.00
Fork, baby, 4 ¼″	15.00
Fork, cocktail, 6 ⅛″	17.00
Fork, salad, 6 ¼″	15.00
Knife, HH, modern blade, 8 ½″	15.00
Knife, steak, 9 ⅛″	20.00
Ladle, gravy, 7 ⅛″	27.00
Ladle, gravy, 7 ⅝″	27.00
Serving Fork, cold meat, 8 ⅝″	27.00
Spoon, baby, straight handle, 4 ¼″	15.00
Spoon, iced tea, 7 ⅝″	15.00
Spoon, infant feeding, 5 ⅝″	15.00
Spoon, soup, oval bowl, 6 ⅞″	15.00
Spoon, sugar, 6″	17.00
Spoon, teaspoon, 6″	15.00

Spoon, teaspoon, 6″	7.00
Spoon, teaspoon, 5 o'clock, 5 ¼″	7.00

Oneida Silversmiths, Michelangelo, Stainless, Heirloom Stainless

Butter Serving Knife, HH, 6 ¾″	$12.00
Butter Spreader, HH, paddled blade, 6 ½″	12.00
Fork, 7 ¼″	10.00
Fork, cocktail, 6″	10.00
Fork, salad, 6 ½″	10.00
Knife, HH, modern blade, 9″	10.00
Ladle, gravy, 6 ¼″	17.00
Ladle, gravy, 6 ⅝″	17.00
Serving Fork, cold meat, 8 ⅜″	17.00

Oneida Silversmiths, Louisiana, Stainless, Community Stainless

Butter Serving Knife, FH, 6 ½″	$10.00
Butter Serving Knife, HH, 6 ½″	10.00
Fork, 7 ¼″	7.00
Fork, cocktail, 6″	10.00
Fork, salad, 6 ¾″	7.00
Knife, HH, modern blade, 9 ⅛″	10.00
Ladle, gravy, 7 ¾″	12.00
Server, pie, 9 ⅝″	15.00
Serving Fork, cold meat, 8 ⅝″	12.00
Serving Spoon, casserole, 8 ⅞″	15.00
Serving Spoon, tablespoon, 8 ½″	12.00
Serving Spoon, tablespoon, pierced, 8 ½″	12.00
Spoon, cream soup, round bowl, 5 ⅞″	10.00
Spoon, iced tea, 7 ½″	7.00
Spoon, soup, oval bowl, 6 ⅞″	7.00
Spoon, sugar, shell-shaped bowl, 6″	12.00

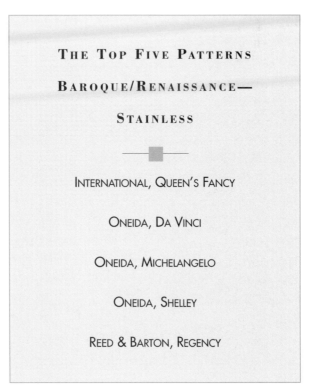

THE TOP FIVE PATTERNS

BAROQUE/RENAISSANCE—

STAINLESS

INTERNATIONAL, QUEEN'S FANCY

ONEIDA, DA VINCI

ONEIDA, MICHELANGELO

ONEIDA, SHELLEY

REED & BARTON, REGENCY

Serving Spoon, casserole,
  shell-shaped bowl, 8 ¾″   12.00
Serving Spoon, tablespoon, 8 ⅜″   17.00
Serving Spoon, tablespoon,
  pierced, 8 ⅜″   17.00
Spoon, demitasse, 4 ¼″   10.00
Spoon, iced tea, 7 ½″   10.00
Spoon, soup, oval bowl, 6 ⅝″   10.00
Spoon, sugar, shell-shaped bowl, 6″ 12.00
Spoon, teaspoon, 6″   10.00

Oneida Silversmiths, Mozart, Stainless, Deluxe Stainless

Butter Serving Knife, FH, 6 ⅝″ $17.00
Fork, cocktail, 6 ⅛″   20.00
Fork, salad, 6 ¾″   20.00
Knife, fish, 7 ⅞″   20.00
Knife, HH, modern blade, 9″   20.00
Knife, modern blade, 9″   22.00
Knife, steak, 9″   20.00
Ladle, gravy, 7 ¾″   22.00
Server, pastry, 8 ¾″   35.00
Serving Fork, cold meat, 8 ½″   25.00
Serving Spoon, tablespoon, 8 ¼″ 27.00
Spoon, bouillon, round bowl, 5 ¾″ 15.00
Spoon, cream soup, round bowl, 6 ¾″ 10.00
Spoon, fruit, 6″   15.00
Spoon, iced tea, 7 ½″   17.00
Spoon, soup, oval bowl, 6 ⅞″   15.00
Spoon, sugar, 6″   17.00
Spoon, sugar, shell-shaped bowl, 6″ 15.00
Spoon, teaspoon   20.00
Spoon, teaspoon, 5 o'clock, 5 ¼″ 12.00

Oneida Silversmiths, My Rose, Stainless

Butter Serving Knife, FH, 6 ¾″ $12.00
Fork, baby, 4 ¼″   12.00
Fork, cocktail, 6 ⅛″   10.00
Fork, salad, 6 ¼″   12.00
Knife, HH, modern blade, 8 ½″   15.00
Knife, modern blade, 8 ½″   15.00
Knife, youth, 6 ¾″   15.00
Serving Fork, cold meat, 8 ⅜″   17.00
Serving Spoon, tablespoon, 8 ¼″ 15.00
Serving Spoon, tablespoon,
  pierced, 8 ¼″   15.00
Spoon, fruit, 6″   10.00
Spoon, iced tea, 7 ½″   10.00
Spoon, jelly, 6 ⅛″   10.00
Spoon, soup, oval bowl, 6 ⅞″   12.00
Spoon, sugar, 6″   12.00
Spoon, teaspoon, 6 ⅛″   10.00
Spoon, youth, 5 ⅛″   12.00

Oneida Silversmiths, Omni, Stainless, Heirloom Stainless

Butter Serving Knife, HH, 7 ⅜″ $20.00
Butter Spreader, HH,
  paddled blade, 7″   22.00
Fork, 7 ½″   20.00
Fork, cocktail, 6″   22.00
Fork, salad, 6 ¾″   17.00

Knife, HH, modern blade, 8 5/8″	22.00
Knife, steak, 9 5/8″	22.00
Ladle, gravy, 7″	30.00
Serving Fork, cold meat, 8 3/4″	32.00
Serving Spoon, casserole, 8 3/4″	32.00
Serving Spoon, tablespoon, 8 1/2″	32.00
Serving Spoon, tablespoon, pierced, 8 1/2″	32.00
Spoon, cream soup, round bowl, 6 1/8″	17.00
Spoon, soup, oval bowl, 6 5/8″	17.00
Spoon, sugar, 6 1/8″	20.00
Spoon, teaspoon	17.00

Spoon, baby, straight handle, 4 1/4″	7.00
Spoon, demitasse, 4 1/2″	7.00
Spoon, fruit, 5 7/8″	7.00
Spoon, iced tea, 7 1/2″	7.00
Spoon, infant feeding, 5 1/2″	7.00
Spoon, soup, oval bowl, 6 3/4″	7.00
Spoon, sugar, 5 7/8″	10.00
Spoon, teaspoon, 6″	7.00
Spoon, teaspoon, 5 o'clock, 5 1/8″	5.00
Youth Set, three pieces	25.00

Oneida Silversmiths, Polonaise, Stainless, Deluxe Stainless

Butter Serving Knife, FH, 6 5/8″	$20.00
Fork, 7 1/4″	17.00
Fork, cocktail, 6″	17.00
Fork, salad, 6 5/8″	17.00
Knife, HH, modern blade, 9″	17.00
Knife, steak, 9″	22.00
Ladle, gravy, 7 1/2″	32.00
Serving Fork, cold meat, 8 3/8″	30.00
Serving Spoon, tablespoon, pierced, 8 1/4″	27.00
Spoon, iced tea, 7 5/8″	17.00
Spoon, soup, oval bowl, 6 7/8″	15.00
Spoon, teaspoon, 6 1/8″	17.00

Oneida Silversmiths, Paul Revere, Stainless, Community Stainless

Baby Set, two pieces	$15.00
Butter Serving Knife, FH, 6 3/8″	10.00
Butter Serving Knife, HH, 6 3/8″	10.00
Butter Spreader, FH, 6 1/4″	10.00
Butter Spreader, HH, paddled blade, 6 1/8″	10.00
Fork, 7 1/4″	7.00
Fork, baby, 4 3/8″	8.00
Fork, cocktail, 6″	10.00
Fork, salad, 6 1/2″	7.00
Fork, youth, 5 3/4″	10.00
Knife, HH, modern blade, 8 1/2″	10.00
Knife, pistol grip, modern blade, 9 1/4″	10.00
Knife, youth, 6 3/8″	10.00
Ladle, gravy, 7 3/8″	12.00
Server, pie, 9 3/4″	15.00
Serving Fork, cold meat, 8 1/2″	12.00
Serving Spoon, casserole, 8 5/8″	15.00
Serving Spoon, tablespoon, 8 1/2″	12.00
Serving Spoon, tablespoon, pierced, 8 1/2″	12.00

Oneida Silversmiths, Rembrandt, Stainless

Butter Serving Knife, HH, 7 1/4″	$20.00
Butter Spreader, HH, paddled blade, 6 7/8″	22.00

Fork	22.00
Fork, salad	22.00
Knife	27.00
Ladle, gravy, 6 ½″	30.00
Serving Fork, cold meat, 8 ½″	30.00
Serving Spoon, tablespoon, 8 ¼″	35.00
Spoon, demitasse, 4 ¼″	20.00
Spoon, soup, oval bowl, 6 ½″	20.00
Spoon, sugar, 6″	20.00
Spoon, sugar, shell-shaped bowl, 6″	20.00
Spoon, teaspoon, 6″	20.00

Oneida Silversmiths, Satinique, Stainless, Community Stainless

Butter Serving Knife, HH, 6 ½″	$10.00
Butter Spreader, HH, paddled blade, 6 ¼″	10.00
Fork, 9″	10.00
Fork, cocktail, 6″	10.00
Fork, salad, 6 ¾″	7.00
Knife, fish, 8″	12.00
Knife, modern blade, 9″	10.00
Knife, modern, HH, 8 ½″	10.00
Knife, modern, HH, 9″	10.00
Knife, youth, 6 ⅜″	10.00
Ladle, gravy, 7 ⅝″	12.00
Server, pie, 9 ⅝″	15.00
Serving Fork, cold meat, 8 ½″	12.00
Serving Spoon, tablespoon, 8 ⅜″	12.00
Serving Spoon, tablespoon, pierced, 8 ⅜″	12.00
Spoon, cream soup, round bowl, 5 ⅞″	10.00
Spoon, fruit, 5 ⅞″	7.00
Spoon, iced tea, 7 ½″	7.00

Photo courtesy of Oneida, Ltd.

Spoon, soup, oval bowl, 6 ⅞″	70.00
Spoon, sugar, shell-shaped bowl, 5 ⅞″	12.00
Spoon, teaspoon, 6″	7.00

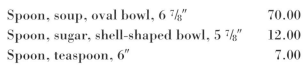

Oneida Silversmiths, Shelley, Stainless, Heirloom Stainless

Butter Serving Knife, HH, 6 ¾″	$22.00
Butter Spreader, HH, paddled blade, 6 ½″	22.00
Fork, salad	22.00
Knife, HH, modern blade, 9 ⅛″	25.00
Ladle, gravy, 6 ¾″	35.00

Serving Fork, cold meat, 8 1/2″	40.00
Serving Spoon, tablespoon, pierced, 8 1/4″	37.00
Spoon, soup, oval bowl, 6 5/8″	20.00
Spoon, sugar, 6″	22.00
Spoon, teaspoon	25.00

Oneida Silversmiths, Toujours, Stainless, Heirloom Stainless

Butter Serving Knife, HH, 6 3/4″	$30.00
Butter Spreader, HH, paddled blade, 6 1/4″	25.00
Fork, salad, 6 5/8″	25.00
Knife, HH, modern blade, 9 1/2″	30.00
Ladle, gravy, 6 3/4″	45.00
Serving Fork, cold meat, 8 1/2″	45.00
Serving Spoon, casserole, shell-shaped bowl, 8 7/8″	50.00
Serving Spoon, tablespoon, 8 3/8″	45.00
Spoon, soup, oval bowl, 6 5/8″	25.00
Spoon, sugar, shell-shaped bowl, 6″	30.00
Spoon, teaspoon, 6 1/8″	25.00

Oneida Silversmiths, Tennyson, Stainless, Community Stainless

Butter Serving Knife, HH, 6 1/2″	$15.00
Butter Spreader, HH, paddled blade, 6 1/4″	10.00
Fork, 7 1/8″	15.00
Fork, 7 1/2″	15.00
Fork, cocktail, 6″	12.00
Fork, salad, 6 3/4″	12.00
Knife, HH, modern blade, 9 1/8″	15.00
Knife, steak, 9″	17.00
Knife, tea, 8″	10.00
Ladle, gravy, 7 3/4″	22.00
Server, pie, 9 5/8″	20.00
Serving Fork, cold meat, 8 1/2″	20.00
Serving Spoon, tablespoon, 8 3/8″	20.00
Serving Spoon, tablespoon, pierced, 8 1/2″	20.00
Spoon, bouillon, round bowl, 5 3/4″	10.00
Spoon, fruit, 5 7/8″	7.00
Spoon, soup, oval bowl, 6 7/8″	12.00
Spoon, sugar, 6″	12.00
Spoon, sugar, shell-shaped bowl, 6″	12.00
Spoon, teaspoon, 6″	12.00

Oneida Silversmiths, Twin Star, Stainless

Butter Serving Knife, FH, 6 3/4″	$12.00
Butter Spreader, FH, 6 3/8″	12.00
Fork, 7 1/4″	12.00
Fork, cocktail, 6 1/8″	10.00
Fork, salad, 6 1/4″	10.00
Fork, youth, 5 7/8″	12.00
Knife, HH, modern blade, 8 5/8″	15.00
Knife, modern blade, 8 1/2″	15.00
Knife, youth, 6 3/4″	15.00
Ladle, gravy, 7 3/8″	17.00
Server, pie, 9 1/2″	20.00
Serving Fork, cold meat, 8 1/2″	15.00

Serving Spoon, tablespoon, 8 ³⁄₈″	15.00
Serving Spoon, tablespoon, pierced, 8 ³⁄₈″	15.00
Spoon, demitasse, 4 ¹⁄₂″	10.00
Spoon, fruit, 6″	10.00
Spoon, iced tea, 7 ¹⁄₂″	10.00
Spoon, jelly, 6 ¹⁄₈″	10.00
Spoon, soup, oval bowl, 6 ³⁄₄″	10.00
Spoon, sugar, 6 ¹⁄₈″	12.00
Spoon, teaspoon, 6 ¹⁄₈″	8.00
Spoon, teaspoon, 5 o'clock, 5 ¹⁄₈″	10.00

Serving Spoon, tablespoon, pierced, 8 ⁵⁄₈″	27.00
Spoon, fruit, 6 ¹⁄₈″	20.00
Spoon, iced tea, 7 ¹⁄₂″	20.00
Spoon, infant feeding, 5 ⁵⁄₈″	15.00
Spoon, soup, oval bowl, 6 ⁷⁄₈″	15.00
Spoon, sugar, 5 ⁷⁄₈″	15.00
Spoon, teaspoon, 6 ¹⁄₈″	20.00

Oneida Silversmiths, Venetia, Stainless, Community Stainless

Butter Serving Knife, FH, 6 ¹⁄₂″	$20.00
Butter Serving Knife, HH, 6 ⁵⁄₈″	20.00
Butter Spreader, FH, 6 ¹⁄₂″	20.00
Butter Spreader, HH, paddled blade, 6 ¹⁄₄″	20.00
Fork, cocktail, 6 ¹⁄₈″	20.00
Fork, salad, 6 ³⁄₄″	20.00
Fork, youth, 6 ¹⁄₂″	17.00
Knife, HH, modern blade, 9 ¹⁄₈″	20.00
Knife, steak, 9 ¹⁄₈″	25.00
Knife, youth, 6 ¹⁄₂″	17.00
Ladle, gravy, 7 ¹⁄₂″	30.00
Ladle, gravy, 8″	30.00
Server, pie, 9 ⁵⁄₈″	40.00
Serving Fork, cold meat, 8 ⁵⁄₈″	30.00
Serving Spoon, tablespoon, 8 ⁵⁄₈″	25.00

Oneida Silversmiths, Will 'O' Wisp, Stainless, Heirloom Stainless

Butter Serving Knife, HH, 6 ³⁄₄″	$20.00
Butter Spreader, HH, paddled blade, 6 ¹⁄₂″	22.00
Carving Fork, 9 ¹⁄₈″	40.00
Fork, 7 ¹⁄₂″	22.00
Fork, cocktail, 6 ¹⁄₈″	22.00
Fork, salad, 6 ³⁄₄″	20.00
Knife, HH, modern blade, 9 ¹⁄₄″	22.00
Ladle, gravy, 6 ⁵⁄₈″	30.00
Serving Fork, cold meat, 8 ⁵⁄₈″	32.00
Serving Spoon, casserole, 8 ⁷⁄₈″	30.00
Serving Spoon, tablespoon, 8 ¹⁄₂″	32.00
Serving Spoon, tablespoon, pierced, 8 ¹⁄₂″	32.00
Spoon, fruit, 6 ¹⁄₈″	20.00
Spoon, iced tea, 7 ¹⁄₂″	20.00
Spoon, soup, oval bowl, 6 ⁷⁄₈″	15.00
Spoon, sugar, 6 ¹⁄₈″	20.00
Spoon, teaspoon, 6 ¹⁄₈″	20.00

Reed & Barton traces its heritage to the firm of Babbitt & Crossman, established by Isaac Babbitt and William W. Crossman in 1824 to manufacture Britannia ware. Hedging their bets, they also continued to operate a small jewelry store that Babbitt opened in 1822 and produced a line of pewter ware.

By 1826, Babbitt and Crossman constructed a new factory on Fayette Street in Taunton, Massachusetts, which included steam-powered machinery designed and manufactured by Nathaniel Leonard of Taunton. William West was brought into the business in 1827 when a need for new capital arose. Babbitt, Crossman & Company, a new firm, was created. Babbitt sold his interest in February 1829 to Zephaniah A. Leonard. Once again, the firm's name was changed, this time to Crossman, West & Leonard. A year and a half later, the company was dissolved. The Taunton Britannia Manufacturing Company, a joint partnership, evolved in August 1830. Less than three years later, it experienced financial difficulties.

Three employees were determined that the business would not die. Charles E. Barton, a solderer, was the brother-in-law of William Crossman. Henry Good Reed was a fifth-generation member of a prominent Taunton family. Benjamin Pratt was the company's sales agent. The Taunton Britannia Manufacturing Company was back in business on April 1, 1835. Barton and Reed rented the old company's tools and equipment. Pratt concentrated on selling products and collecting back debts. By 1836, the company was once again on sound financial footing.

Barton, Reed, and Pratt did not have ownership rights in the company. Eventually an agreement was reached whereby Reed and Barton obtained one-third ownership in the tools and equipment and one-third interest in the property. The Taunton Britannia Manufacturing Company became nothing more than a landlord.

Leonard, Reed & Barton, established on February 20, 1837, became the new operating company. The company survived the 1837 depression. By 1840, Barton and Reed purchased Leonard's interest in the firm. Objects made between 1840 and 1847 bore one of two marks—Leonard, Reed & Barton or Reed & Barton. Silver-plated flatware joined the company's product line around 1848.

By the time of the Civil War, two-thirds of the products manufactured by Reed & Barton were purchased by retailers and jobbers who operated their own plating shops. These firms applied the plating and added their own trademarks. Rogers & Brothers was a major purchaser of hollowware. As such, Reed & Barton found itself on occasion competing against it-

ENTERTAINING ESSENTIALS

Whether your entertaining needs are large or small, Reed & Barton offers a full complement of serving pieces in sterling silver, silverplate and 18/8 stainless to add to your collection. A wide range of pieces is available in all patterns to satisfy your most common serving needs. Shown here are the most frequently used pieces in sterling silver. (Not all pieces are available in all metals in all patterns.)

1. Lemon Fork
2. Cocktail/Oyster Fork
3. Olive/Pickle Fork
4. Coffee Spoon
5. Cream Soup Spoon
6. Jelly Server
7. Sugar Spoon
8. Cream/Sauce Ladle
9. Gravy Ladle
10. Butter Serving Knife
11. Cheese Serving Knife
12. Steak Knife
13. Letter Opener
14. Cold Meat Fork
15. Tablespoon
16. Pierced Tablespoon
17. Tomato/Flat Server
18. Pie Server
19. Bread/Cake Knife
20. Roast Carving Knife
21. Roast Carving Fork
22. Pasta Scoop
23. Olivewood Salad Fork
24. Olivewood Salad Spoon
25. Lasagna Server
26. Pastry Server
27. Cheese Plane
28. Serving Fork
29. Serving Spoon

From the Reed & Barton brochure, "Entertaining Essentials," this photo pictures twenty-nine of the most frequently used serving pieces in the eighteenth-century sterling silver pattern.

self. However, Reed & Barton also followed this practice, buying most of the flatware they sold from Rogers & Brothers and the Hartford Manufacturing Company.

Charles Barton died on September 3, 1867, with Henry Reed by his bedside. Henry Reed,

George Brabrook, and Henry Fish formed a new partnership in 1868, retaining the Reed & Barton name. The company was incorporated in 1888.

George Brabrook, in addition to Henry Reed, deserves a major share of the credit for Reed & Barton's success in the last half of the nineteenth century. Brabrook was a super salesman. By the 1870s, he had established Reed & Barton as a primary supplier of silver-plated ware to the hotel market. He was responsible for Reed & Barton's detailed, highly illustrated catalogs.

Henry Reed's career with Reed & Barton lasted seventy-three years, from 1828 to 1901. William Dowse, Reed's son-in-law, succeeded him. Dowse became actively involved in design. When he retired in 1923, he was replaced by Sinclair Weeks, husband of Beatrice Dowse.

Reed & Barton introduced the production of sterling silverware in 1889. By 1904, sterling silverware outsold the company's plated ware. In 1903, the company offered a line of reproduction pewter that retained its popularity through the late 1930s.

Reed & Barton purchased Dominick & Haff Company of Newark, New Jersey, in 1928. The Webster Company was acquired in 1949 and sold in the mid-1960s to Towle. Reed & Barton also owns Eureka Manufacturing Company, a maker of silverware chests, and Sheffield Silver Co., a maker of silver-plated wares.

Reed & Barton developed and manufactured approximately 110 flatware patterns. Francis First, three years in development, has been popular for almost a century. Serenade and Jubilee were introduced in the 1930s, and Burgundy, a new Florentine Lace, La Parisienne, and Les Six Fleurs date from the 1950s. Approximately seventy Dominick & Haff patterns remain in production.

In 1989, Reed & Barton introduced its line of Sterling II flatware with its sterling handles and stainless steel blades, bowls, and tines. The company also entered the heirloom market with a line of Christmas ornaments.

Sinclair Weeks Jr. followed in the footsteps of his father. Reed & Barton continues to remain a privately held company. Today, the firm manufactures Damascene, jewelry, pewter hollowware, stainless flatware, and sterling flatware and hollowware.

FRANCIS FIRST

Photo courtesy of Reed & Barton.

Ernest Meyer, a brilliant French designer, created Reed & Barton's Francis First pattern. The creative process took three years. Meyer's goal was to create a solid silver pattern that rivaled the beauty and opulence of works created by the great Italian Renaissance masters for the French court of Francis I.

The Francis First pattern consists of fifteen different designs. There are subtle variations of the fruit cluster in the center panel of the different handles. Meyer personally supervised the complex handle carving of each of the manifold steel dies required to create this richly sculptured service.

Francis First was introduced in 1906, and it was an immediate success. Royalty from all over the world purchased it. Three American presidents also have owned the pattern.

The tremendous popularity of Francis First led to a demand for matching service pieces. Reed & Barton responded by creating over 100 matching hollowware pieces, which are available in sterling, silver plate, or both. The silver plate line is marketed as King Francis. Each serving piece mirrors the flatware's luxurious fruit-and-flowers motif, depth of design, and intricate sculptural beauty.

STERLING

Spoon, soup, oval bowl, 6 3/4″	40.00
Spoon, sugar, 6 1/4″	40.00
Spoon, sugar, shell-shaped bowl, 6 1/4″	40.00
Spoon, teaspoon, 6″	25.00

Reed & Barton, 18th Century, Sterling Silver

Butter Serving Knife, HH, 7 1/2″	$45.00
Fork, 7 1/2″	60.00
Fork, baby, 4 1/2″	40.00
Fork, salad, 6 1/2″	45.00
Fork, youth, 6 1/4″	45.00
Knife, HH, modern blade, 9″	32.00
Knife, HH, modern blade, 10″	45.00
Knife, youth, 7 1/2″	40.00
Server, pie/cake, ST blade, 11″	60.00
Serving Spoon, tablespoon, 8 3/4″	100.00
Spoon, baby, straight handle, 4 5/8″	40.00
Spoon, cream soup, round bowl, 6″	50.00
Spoon, soup, oval bowl, 6 3/4″	50.00
Spoon, sugar, shell-shaped bowl, 6 1/4″	50.00

Reed & Barton, Burgundy, Sterling Silver

Butter Spreader, FH, 5 7/8″	$32.00
Butter Spreader, HH, paddled ST blade, 6 1/4″	30.00
Carving Knife, ST blade, 10 3/8″	65.00
Creamer	1,000.00
Fork, 7 1/8″	50.00
Fork, 7 7/8″	80.00
Fork, baby, 4 1/2″	40.00
Fork, salad, 6 1/2″	45.00
Knife, HH, modern blade, 8 7/8″	35.00
Knife, HH, New French blade, 9 1/8″	35.00
Knife, HH, New French blade, 9 5/8″	50.00
Knife, youth, 7 7/8″	40.00
Ladle, gravy, 6 1/2″	90.00
Salad Set, two pieces, ST bowl	110.00
Salad Set, two pieces	350.00
Serving Fork, cold meat, 8″	95.00
Serving Fork, cold meat, 9 1/4″	90.00
Serving Spoon, tablespoon, 8 3/8″	90.00
Spoon, cream soup, round bowl, 6 3/8″	45.00
Spoon, fruit, 5 7/8″	45.00
Spoon, iced tea, 7 3/4″	50.00
Spoon, soup, oval bowl, 6 3/4″	45.00
Spoon, teaspoon, 6″	25.00
Sugar Bowl, covered	1,700.00

Reed & Barton, Autumn Leaves, Sterling Silver

Bowl, bonbon, 6″	$50.00
Butter Serving Knife, HH, 7 3/8″	40.00
Butter Spreader, HH, modern ST blade, 6 3/4″	25.00
Fork, 7 1/2″	60.00
Fork, pickle, short handle, 5 3/4″	32.00
Fork, salad, 6 3/4″	45.00
Knife, HH, modern blade, 9″	35.00
Ladle, gravy, 6 3/4″	85.00
Serving Spoon, tablespoon, 8 5/8″	85.00

Reed & Barton, Classic Rose, Sterling Silver

Butter Serving Knife, HH, 6 7/8″	$40.00
Butter Spreader, FH, 6 1/8″	30.00
Fork, 7 1/2″	60.00
Fork, baby, 4 1/2″	45.00
Fork, salad, 6 5/8″	50.00
Fork, youth, 6 3/8″	50.00
Knife, HH, modern blade, 9 1/8″	40.00
Ladle, gravy, 6 7/8″	95.00
Salt and Pepper Shakers, pair, 3 1/2″	200.00
Serving Spoon, tablespoon, 8 5/8″	90.00
Spoon, baby, straight handle, 4 1/2″	45.00
Spoon, bonbon, 5″	45.00
Spoon, jelly, 6 3/8″	40.00
Spoon, soup, oval bowl, 6 5/8″	45.00
Spoon, sugar, 6″	40.00
Spoon, teaspoon	25.00

Reed & Barton, English Chippendale, Sterling Silver

Butter Serving Knife, HH, 7 3/8″	$40.00
Cheese Plane, ST plane, 9 1/2″	40.00
Fork, 7 1/2″	60.00
Fork, salad, 6 5/8″	45.00
Knife, fish, ST blade, 8 1/8″	40.00
Knife, fruit, ST blade, 7 5/8″	35.00
Knife, HH, modern blade, 9″	30.00
Ladle, soup, ST bowl, 11 1/4″	70.00
Server, pie/cake, ST blade, 11″	60.00
Serving Fork, cold meat, 8 3/4″	95.00
Serving Fork, salad, ST tines, 9 1/4″	40.00

Serving Spoon, tablespoon, 8 7/8″	90.00
Serving Spoon, tablespoon, pierced, 8 7/8″	95.00
Spoon, soup, oval bowl, 6 7/8″	45.00
Spoon, teaspoon, 6 1/4″	30.00

Reed & Barton, English Provincial, Sterling Silver

Butter Serving Knife, HH, 7 3/8″	$32.00
Butter Spreader, HH, modern ST blade, 6 3/4″	20.00
Fork, 7 5/8″	45.00

Photo courtesy of Reed & Barton.

Fork, salad	35.00	Butter Serving Knife, FH, 7 1/8″	50.00
Knife	30.00	Butter Serving Knife, HH, 7″	42.00
Spoon, cream soup, round bowl, 6″	40.00	Butter Spreader, FH, 5 7/8″	32.00
Spoon, iced tea, 7 1/4″	40.00	Butter Spreader, HH,	
Spoon, sugar, shell-shaped bowl, 6 1/4″	35.00	modern ST blade, 6 3/8″	32.00
Spoon, teaspoon	22.00	Carving Fork, ST tines, 8 7/8″	75.00
		Carving Set, two pieces, ST blade	150.00
		Centerpiece, 12 3/4″	825.00
		Cheese Plane, ST plane, 9″	75.00

Reed & Barton, Florentine Lace, Sterling Silver

		Compote, 4 1/4″	700.00
		Fork, 7 1/8″	50.00
		Fork, 7 3/4″	75.00
		Fork, baby, 4 3/8″	40.00
		Fork, cocktail, 5 5/8″	40.00
		Fork, lemon, 4 7/8″	40.00
Butter Spreader, FH, 6″	$35.00	Fork, pickle, short handle, 6″	40.00
Butter Spreader, HH,		Fork, salad, 6 1/8″	50.00
modern ST blade, 6 3/8″	37.00	Ice Cream Slicer, 12 1/2″	200.00
Butter Spreader, HH,		Knife, cheese, ST blade, 7 1/4″	55.00
paddled ST blade, 6 1/4″	37.00	Knife, HH, modern blade, 8 7/8″	50.00
Fork, 7 3/8″	60.00	Knife, HH, modern blade, 9 1/2″	60.00
Fork, salad	60.00	Knife, HH, New French blade, 9 1/4″	50.00
Fork, youth, 6 1/8″	55.00	Knife, HH, New French blade, 9 1/2″	60.00
Knife, HH, modern blade, 9″	45.00	Knife, steak, 8 7/8″	60.00
Knife, youth, 7 3/4″	50.00	Knife, wedding cake, ST blade, 12 5/8″	55.00
Plate, sandwich, 9 1/2″	180.00	Knife, youth, 7 1/8″	40.00
Server, pie, ST blade, 10 1/8″	80.00	Knife, youth, 7 7/8″	40.00
Server, tomato, 7 3/4″	130.00	Ladle, cream sauce, 5 3/4″	55.00
Serving Spoon, tablespoon, 8 1/2″	110.00	Ladle, gravy, 6 7/8″	100.00
Spoon, demitasse, 4 1/2″	32.00	Ladle, punch, 15 1/2″	475.00
Spoon, teaspoon, 6″	35.00	Ladle, soup, 11 1/2″	300.00
Spoon, youth, 5 7/8″	50.00	Ladle, soup, ST bowl, 11″	150.00
		Letter Opener, ST blade, 7 7/8″	40.00
		Nut Dish, 3 3/8″	95.00
		Salad Set, two pieces	350.00
		Salad Set, two pieces, ST bowl, 8 5/8″	90.00
		Server, asparagus, 9 7/8″	300.00
		Server, asparagus, 10″	365.00

Reed & Barton, Francis I, Sterling Silver

		Server, cake, 9 3/4″	150.00
		Server, cheese, ST blade, 6 3/4″	55.00
Bowl, bonbon, footed, 7 3/4″	$675.00	Server, fish, 12″	290.00
Bowl, vegetable, round, 11 1/2″	675.00	Server, ice cream, 11 1/4″	300.00

Server, lasagna, ST blade, 10″	70.00
Server, macaroni, 10 ½″	300.00
Server, pie, ST blade, 9 ⅝″	70.00
Server, pie/cake, ST blade, 10 ⅜″	50.00
Server, sardine, 6 ⅛″	175.00
Server, toast, 10 ⅛″	360.00
Serving Fork, cold meat, 7 ⅞″	100.00
Serving Fork, cold meat, 9 ¼″	150.00
Serving Fork, salad, 9 ½″	175.00
Serving Set, fish, pierced	600.00
Serving Spoon, rice, pierced, ST bowl, 8 ⅝″	50.00
Serving Spoon, tablespoon, 8 ⅜″	100.00
Serving Spoon, tablespoon, pierced, 8 ⅜″	100.00
Spoon, bonbon, 4 ⅝″	50.00
Spoon, cream soup, round bowl, 6″	42.00
Spoon, iced tea, 7 ⅝″	50.00
Spoon, jelly, 6 ¼″	40.00
Spoon, sugar, 5 ⅞″	45.00
Spoon, teaspoon, 6″	40.00
Spoon, teaspoon, 5 o'clock, 5 ½″	30.00
Sugar Tongs, 4 ⅛″	70.00
Tea Set, three pieces	7,000.00
Tea Set, four pieces, with tray, mini	6,400.00

Reed & Barton, French Renaissance, Sterling Silver

Butter Spreader, FH, 6″	$30.00
Fork, 7 ⅛″	60.00
Fork, cocktail, 5 ⅝″	35.00
Fork, ice cream, 5 ½″	60.00
Fork, salad	55.00
Knife, HH, New French blade, 9″	40.00
Knife, HH, New French blade, 9 ¾″	50.00
Knife Sharpener, steel sharpener	75.00
Ladle, gravy, 6 ¼″	95.00

Serving Fork, salad, 8 ⅞″	110.00
Serving Spoon, tablespoon, 8 ¼″	95.00
Spoon, fruit, 5 ¾″	45.00
Spoon, iced tea, 7 ½″	40.00
Spoon, sugar, 6″	50.00
Spoon, sugar, shell-shaped bowl, 6 ⅛″	50.00
Spoon, teaspoon	32.00
Spoon, teaspoon, 5 o'clock, 5 ⅜″	27.00

Reed & Barton, Georgian Rose, Sterling Silver

Butter Serving Knife, FH, 7 ¼″	$35.00
Butter Spreader, FH, 6″	22.00
Butter Spreader, HH, modern ST blade, 6 ¼″	27.00
Fork, 8 ½″	40.00
Fork, salad, 6 ¼″	30.00
Knife, HH, New French blade, 9 ⅛″	35.00
Ladle, gravy, 5 ¾″	80.00
Serving Spoon, tablespoon, 8 ½″	65.00
Serving Spoon, tablespoon, pierced, 8 ½″	95.00
Spoon, demitasse, 4 ¼″	25.00
Spoon, jelly, 6″	40.00
Spoon, soup, oval bowl, 6 ⅞″	45.00
Spoon, sugar, shell-shaped bowl, 6 ¼″	40.00
Spoon, teaspoon, 6″	20.00
Tea Set, three pieces	2,300.00

Reed & Barton, Grande Renaissance, Sterling Silver

Butter Serving Knife, HH, 7″	$37.00
Fork, 7 ⅜″	45.00

Fork, 8″   60.00
Fork, salad, 6 3/8″   37.00
Knife, HH, modern blade, 9″   45.00
Knife, HH, modern blade, 9 3/4″   35.00
Serving Spoon, tablespoon, 8 5/8″   80.00
Spoon, iced tea, 7 1/4″   40.00
Spoon, sugar, shell-shaped bowl, 6 1/8″   40.00
Spoon, teaspoon, 6″   25.00

Reed & Barton, Lark, Sterling Silver

Butter Serving Knife, HH, 7 3/8″	$40.00
Butter Spreader, HH, modern ST blade, 7″	25.00
Cake Breaker, SP tines, 11 1/8″	40.00
Fork, 7 5/8″	60.00
Fork, cocktail, 6 1/8″	32.00
Fork, lemon, 4 3/4″	32.00
Fork, pickle, short handle, 6 3/8″	32.00
Fork, salad, 7 1/8″	50.00
Knife, cheese, ST blade, 7 5/8″	45.00
Knife, HH, modern blade, 9 1/8″	35.00
Ladle, cream sauce, 6″	45.00
Server, pie/cake, ST blade, 10 3/4″	65.00
Server, tomato, 8 3/8″	95.00
Serving Fork, cold meat, 8 1/2″	80.00
Serving Fork, salad, 8 1/2″	10.00
Serving Spoon, casserole, 8 1/4″	130.00
Serving Spoon, tablespoon, 8 1/2″	80.00
Serving Spoon, tablespoon, pierced, 8 1/2″	85.00
Spoon, demitasse, 4 3/4″	25.00
Spoon, iced tea, 7 1/2″	45.00
Spoon, jelly, 6 1/2″	40.00
Spoon, soup, oval bowl, 7″	50.00
Spoon, sugar, 6 1/8″	40.00
Spoon, teaspoon, 6 1/4″	25.00
Sugar Tongs, 4 1/2″	65.00

Reed & Barton, Hampton Court, Sterling Silver

Butter Serving Knife, HH, 7″	$35.00
Fork, 7 1/2″	55.00
Fork, baby, 4 3/8″	37.00
Fork, cocktail, 5 5/8″	32.00
Fork, pickle, short handle, 5 3/4″	30.00
Fork, salad	35.00
Fork, strawberry, 5″	37.00
Fork, youth, 6 1/4″	40.00
Knife, HH, modern blade, 9 1/8″	32.00
Knife, steak, 9 1/4″	45.00
Knife, youth, 7 1/8″	35.00
Server, pie/cake, ST blade, 10 1/2″	60.00
Serving Spoon, tablespoon, 8 5/8″	80.00
Serving Spoon, tablespoon, pierced, 8 5/8″	85.00
Spoon, bonbon, 4 7/8″	40.00
Spoon, demitasse, 4 3/8″	22.00
Spoon, fruit, 5 7/8″	37.00
Spoon, sugar, shell-shaped bowl, 6 1/4″	40.00
Spoon, teaspoon	25.00

163

Spoon, cracker, 8 ³/₄″   230.00
Spoon, cream soup, round bowl, 6″   110.00
Spoon, infant feeding, 5 ³/₄″   80.00
Spoon, soup, oval bowl, 7 ¹/₄″   100.00
Spoon, teaspoon   80.00

Reed & Barton, Love Disarmed, Sterling Silver

Fork, 7 ¹/₈″	$125.00
Fork, 7 ³/₄″	160.00
Fork, baby, 4 ³/₈″	80.00
Fork, ice cream, 5 ¹/₈″	100.00
Fork, ice cream, 5 ³/₈″	100.00
Fork, salad	100.00
Fork, strawberry, 4 ⁷/₈″	70.00
Ice Cream Slicer, 13 ¹/₄″	375.00
Knife, HH, New French blade, 9 ¹/₄″	95.00
Knife, HH, New French blade, 9 ³/₄″	110.00
Knife, steak 9 ¹/₈″	110.00
Knife, wedding cake, ST blade, 12 ³/₄″	175.00
Ladle, gravy, 6 ³/₄″	175.00
Salad Set, two pieces	675.00
Server, asparagus, 11 ¹/₂″	500.00
Server, cake, 10 ¹/₈″	260.00
Server, fish, 13″	400.00
Server, ice cream, 12 ¹/₂″	375.00
Server, macaroni, 11 ¹/₂″	400.00
Server, sardine, 6 ¹/₄″	225.00
Server, toast, 11 ¹/₄″	375.00
Server, tomato, 8″	200.00
Server, waffle, pierced, 11″	400.00
Serving Fork, asparagus, 10 ⁷/₈″	390.00
Serving Fork, cold meat, 7 ⁷/₈″	175.00
Serving Fork, cold meat, 10 ⁷/₈″	375.00
Serving Fork, salad, 10 ³/₄″	335.00
Serving Set, fish, pierced	800.00
Serving Spoon, salad, 10 ⁵/₈″	335.00
Serving Spoon, tablespoon, 8 ¹/₄″	200.00
Serving Spoon, tablespoon, pierced, 8 ¹/₄″	200.00
Spoon, baby, straight handle, 4 ¹/₂″	80.00
Spoon, bouillon, round bowl, 5 ³/₈″	70.00

Reed & Barton, Marlborough, Sterling Silver

Butter Spreader, FH, 5 ⁷/₈″	$30.00
Carving Fork, ST tines, 9 ¹/₈″	70.00
Carving Knife, ST blade, 10 ³/₈″	70.00
Carving Set, two pieces, ST blade	140.00
Fork, 7 ¹/₄″	45.00
Fork, 7 ³/₄″	60.00
Fork, cocktail, 5 ¹/₂″	30.00
Fork, joint, 11 ⁵/₈″	110.00
Fork, salad, 6 ¹/₈″	45.00
Knife, cheese, ST blade, 7 ¹/₄″	45.00
Knife, HH, modern blade, 8 ⁷/₈″	40.00
Knife, HH, New French blade, 9 ¹/₈″	40.00
Knife, HH, New French blade, 9 ⁵/₈″	50.00
Ladle, gravy, 6 ⁵/₈″	95.00
Server, cheese, ST blade, 6 ⁷/₈″	50.00
Server, tomato, 7 ³/₄″	110.00
Serving Fork, cold meat, 9 ¹/₈″	110.00
Serving Spoon, tablespoon, 8 ¹/₄″	90.00
Spoon, demitasse, 4 ¹/₄″	25.00
Spoon, iced tea, 7 ⁵/₈″	45.00
Spoon, teaspoon	25.00
Spoon, teaspoon, 5 o'clock, 5 ³/₈″	25.00
Sugar Tongs, 4 ⁵/₈″	65.00

Reed & Barton, Pointed Antique, Sterling Silver

Butter Serving Knife, HH, 7″	$50.00
Butter Spreader, FH, 5 3/4″	35.00
Butter Spreader, HH, modern ST blade, 6 3/8″	35.00
Butter Spreader, HH, paddled blade, 5 1/2″	45.00
Butter Spreader, HH, paddled ST blade, 5 1/2″	35.00
Carving Set, two pieces, ST blade	150.00
Fork, baby, 4 1/4″	50.00
Fork, salad	60.00
Knife, cheese, ST blade, 7 1/4″	55.00
Knife, HH, modern blade, 9″	45.00
Knife, HH, New French blade, 8 3/4″	45.00
Knife, HH, New French blade, 9 1/2″	60.00
Knife, HH, Old French blade, 8 1/2″	45.00
Knife, HH, Old French blade, 9 1/2″	60.00
Knife, wedding cake, ST blade, 12 3/4″	95.00
Server, pastry, ST bowl, 9 3/4″	80.00
Server, pie, ST blade, 9 5/8″	80.00
Server, pie, ST blade, 10″	80.00
Server, pie/cake, ST blade, 10 1/2″	80.00
Spoon, dessert, 6 3/4″	50.00
Spoon, teaspoon, 6″	40.00

Reed & Barton, Rose Cascade, Sterling Silver

Butter Serving Knife, HH, 6 7/8″	$50.00
Butter Spreader, HH, modern ST blade, 6 3/8″	35.00

Fork, 7 3/8″	60.00
Fork, cocktail, 5 5/8″	40.00
Fork, lemon, 5″	37.00
Fork, pickle, short handle, 5 7/8″	37.00
Fork, salad	60.00
Knife, HH, modern blade, 9 1/4″	45.00
Ladle, gravy, 6 3/4″	110.00
Serving Spoon, tablespoon, 8 5/8″	105.00
Serving Spoon, tablespoon, pierced, 8 5/8″	110.00
Spoon, bonbon, 4 3/4″	50.00
Spoon, sugar, shell-shaped bowl, 6 1/4″	50.00
Spoon, teaspoon, 6″	35.00

Reed & Barton, Savannah, Sterling Silver

Fork, 7 3/8″	$75.00
Fork, ice cream, 5 3/4″	70.00
Fork, lemon, 5″	45.00
Fork, salad, 6 1/2″	70.00
Fork, youth, 6 1/8″	70.00
Knife, HH, modern blade, 9 1/8″	60.00
Knife, youth, 7 7/8″	60.00
Ladle, cream sauce, 5 1/2″	70.00
Server, pie/cake, ST blade, 10 1/2″	100.00
Server, tomato, 8 1/8″	130.00
Serving Fork, cold meat, 8 1/2″	110.00
Serving Spoon, casserole, shell-shaped bowl, 9″	200.00
Serving Spoon, salad, 9 3/8″	150.00
Spoon, bonbon, 4 7/8″	60.00
Spoon, jelly, 6 1/8″	60.00
Spoon, sugar, shell-shaped bowl, 6 1/8″	60.00
Spoon, teaspoon, 6″	45.00

Reed & Barton, Silver Sculpture, Sterling Silver

Bowl, vegetable, oval, 9 1/4″	$300.00
Butter Serving Knife, HH, 7 3/8″	40.00
Butter Spreader, HH, modern ST blade, 6 3/4″	25.00
Butter Spreader, HH, paddled ST blade, 6 5/8″	25.00
Carving Knife, ST blade, 10 1/2″	70.00
Carving Set, two pieces, ST blade	150.00
Fork, 7 3/8″	50.00
Fork, cocktail, 5 5/8″	30.00
Fork, lemon, 4 3/4″	30.00
Fork, pickle, short handle, 5 3/4″	30.00
Fork, salad, 6 5/8″	50.00
Fork, youth, 6 1/2″	50.00
Knife, cheese, ST blade, 7 1/2″	45.00
Knife, HH, modern blade, 9″	35.00
Ladle, gravy, 6 5/8″	90.00
Salt Dish, open, 3 7/8″	40.00
Server, pie/cake, ST blade, 11″	70.00
Serving Fork, cold meat, 8 1/4″	95.00
Serving Spoon, tablespoon, 8 5/8″	85.00
Serving Spoon, tablespoon, pierced, 8 5/8″	90.00
Spoon, bonbon, 4 7/8″	45.00
Spoon, demitasse, 4 1/2″	25.00
Spoon, jelly, 6 1/2″	35.00
Spoon, soup, oval bowl, 6 5/8″	45.00
Spoon, sugar, 6 1/4″	40.00
Spoon, teaspoon, 6 1/8″	27.00

Reed & Barton, Silver Wheat, Sterling Silver

Butter Serving Knife, HH, 7″	$35.00
Butter Spreader, FH, 5 3/4″	25.00
Butter Spreader, HH, paddled ST blade, 6 1/4″	22.00
Carving Fork, ST tines, 8 1/2″	60.00
Carving Set, two pieces, ST blade	120.00
Fork, 7 3/8″	45.00
Fork, 7 5/8″	60.00
Fork, cocktail, 5 3/4″	30.00
Fork, lemon, 5″	30.00
Fork, pickle, short handle, 5 3/4″	30.00
Fork, salad	40.00
Fork, youth, 6 3/8″	45.00
Knife	35.00
Knife, cheese, ST blade, 7 1/8″	45.00
Knife, youth, 7 7/8″	40.00
Ladle, cream sauce, 5 1/4″	45.00
Ladle, gravy, 6 3/4″	80.00
Salad Set, two pieces, plastic bowl	90.00
Salad Set, two pieces, wooden bowl	70.00
Server, pastry, ST bowl, 10″	60.00
Server, pie, ST blade, 10″	60.00
Serving Spoon, salad, plastic bowl, 12″	35.00
Serving Spoon, tablespoon, 8 5/8″	70.00
Spoon, bonbon, 5″	40.00
Spoon, cream soup, round bowl, 6 3/8″	40.00
Spoon, demitasse, 4 1/2″	22.00
Spoon, jelly, 6 1/2″	30.00
Spoon, soup, oval bowl, 6 5/8″	40.00
Spoon, sugar, 6 3/8″	40.00
Spoon, sugar, shell-shaped bowl, 6 3/8″	40.00
Spoon, teaspoon	25.00
Sugar Tongs, 4″	60.00

Reed & Barton, Spanish Baroque, Sterling Silver

Butter Serving Knife, HH, 7″	$40.00
Butter Spreader, HH, modern ST blade, 6 ½″	30.00
Fork, 7 ½″	50.00
Fork, salad, 6 ½″	45.00
Knife, HH, modern blade, 9 ¼″	35.00
Knife, HH, modern blade, 9 ¾″	50.00
Knife, youth, 7 ⅛″	40.00
Spoon, iced tea, 7 ¼″	45.00
Spoon, soup, oval bowl, 6 ¾″	45.00
Spoon, sugar, shell-shaped bowl, 6 ¼″	45.00
Spoon, teaspoon, 6″	25.00

Reed & Barton, Tara, Sterling Silver

Butter Serving Knife, HH, 7″	$40.00
Butter Spreader, HH, modern ST blade, 6 ½″	30.00
Butter Spreader, HH, paddled ST blade, 6 ¼″	30.00
Carving Fork, ST tines, 11 ⅛″	75.00
Carving Set, two pieces, ST blade	150.00
Fork, 7 ½″	60.00
Fork, baby, 4 ⅜″	40.00
Fork, ice cream, 5 ⅝″	60.00
Fork, ice cream, 5 ¾″	60.00
Fork, lemon, 5″	37.00
Fork, pickle, short handle, 5 ⅞″	37.00
Fork, salad, 6 ½″	50.00
Fork, youth, 6 ¼″	50.00

Knife, HH, modern blade, 9 ⅛″	40.00
Knife, youth, 7 ⅛″	40.00
Knife, youth, 7 ⅞″	40.00
Knife Sharpener, steel sharpener, 14 ⅝″	75.00
Ladle, gravy, 6 ⅝″	90.00
Salad Set, two pieces, plastic bowl	100.00
Serving Fork, cold meat, 8 ½″	90.00
Serving Spoon, tablespoon, 8 ½″	110.00
Serving Spoon, tablespoon, pierced, 8 ½″	120.00
Spoon, jelly, 6 ¼″	40.00
Spoon, soup, oval bowl, 6 ⅝″	50.00
Spoon, sugar, shell-shaped bowl, 6 ⅛″	45.00
Spoon, teaspoon, 6″	30.00
Sugar Tongs, 4″	70.00

Reed & Barton, Woodwind, Sterling Silver

Butter Serving Knife, HH, 7″	$45.00
Carving Set, two pieces, ST blade	140.00
Fork, 7 ½″	60.00
Fork, salad, 6 ½″	50.00
Knife, cheese, ST blade, 7 ¼″	45.00
Knife, cheese, ST blade, 9 ⅜″	60.00
Knife, HH, modern blade, 9″	40.00
Server, pie/cake, ST blade, 11″	70.00
Serving Fork, salad, ST tines, 9 ¼″	45.00
Serving Spoon, casserole, ST bowl, 10 ½″	70.00
Spoon, rice, pierced, ST bowl, 9 ⅛″	60.00
Spoon, soup, oval bowl, 6 ¾″	60.00
Spoon, teaspoon	30.00

SILVER PLATE

Reed & Barton, Dresden Rose, Silver Plate

Butter Serving Knife, FH, 7 ¼″	$20.00
Butter Serving Knife, HH, 7″	20.00
Butter Spreader, FH, 6 ⅛″	12.00
Butter Spreader, HH, modern ST blade, 6 ⅜″	17.00
Fork, 7 ½″	17.00
Fork, cocktail, 5 ½″	15.00
Fork, salad, 6 ⅝″	15.00
Knife, HH, modern blade, 9″	20.00
Ladle, gravy, 6 ½″	30.00
Server, pie, 9 ¼″	60.00

Server, pie, ST blade, 10 ¼″	60.00
Server, pie/cake, ST blade, 10 ½″	30.00
Serving Fork, cold meat, 8″	22.00
Serving Spoon, tablespoon, 8 ½″	20.00
Serving Spoon, tablespoon, pierced, 8 ½″	20.00
Spoon, demitasse, 4 ½″	12.00
Spoon, grapefruit, round bowl, 7 ⅛″	15.00
Spoon, iced tea, 7 ¾″	15.00
Spoon, jelly, 6 ⅜″	20.00
Spoon, soup, oval bowl, 6 ⅝″	15.00
Spoon, sugar, shell-shaped bowl, 6 ⅛″	17.00
Spoon, teaspoon, 6″	12.00

THE TOP FIVE PATTERNS

TRADITIONAL—

SILVER PLATE

INTERNATIONAL, OLD COLONY

INTERNATIONAL, REFLECTION

ONEIDA, LADY HAMILTON

REED & BARTON, DRESDEN ROSE

REED & BARTON, FRENCH CHIPPENDALE

Reed & Barton, French Chippendale, Silver Plate

Butter Serving Knife, HH, 7 ½″	$20.00
Butter Spreader, HH, modern ST blade, 6 ¾″	17.00
Fork, 7 ½″	17.00
Fork, cocktail, 5 ½″	15.00
Fork, salad, 6 ⅜″	15.00
Knife, HH, modern blade, 9 ⅛″	20.00
Server, pie/cake, ST blade, 11″	30.00
Serving Fork, cold meat, 8 ¼″	22.00
Serving Fork, cold meat, 8 ½″	22.00
Serving Spoon, tablespoon, 8 ½″	20.00
Serving Spoon, tablespoon, pierced, 8 ½″	20.00
Spoon, iced tea, 7 ⅜″	15.00
Spoon, soup, oval bowl, 6 ¾″	15.00
Spoon, sugar, shell-shaped bowl, 6 ¼″	17.00
Spoon, teaspoon, 6 ⅛″	12.00

STAINLESS

Reed & Barton, 1800, Stainless

Butter Serving Knife, HH, 7 ½″	$15.00
Fork, 7 ⅝″	10.00
Fork, baby, 4 ½″	10.00
Fork, cocktail, 5 ⅞″	10.00
Fork, salad, 6 ½″	10.00
Knife, HH, modern blade, 9″	17.00
Ladle, gravy, 6 ⅝″	20.00
Serving Fork, cold meat, 8 ¾″	15.00
Serving Spoon, tablespoon, 8 ⅞″	15.00
Serving Spoon, tablespoon, pierced, 8 ⅞″	15.00
Spoon, baby, straight handle, 4 ⅝″	10.00
Spoon, iced tea, 7 ½″	10.00
Spoon, infant feeding, 5 ¾″	10.00
Spoon, soup, oval bowl, 6 ⅞″	10.00
Spoon, sugar, shell-shaped bowl, 6 ½″	10.00
Spoon, teaspoon, 6 ⅛″	7.00

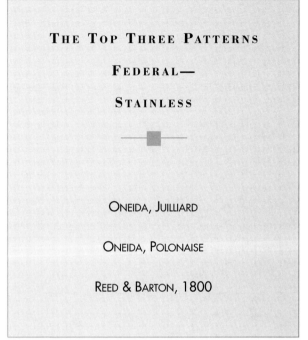

THE TOP THREE PATTERNS

FEDERAL—

STAINLESS

ONEIDA, JUILLIARD

ONEIDA, POLONAISE

REED & BARTON, 1800

Serving Spoon, tablespoon, pierced, 8 ½″	15.00
Spoon, iced tea, 7 ½″	10.00
Spoon, soup, oval bowl, 6 ⅞″	10.00
Spoon, sugar, shell-shaped bowl, 6 ⅛″	10.00
Spoon, teaspoon, 6″	7.00

Reed & Barton, Colonial Shell, Stainless

Butter Serving Knife, HH, 7″	$12.00
Fork, 7 ⅜″	10.00
Fork, salad, 6 ⅝″	10.00
Knife, HH, modern blade, 8 ½″	17.00
Ladle, gravy, 6 ¾″	20.00
Ladle, gravy, 7 ⅜″	20.00
Serving Fork, cold meat, 8 ¾″	15.00
Serving Spoon, tablespoon, 8 ½″	15.00

Reed & Barton, Country French, Stainless

Butter Spreader, HH, 6 ⅞″	$15.00
Fork, 7 ½″	10.00
Fork, cocktail, 5 ⅜″	10.00
Fork, salad, 6 ¼″	10.00
Knife, HH, modern blade, 9″	17.00
Ladle, gravy, 6 ⅜″	20.00
Serving Fork, cold meat, 8 ¼″	15.00
Serving Spoon, tablespoon, 8 ½″	17.00

Serving Spoon, tablespoon,
   pierced, 8 ¼″   17.00
Serving Spoon, tablespoon,
   pierced, 8 ½″   17.00
Spoon, iced tea, 7 ⅜″   12.00
Spoon, soup, oval bowl, 6 ¾″   10.00
Spoon, sugar, shell-shaped bowl, 6″   10.00
Spoon, teaspoon, 6″   7.00

Photo courtesy of Reed & Barton.

Reed & Barton, Modern Provincial, Stainless

Butter Serving Knife, FH, 7 ¼″	$32.00
Butter Spreader, FH, 6 ½″	25.00
Fork	30.00
Fork, salad	25.00
Knife, HH, modern blade, 8 ⅞″	30.00
Ladle, gravy, 6 ⅝″	65.00
Serving Fork, cold meat, 8 ⅜″	65.00
Serving Spoon, tablespoon, 8 ⅜″	50.00
Serving Spoon, tablespoon, pierced, 8 ⅜″	50.00
Spoon, soup, oval bowl, 6 ⅝″	30.00
Spoon, sugar, 6″	32.00
Spoon, teaspoon	25.00

Reed & Barton, Regency, Stainless

Butter Serving Knife, HH, 7″	$22.00
Butter Spreader, HH, modern blade, 6 ⅜″	25.00
Fork, salad	20.00
Knife	22.00
Ladle, gravy, 6 ½″	35.00
Ladle, gravy, 6 ¾″	35.00
Serving Fork, cold meat, 8 ⅞″	35.00
Spoon, sugar, shell-shaped bowl, 6 ¼″	20.00
Spoon, teaspoon	20.00

Empire Crafts Corporation, Newark, New Jersey, was one of many companies that specialized in selling directly to consumers. Its product line included three flatware patterns—Castle Rose (1942), Promise (1948), and Wildflower (1942)—manufactured by Oneida Ltd.

Royal Crest, Castle Rose, Sterling Silver

Butter Serving Knife, FH, 6 ⁷⁄₈″	$27.00
Butter Spreader, FH, 5 ⁷⁄₈″	20.00
Fork, 7 ¹⁄₄″	35.00
Fork, baby, 4 ¹⁄₄″	35.00
Fork, cocktail, 5 ³⁄₈″	22.00
Fork, grille, 7 ⁵⁄₈″	35.00
Fork, salad, 6 ³⁄₈″	30.00
Knife	27.00
Knife, grille, HH, modern blade, 8 ³⁄₈″	25.00
Ladle, gravy, 6 ¹⁄₄″	70.00
Salad Set, two pieces, plastic bowl	60.00
Server, pie, ST blade, 9 ³⁄₄″	45.00
Serving Spoon, casserole, 8 ¹⁄₂″	75.00
Serving Spoon, tablespoon, 8 ¹⁄₈″	65.00
Spoon, cream soup, round bowl, 6 ¹⁄₄″	27.00
Spoon, iced tea, 7 ¹⁄₂″	30.00
Spoon, soup, oval bowl, 7″	30.00
Spoon, sugar, 6 ¹⁄₈″	30.00
Spoon, teaspoon, 6 ¹⁄₈″	17.00

Oneida Ltd. produced three patterns—Formality (1942), Inaugural (1942), and Stately (1948)—for State House Sterling.

State House Sterling was a division of Home Decorators, Inc., headquartered in Newark, New York. The company sold its products through Silver Counselors who visited potential customers in their own homes. Silver Counselors carried full place settings of each pattern and used them to create place settings on the table so the customer could "see for yourself."

State House Sterling offered a free consultation service, directed by Emily Post and a staff of trained assistants, to purchasers of State House Sterling. The consultation service responded to any questions about party planning and entertaining etiquette.

Silver Counselors encouraged the use of State House Sterling's Co-operative Club Plan described in a 1947 sales brochure as "No need to buy one piece at a time—you start with a *complete* silver service for, say, four or six. And through the Co-operative Club Plan, you may build it up to a service for eight or twelve! You actually *earn* these extra place-settings consisting of a knife, fork and teaspoon—at no extra cost to you!"

The 1947 brochure also offered the following advice from Emily Post on selecting a silver service: "THE most important table appointment is silver. The bride who would have a perfectly appointed table must be very conservative. Choose reproductions, rather than new designs. Every woman interested in the setting of her table should remember that she must like her silver—not just at first sight . . . but for always."

State House Sterling, Stately, Sterling Silver

Butter Serving Knife, FH, 6 3/4"	$32.00	Fork, 7 1/8"	40.00
Butter Spreader, FH, 5 3/4"	22.00	Fork, cocktail, 5 3/8"	25.00
Carving Set, two pieces, ST blade	110.00	Fork, grille, 7 5/8"	40.00
Carving Set, three pieces, ST blade	160.00	Fork, lemon, 5 3/8"	30.00
		Knife, grille, HH, modern blade, 8 3/8"	27.00
		Knife, HH, modern blade, 9 1/4"	27.00
		Knife Sharpener, steel sharpener, 10 3/4"	50.00
		Ladle, gravy, 6 1/4"	70.00
		Server, pie, ST blade, 9 7/8"	60.00
		Serving Fork, cold meat, 8 1/8"	75.00
		Serving Spoon, casserole, 8 1/2"	85.00

Serving Spoon, tablespoon, 8 1/4″	70.00	Spoon, jelly, 6 1/4″	30.00
Spoon, cream soup, round bowl, 6 1/4″	35.00	Spoon, soup, oval bowl, 7 1/8″	35.00
Spoon, demitasse, 4 1/8″	20.00	Spoon, sugar, 6 1/8″	35.00
Spoon, iced tea, 7 5/8″	35.00	Spoon, teaspoon, 6 1/8″	20.00

Charles L. Tiffany and John B. Young founded Tiffany & Young, a stationery and gift store, in 1837. Tiffany & Young offered a wide variety of goods, from desks to umbrellas. It purchased most of the silverware they sold from John C. Moore, a firm founded in 1827, based in New York City. Between 1832 and 1836, the firm was known as Eoff & Moore. When Edward C. Moore, John's son, was taken into partnership, the firm became John C. Moore & Sons. Moore also supplied silverware to Marquand & Co. and its successor, Ball, Thompkins & Black.

In 1841, Tiffany & Young became Tiffany, Young & Ellis. The name was changed to Tiffany & Company in 1853.

In 1852, Tiffany insisted that its silver comply with the English sterling silver standard of 925/1000. Charles Lewis Tiffany was one of the leaders in the fight, which resulted in the federal government eventually adopting this standard, passing a 1906 statute that set 925/1000 as the minimum requirement for articles marked "Sterling Silver."

During the 1850s, Tiffany & Company produced some electroplated wares. Production increased significantly following the Civil War. A variety of marks appeared on Tiffany's electroplated wares, from the company name to more complex marks similar to those found on Tiffany silver. The manufacture of electroplated ware ended in 1931.

Tiffany achieved international recognition in 1867 when its designs won the coveted Gold Medal for silver craftsmanship at the Paris Exposition Universelle. Due to this recognition, Tiffany become the silversmith and goldsmith to seventeen crowned heads of Europe.

Tiffany did not manufacture its own flatware between 1850 and 1860. Instead, it retailed the flatware of other makers. Flatware sold by Tiffany contained the touch mark of its manufacturer and "Tiffany, Young & Ellis" (prior to 1853) or "Tiffany & Co." (after 1853).

Tiffany incorporated as Tiffany & Co., Inc., in 1868. It also acquired in 1868 the Moore silverware factory, making Edward C. Moore, son of John Moore, a director. Edward Moore became head of Tiffany's silver studio, which became America's first school of design. Moore encouraged apprentices to observe and sketch nature, a theme that dominated many Tiffany designs in the last half of the nineteenth century.

Beginning in 1868, Tiffany silverware was marked with "Tiffany & Co." and the letter "M." When Edward C. Moore died in 1891, the company continued marking its silverware with the initial of its incumbent president, until the practice was discontinued in 1965.

It was Tiffany's jewelry, especially its botanical brooches and use of semiprecious gemstones, that captured the world's attention at the Paris Exposition Universelle in 1878. This also marked the year when the famed Tiffany Diamond, 128.54 carats with 90 facets, was cut by gemologist George Frederick Kunz.

Louis Comfort Tiffany, son of Charles Tiffany, became the company's first design director. Under his leadership, the company manufactured a wealth of Art Nouveau objects, especially jewelry.

Recognized as one of the world's most respected sources of diamonds and other jewelry, Tiffany craftsmanship extends to a broad range of items, including fine china, clocks, flatware, leather goods, perfume, scarves, silver, stationery, and watches. Tiffany opened its New York corporate division in 1960. The Vince Lombardi Trophy for the National Football League Super Bowl Championship is one of its most famous commissions. Thus far, Tiffany has established ten additional corporate sales offices with more openings scheduled for future years.

Tiffany & Company, Inc., Audubon, Sterling Silver

Butter Spreader, FH	$70.00
Butter Spreader, HH	75.00
Fork	95.00
Fork, salad	95.00
Knife	80.00
Serving Fork	150.00
Serving Spoon	150.00
Spoon, grapefruit, round bowl, 7"	115.00
Spoon, teaspoon	70.00

Tiffany & Company, Inc., Chrysanthemum, Sterling Silver

Photo courtesy of Tiffany & Co.

Butter Spreader, FH	$90.00	Fork, salad	135.00
Butter Spreader, HH	95.00	Knife	100.00
Fork	130.00	Serving Fork	200.00
Fork, ice cream, 5 5/8"	135.00	Serving Spoon	200.00
		Spoon, teaspoon	85.00

175

**Tiffany & Company, Inc., English King,
Sterling Silver**

Carving Set, two pieces, ST blade $360.00

Fork, 6 7/8″	130.00
Fork, 7 5/8″	180.00
Fork, salad	130.00
Knife, HH, blunt blade, 9 1/4″	100.00
Knife, HH, blunt blade, 10 1/4″	130.00
Serving Spoon, casserole, 7 3/4″	250.00
Serving Spoon, tablespoon, 8 5/8″	210.00
Spoon, bouillon, round bowl, 5 1/4″	125.00
Spoon, soup, oval bowl, 7″	150.00
Spoon, teaspoon, 5 7/8″	85.00

TOWLE

Like Rogers, Lunt, and Bowlen (Lunt Silversmiths), Towle Silversmiths of Newburyport, Massachusetts, traces it lineage to William Moulton II (1664–1732), who left the family farm in Hampton, New Hampshire, in 1682 and settled in Old Newbury, now Newburyport, on Massachusetts's Merrimac River. Moulton began working as a silversmith in 1690. Six consecutive generations of Moultons, followed by generations of Towles, followed in his footsteps. William was succeeded by Joseph I, William III, Joseph II, Ebenezer, William IV, Enoch, Abel, and Joseph IV.

Anthony F. Towle and William P. Jones were apprentices under William Moulton IV. In 1857, the two founded Towle & Jones, ultimately buying the business of William IV and Joseph IV. Anthony F. Towle and Edward F. Towle, Anthony's son, established A. F. Towle & Sons in 1873. Seven years later, the company became A. F. Towle & Son, Inc. Anthony and Edward left the company three years later and created a rival firm, A. F. Towle & Sons Company (see Lunt Silversmiths). A. F. Towle & Son, Inc., became the Towle Manufacturing Company.

Around 1890, Towle introduced its famous trademark of a lion standing inside the letter "T." Richard Dimes, who would eventually establish his own silverware manufacturing business with Frank W. Smith, supervised the introduction of the manufacture of hollowware at Towle.

Towle manufactured plated flatware between 1906 and 1909. Chester was the last pattern it introduced. As the decade ended, Samuel Weare purchased the remaining stock.

Towle's Old Master, produced for over fifty years, is one of the company's most popular patterns. The Colonial, Benjamin Franklin, and William and Mary patterns also are proven favorites with individuals who seek a simple, traditional pattern. The King Richard, Orchid, and Princess patterns are purchased by individuals who want an intricate, complex pattern. A display that includes an example of every sterling pattern made by Towle appears at the company's Newburyport manufacturing facility.

Beginning in the 1940s, Towle acquired a number of silverware companies, including the Mueck-Gary Company and its trademark. Carvel Hill, a subsidiary in Crisfield, Maryland, made fine cutlery. At one point, the company bought fourteen businesses in a five-year period.

Leonard Florence became chairman of the board when Towle acquired the Leonard Silver Manufacturing Company in 1978. Despite marketing and manufacturing changes, Towle filed for Chapter 11 bankruptcy protection in 1986. Many divisions were sold and the business was restructured to focus on the sterling flatware line. When Towle emerged from bankruptcy in 1987, the company was purchased by the First Republic Corporation of America, a New

York–based conglomerate with holdings in seafood, textiles, and real estate. A gradual decline in the quality of its ware and a host of distribution problems forced Towle to again file for bankruptcy protection in 1990.

Syratech Corporation acquired certain Towles assets, including the Towle® brand name, as well as tools, dies, proprietary patterns, copyrights, trademarks, and patent rights. Once again, the company is manufacturing sterling flatware, stainless and silver-plated flatware, sterling and silver-plated hollowware and giftware, holiday ornaments, accessories, and cutlery.

STERLING

Towle, Candlelight, Sterling Silver

Bar Knife, 8 ½″	$40.00
Butter Serving Knife, FH, 6 ¾″	32.00
Butter Spreader, FH, 5 ⅞″	25.00
Butter Spreader, HH, modern ST blade, 6 ⅛″	30.00
Butter Spreader, HH, paddled ST blade, 5 ⅝″	30.00
Carving Fork, ST tines, 8 ½″	40.00
Carving Set, two pieces, large, ST blade	85.00
Carving Set, two pieces, small, ST blade	75.00
Fork, 7 ¼″	35.00
Fork, 7 ¾″	50.00
Fork, baby, 4 ¼″	30.00
Fork, cocktail, 5 ¾″	25.00
Fork, ice cream, 5 ⅝″	45.00
Fork, lemon, 5 ⅜″	30.00
Fork, pickle, short handle, 5 ⅞″	30.00

Fork, salad, 6 ⅜″	35.00
Fork, strawberry, 5 ½″	40.00
Fork, youth, 6″	40.00
Knife, cheese, ST blade, 6 ⅞″	45.00
Knife, HH, modern blade, 8 ½″	30.00
Knife, HH, New French blade, 8 ¾″	30.00
Knife, HH, New French blade, 9 ½″	40.00
Knife, youth, 6 ⅞″	40.00
Ladle, gravy, 6 ¾″	90.00
Salad Set, two pieces, wooden bowl, 10 ¾″	80.00
Server, tomato, 7 ½″	115.00
Serving Fork, cold meat, 7 ⅞″	90.00
Serving Spoon, casserole, 9 ¼″	120.00
Serving Spoon, tablespoon, 8 ½″	80.00
Spoon, baby, straight handle, 4 ⅜″	30.00
Spoon, bonbon, 5 ½″	40.00
Spoon, bouillon, round bowl, 5 ⅛″	40.00
Spoon, cream soup, round bowl, 6 ¼″	40.00
Spoon, demitasse, 4 ¼″	22.00
Spoon, fruit, 5 ¾″	35.00
Spoon, fruit, 6″	35.00
Spoon, iced tea, 8 ⅛″	35.00
Spoon, jelly, 6 ½″	40.00
Spoon, relish, 6″	45.00
Spoon, soup, oval bowl, 6 ¾″	40.00
Spoon, sugar, 5 ⅞″	30.00
Spoon, teaspoon, 6″	22.00
Sugar Tongs, 4″	55.00

Towle, Chippendale, Sterling Silver

Bar Knife, 9″	$35.00
Bottle Opener, 5 ⁷/₈″	35.00
Butter Serving Knife, FH, 6 ⁷/₈″	37.00
Butter Spreader, FH, 5 ⁷/₈″	27.00
Butter Spreader, HH, paddled ST blade, 5 ⁵/₈″	30.00
Carving Fork, ST tines, 8 ¹/₂″	65.00
Carving Knife, ST blade, 10″	65.00
Carving Knife, ST blade, 10 ¹/₂″	65.00
Carving Set, two pieces, ST blade	130.00
Cheese Cleaver, ST blade, 6 ¹/₄″	40.00
Cheese Plane, ST plane, 9 ¹/₂″	60.00
Fork, 7 ³/₈″	50.00
Fork, 8″	65.00
Fork, baby, 4 ¹/₄″	40.00
Fork, cocktail, 5 ³/₄″	30.00
Fork, fish, ST tines, 7 ¹/₂″	35.00
Fork, ice cream, 5 ⁵/₈″	45.00
Fork, lemon, 5 ¹/₂″	30.00
Fork, salad, 6 ³/₄″	45.00
Fork, strawberry, 5 ¹/₂″	40.00
Fork, youth, 6 ¹/₈″	45.00
Knife, cheese, ST blade, 6 ¹/₄″	40.00
Knife, fish, ST blade, 8″	70.00
Knife, HH, modern blade, 8 ³/₄″	35.00
Knife, HH, New French blade, 8 ⁷/₈″	35.00
Knife, HH, New French blade, 9 ³/₄″	50.00
Knife, steak, 8 ⁷/₈″	45.00
Knife, youth, 6 ³/₄″	40.00
Ladle, cream sauce, 5 ⁵/₈″	50.00
Ladle, gravy, 7″	90.00
Ladle, punch, 15 ¹/₄″	250.00
Letter Opener, ST blade, 7 ¹/₂″	37.00
Magnifying Glass, 6″	40.00

Scoop, ice cream, ST bowl, 8 ¹/₈″	60.00
Server, fish, ST blade, 11 ¹/₄″	60.00
Server, pasta, ST bowl, 10 ⁵/₈″	60.00
Server, pie, ST blade, 9 ³/₄″	60.00
Server, pie, ST blade, 10 ¹/₈″	60.00
Server, pie, ST blade, 10 ¹/₂″	60.00
Server, pie/cake, ST blade, 10 ³/₈″	60.00
Serving Fork, cold meat, 8″	90.00
Serving Spoon, casserole, 9 ¹/₄″	100.00
Serving Spoon, casserole, shell-shaped ST bowl, 9 ³/₄″	60.00
Serving Spoon, salad, plastic bowl, 11 ⁷/₈″	45.00
Serving Spoon, tablespoon, 8 ¹/₂″	85.00
Serving Spoon, tablespoon, pierced, 8 ¹/₂″	90.00
Spoon, baby, straight handle, 4 ³/₈″	40.00
Spoon, bonbon, 4 ⁷/₈″	40.00
Spoon, bonbon, 5 ⁵/₈″	40.00
Spoon, cream soup, round bowl, 6 ¹/₂″	50.00
Spoon, demitasse, 4 ¹/₄″	25.00
Spoon, fruit, 6″	40.00
Spoon, iced tea, 8″	40.00
Spoon, jelly, 6 ⁵/₈″	35.00
Spoon, salt, 2 ¹/₂″	15.00
Spoon, soup, oval bowl, 6 ⁷/₈″	50.00
Spoon, sugar, 5 ⁷/₈″	40.00
Spoon, teaspoon, 6 ¹/₈″	25.00
Spoon, teaspoon, 5 o'clock, 5 ¹/₂″	22.00
Sugar Tongs, 4″	60.00

Towle, Contour, Sterling Silver

Butter Serving Knife, HH, 7″	$32.00
Butter Spreader, HH, paddled ST blade, 6″	20.00

Serving Spoon, casserole, 9 3/8″	90.00
Serving Spoon, tablespoon, 8 3/4″	60.00
Serving Spoon, tablespoon, pierced, 8 3/4″	75.00
Spoon, bonbon, 4 1/4″	35.00
Spoon, demitasse, 4 1/2″	20.00
Spoon, iced tea, 8″	35.00
Spoon, jelly, 7″	32.00
Spoon, salt, 2 1/2″	15.00
Spoon, soup, oval bowl, 7″	35.00
Spoon, sugar, 5 7/8″	32.00
Spoon, teaspoon, 6 1/2″	20.00
Sugar Tongs, 4 1/4″	55.00

THE TOP FIVE PATTERNS

MODERN—

STERLING

GORHAM, CELESTE

INTERNATIONAL, PINE SPRAY

INTERNATIONAL, VALENCIA

REED & BARTON, SILVER SCULPTURE

TOWLE, CONTOUR

Carving Fork, ST tines, 8 7/8″	60.00
Carving Set, two pieces, large, ST blade	120.00
Carving Set, two pieces, small, ST blade	120.00
Fork, 7 3/4″	50.00
Fork, cocktail, 6 1/8″	25.00
Fork, ice cream, 5 1/2″	35.00
Fork, pickle, short handle, 6 1/4″	25.00
Fork, salad, 6 3/4″	32.00
Knife, cheese, ST blade, 7 1/4″	35.00
Knife, HH, modern blade, 8 3/4″	32.00
Knife, steak, 8 7/8″	40.00
Ladle, cream sauce, 5 3/4″	40.00
Ladle, gravy, 6 3/8″	70.00
Salad Set, two pieces, plastic bowl	70.00
Salt Dish, open, 2 5/8″	50.00
Server, pie/cake, ST blade, 10 7/8″	55.00
Server, tomato, 7 5/8″	70.00
Serving Fork, cold meat, 9 1/2″	85.00
Serving Spoon, casserole, 7 1/4″	35.00

Towle, Craftsman, Sterling Silver

Bar Knife, 8 5/8″	$30.00
Butter Serving Knife, HH, 6 5/8″	30.00
Butter Spreader, FH, 6″	25.00
Butter Spreader, HH, modern ST blade, 6 1/4″	25.00
Butter Spreader, HH, paddled ST blade, 5 3/4″	25.00
Carving Set, two pieces, ST blade	90.00
Cheese Pick, 8″	30.00
Fork, 7 3/8″	40.00
Fork, 8 1/8″	50.00
Fork, baby, 4 1/8″	25.00
Fork, cocktail, 5 3/4″	25.00
Fork, ice cream, 5 5/8″	45.00
Fork, lemon, 5 1/2″	30.00
Fork, pickle, short handle, 6″	30.00
Fork, salad, 6 1/2″	37.00
Fork, youth, 6 1/8″	40.00
Knife, cheese, ST blade, 6 7/8″	40.00

Knife, HH, modern blade, 8 3/4″	32.00	Fork, 8″	80.00
Knife, HH, New French blade, 8 7/8″	32.00	Fork, lemon, 5 1/2″	40.00
Ladle, cream sauce, 5 3/4″	40.00	Fork, pickle, short handle, 5 3/4″	40.00
Ladle, gravy, 6 5/8″	90.00	Fork, salad, 6 5/8″	65.00
Letter Opener, ST blade, 7 3/8″	35.00	Fork, youth, 6 1/4″	50.00
Server, cheese, ST blade, 6 1/4″	40.00	Knife, HH, modern blade, 9″	50.00
Server, pie, ST blade, 10″	40.00	Knife, HH, modern blade, 9 1/2″	60.00
Server, pie/cake, ST blade, 10 1/2″	40.00	Server, pie/cake, ST blade, 11 1/8″	80.00
Server, tomato, 7 1/2″	110.00	Serving Fork, cold meat, 8 1/2″	130.00
Serving Fork, cold meat, 8″	90.00	Serving Spoon, tablespoon, 8 3/4″	100.00
Serving Spoon, casserole, 7 7/8″	110.00	Spoon, bonbon, 5 1/2″	60.00
Serving Spoon, tablespoon, 8 1/2″	80.00	Spoon, jelly, 6 7/8″	45.00
Serving Spoon, tablespoon, pierced, 8 1/2″	100.00	Spoon, salt, 2 1/2″	15.00
Spoon, bonbon, 5 1/2″	40.00	Spoon, soup, oval bowl, 6 5/8″	60.00
Spoon, bouillon, round bowl, 5 1/8″	40.00	Spoon, sugar, 6″	50.00
Spoon, cream soup, round bowl, 6 1/2″	40.00	Spoon, teaspoon, 6″	32.00
Spoon, demitasse, 4 1/4″	20.00		
Spoon, infant feeding, 5″	25.00		
Spoon, jelly, 6 5/8″	40.00		
Spoon, relish, 6″	40.00		
Spoon, salt, 2 1/2″	12.00		
Spoon, soup, oval bowl, 7″	45.00		
Spoon, sugar, 6″	30.00		
Spoon, teaspoon, 6″	25.00		
Spoon, teaspoon, 5 o'clock, 5 5/8″	20.00		
Spoon, youth, 5 3/8″	25.00		
Sugar Tongs, 4″	45.00		

Towle, El Grandee, Sterling Silver

Butter Serving Knife, HH, 7 1/8″	$40.00
Fork, 7 1/2″	45.00
Fork, cocktail, 5 5/8″	37.00
Fork, fish, ST tines, 8 1/4″	50.00
Fork, ice cream, 5 1/4″	45.00
Fork, lemon, 5 5/8″	40.00
Fork, pickle, short handle, 5 7/8″	40.00
Fork, salad, 6 7/8″	50.00
Fork, strawberry, 5 5/8″	45.00
Knife, cheese, ST blade, 7 3/8″	50.00
Knife, fish, ST blade, 8 1/2″	50.00
Knife, HH, modern blade, 8 3/4″	40.00
Knife, steak, 8 7/8″	40.00
Salad Set, two pieces, plastic bowl	100.00
Server, pie/cake, ST blade, 10 3/4″	55.00

Towle, Debussy, Sterling Silver

Butter Spreader, HH, modern ST blade, 6 1/2″	$35.00
Fork, 7 3/8″	60.00

Server, tomato, 8 1/8″	105.00		Ladle, gravy, 6 1/4″	95.00
Serving Spoon, tablespoon, pierced, 8 5/8″	105.00		Server, pie, ST blade, 10″	70.00
			Server, pie/cake, ST blade, 10 1/4″	70.00
Spoon, bonbon, 6″	50.00		Serving Fork, cold meat, 7 1/2″	110.00
Spoon, iced tea, 8 1/8″	50.00		Serving Fork, cold meat, ST tines, 9 3/4″	70.00
Spoon, salt, 2 1/2″	15.00		Serving Spoon, casserole, 7 3/4″	125.00
Spoon, sugar, 6 1/4″	40.00		Serving Spoon, tablespoon, 8 1/8″	105.00
Spoon, teaspoon, 6 1/8″	30.00		Spoon, bouillon, round bowl, 5 1/4″	40.00
			Spoon, cream soup, round bowl, 5 5/8″	45.00
			Spoon, demitasse, 4 3/8″	30.00
			Spoon, sugar, 5 3/4″	50.00
			Spoon, teaspoon, 5 3/4″	40.00
			Sugar Tongs, 4 1/8″	80.00

Towle, Fiddle Thread, Sterling Silver

Bar Knife, 8 3/8″	$50.00
Butter Serving Knife, FH, 7 1/8″	50.00
Butter Spreader, FH, 5 7/8″	35.00
Butter Spreader, HH, paddled ST blade, 6″	35.00
Carving Set, two pieces, large, ST blade	180.00
Carving Set, two pieces, small, ST blade	170.00
Fork, 7 1/8″	60.00
Fork, 7 1/2″	80.00
Fork, fish, ST tines, 7 1/2″	45.00
Fork, ice cream, 5 1/2″	60.00
Fork, pickle, short handle, 6″	40.00
Fork, salad	60.00
Fork, strawberry, 5 1/8″	45.00
Knife, fish, SP blade, 7 7/8″	50.00
Knife, fish, ST blade, 7 7/8″	50.00
Knife, HH, New French blade, 8 1/2″	50.00
Knife, HH, New French blade, 8 3/4″	50.00
Knife, steak, 8″	60.00
Knife, steak, 8 3/4″	60.00
Knife, wedding cake, ST blade, 12 1/8″	100.00

Towle, Fontana, Sterling Silver

Butter Serving Knife, HH, 6 7/8″	$32.00
Butter Spreader, HH, modern ST blade, 6 5/8″	30.00
Carving Knife, ST blade, 11″	40.00
Cheese Cleaver, ST blade, 7″	40.00
Fork, 7 1/4″	40.00
Fork, 7 3/4″	50.00
Fork, baby, 4 1/8″	25.00
Fork, cocktail, 5 1/2″	30.00
Fork, ice cream, 5 1/4″	40.00
Fork, ice cream, 5 3/4″	40.00
Fork, lemon, 5 1/8″	30.00
Fork, pickle, short handle, 5 5/8″	30.00
Fork, salad, 6 1/2″	40.00
Fork, youth, 6 1/4″	35.00
Knife, cheese, ST blade, 7″	40.00
Knife, cheese, ST blade, 7 1/4″	40.00
Knife, fruit, ST blade, 7″	35.00

Knife, HH, modern blade, 9″	32.00	Cheese Pick, 8 1/8″	30.00
Knife, HH, modern blade, 9 5/8″	40.00	Fork, 7 1/4″	40.00
Knife, youth, 6 5/8″	30.00	Fork, baby, 4 1/4″	25.00
Ladle, cream sauce, 5 3/8″	50.00	Fork, cocktail, 5 5/8″	27.00
Ladle, gravy, 6 1/4″	90.00	Fork, fish, ST tines, 7 3/4″	40.00
Letter Opener, ST blade, 7 3/4″	35.00	Fork, ice cream, 5 5/8″	45.00
Salad Set, two pieces, plastic bowl	90.00	Fork, lemon, 5 1/2″	30.00
Server, pie/cake, ST blade, 11″	45.00	Fork, pickle, short handle, 6″	30.00
Serving Fork, cold meat, 9 1/4″	110.00	Fork, salad, 6 3/8″	40.00
Serving Spoon, tablespoon, 8 5/8″	90.00	Fork, strawberry, 5 1/2″	30.00
Serving Spoon, tablespoon, pierced, 8 5/8″	100.00	Fork, youth, 6″	35.00
Spoon, bonbon, 5 3/8″	45.00	Knife, cheese, ST blade, 7 1/8″	40.00
Spoon, demitasse, 4 1/4″	22.00	Knife, fish, ST blade, 8 1/8″	40.00
Spoon, fruit, 6 1/8″	32.00	Knife, fruit, ST blade, 6 5/8″	35.00
Spoon, iced tea, 7 7/8″	40.00	Knife, HH, modern blade, 8 7/8″	32.00
Spoon, infant feeding, 5 3/8″	25.00	Knife, HH, New French blade, 8 7/8″	32.00
Spoon, jelly, 6 3/8″	40.00	Ladle, cream sauce, 5 3/4″	40.00
Spoon, salt, 2 1/2″	12.00	Ladle, gravy, 6 3/4″	85.00
Spoon, soup, oval bowl, 6 5/8″	50.00	Salad Set, two pieces, plastic bowl	90.00
Spoon, sugar, 5 1/4″	30.00	Server, cheese, ST blade, 6 5/8″	40.00
Spoon, teaspoon	25.00	Server, pasta, ST bowl, 10 5/8″	40.00
Spoon, youth, 5 1/4″	25.00	Server, pie/cake, ST blade, 10 3/8″	40.00
		Server, tomato, 7 3/8″	110.00
		Serving Fork, cold meat, 8 1/4″	90.00
		Serving Spoon, casserole, 8 1/8″	100.00

Towle, French Provincial, Sterling Silver

Bar Knife, 8 7/8″	$35.00
Butter Serving Knife, FH, 6 7/8″	35.00
Butter Serving Knife, HH, 6 7/8″	35.00
Butter Spreader, FH, 5 3/4″	30.00
Butter Spreader, HH, modern ST blade, 6 1/2″	27.00
Butter Spreader, HH, paddled ST blade, 6″	27.00
Carving Set, two pieces, ST blade	100.00

Photo courtesy of Towle Silversmiths/Syratech Corporation.

Serving Spoon, tablespoon, 8 ½″	80.00	Knife, HH, New French blade, 9″	40.00
Serving Spoon, tablespoon, pierced, 8 ½″	90.00	Ladle, gravy, 7 ¼″	90.00
		Letter Opener, ST blade, 8 ½″	40.00
Spoon, bonbon, 5 ½″	40.00	Server, fish, ST blade, 11″	50.00
Spoon, cream soup, round bowl, 6 ¼″	45.00	Server, pie, ST blade, 9 ½″	50.00
Spoon, demitasse, 4 ¼″	20.00	Server, pie/cake, ST blade, 10 ⅝″	50.00
Spoon, fruit, 6″	35.00	Serving Fork, cold meat, 8 ⅛″	100.00
Spoon, iced tea, 7 ⅞″	35.00	Serving Spoon, tablespoon, 8 ⅝″	90.00
Spoon, jelly, 6 ½″	40.00	Spoon, bonbon, 5 ⅞″	45.00
Spoon, relish, 6″	45.00	Spoon, cream soup, round bowl, 6 ⅛″	50.00
Spoon, salt, 2 ½″	12.00	Spoon, demitasse, 4 ½″	25.00
Spoon, soup, oval bowl, 6 ½″	45.00	Spoon, iced tea, 8 ¼″	45.00
Spoon, sugar, 5 ⅞″	30.00	Spoon, jelly, 6 ⅞″	50.00
Spoon, teaspoon, 6″	25.00	Spoon, mustard, 5 ¼″	40.00
Spoon, teaspoon, 5 o'clock, 5 ⅜″	25.00	Spoon, salt, 2 ½″	15.00
Sugar Tongs, 4″	50.00	Spoon, soup, oval bowl, 7 ¼″	50.00
		Spoon, sugar, 5 ¾″	40.00
		Spoon, teaspoon, 6″	30.00
		Spoon, teaspoon, 5 o'clock, 5 ½″	25.00
		Tea Strainer, 7 ⅜″	45.00

Towle, King Richard, Sterling Silver

Bar Knife, bar, 8 ¾″	$40.00
Butter Serving Knife, HH, 6 ½″	40.00
Butter Spreader, HH, modern ST blade, 6 ¼″	40.00
Butter Spreader, HH, paddled blade, 5 ¾″	40.00
Carving Set, two pieces, ST blade	100.00
Fork, 7 ⅜″	45.00
Fork, 7 ⅞″	60.00
Fork, baby, 4 ¼″	40.00
Fork, cocktail, 5 ¾″	35.00
Fork, lemon, 5″	40.00
Fork, pickle, short handle, 6 ⅛″	40.00
Fork, salad, 6 ½″	45.00
Fork, strawberry, 5 ¼″	40.00
Knife, HH, modern blade, 8 ¾″	40.00
Knife, HH, modern blade, 9 ½″	50.00

Photo courtesy of Towle Silversmiths/Syratech Corporation.

Towle, Legato, Sterling Silver		Towle, Louis XIV, Sterling Silver	
Bar Knife, 9 3/8″	$30.00	Bowl, bonbon, 7 3/8″	$100.00
Butter Serving Knife, HH, 6 7/8″	32.00	Butter Serving Knife, FH, 6 7/8″	40.00
Carving Fork, ST tines, 9 1/8″	50.00	Butter Spreader, FH, 5 3/4″	30.00
Fork, 7 3/8″	40.00	Candlestick, 10 1/4″	600.00
Fork, 8″	55.00	Carving Fork, ST tines, 8 7/8″	50.00
Fork, fish, ST tines, 8 3/8″	30.00	Carving Knife, ST blade, 10″	50.00
Fork, ice cream, 5 1/8″	35.00	Carving Set, two pieces, ST blade	100.00
Fork, lemon, 5 3/8″	25.00	Fork, 7 3/8″	45.00
Fork, pickle, short handle, 5 3/4″	25.00	Fork, 7 7/8″	65.00
Fork, salad, 6 5/8″	32.00	Fork, cocktail, 5 1/2″	30.00
Fork, strawberry, 5 1/2″	30.00	Fork, ice cream, 5 1/2″	50.00
Knife, cheese, ST blade, 7 1/8″	35.00	Fork, lemon, 5 3/8″	30.00
Knife, HH, modern blade, 9″	30.00	Fork, pickle, short handle, 5 3/4″	30.00
Knife, HH, modern blade, 9 3/4″	40.00	Fork, pickle, short handle, 6 1/4″	30.00
Knife, steak, 9″	40.00	Fork, salad, 6 1/4″	40.00
Knife, wedding cake, ST blade, 12 1/2″	70.00	Knife, cheese, ST blade, 7″	45.00
Knife, youth, 7 1/8″	32.00	Knife, HH, modern blade, 9 1/8″	40.00
Ladle, gravy, 6 5/8″	70.00	Knife, HH, New French blade, 9 1/2″	50.00
Letter Opener, ST blade, 7 3/4″	32.00	Knife, HH, Old French blade, 9 1/4″	40.00
Server, lasagna, ST blade, 10 1/2″	55.00	Ladle, cream sauce, 5 1/4″	45.00
Server, pie/cake, ST blade, 11″	50.00	Ladle, cream sauce, 5 5/8″	45.00
Serving Fork, cold meat, 9 1/8″	50.00	Ladle, gravy, 6 3/8″	90.00
Serving Spoon, tablespoon, 8 3/8″	70.00	Server, cheese, ST blade, 5 7/8″	50.00
Serving Spoon, tablespoon, pierced, 8 3/8″	80.00	Server, pastry, ST bowl, 8 7/8″	70.00
Spoon, bonbon, 5 1/2″	35.00	Serving Fork, cold meat, 7 5/8″	80.00
Spoon, demitasse, 4 1/4″	22.00	Serving Spoon, casserole, 7 5/8″	110.00
Spoon, iced tea, 7 3/4″	32.00	Serving Spoon, tablespoon, 8 1/4″	70.00
Spoon, infant feeding, 5 1/2″	32.00	Spoon, bouillon, round bowl, 5″	40.00
Spoon, salt, 2 1/2″	12.00	Spoon, demitasse, 4 1/4″	25.00
Spoon, soup, oval bowl, 6 5/8″	40.00	Spoon, fruit, 5 1/2″	40.00
Spoon, sugar, 6″	32.00	Spoon, grapefruit, round bowl, 6 7/8″	45.00
Spoon, teaspoon, 6 1/8″	20.00	Spoon, iced tea, 7 7/8″	40.00
		Spoon, jelly, 6 1/2″	35.00
		Spoon, relish, 6 3/8″	40.00

Spoon, sugar, 5 5/8"	40.00
Spoon, teaspoon, 5 7/8"	22.00
Spoon, teaspoon, 5 o'clock, 5 1/2"	20.00
Spoon, youth, 5 1/4"	40.00
Sugar Tongs, 4"	65.00
Sugar Tongs, 4 3/4"	65.00

Spoon, bonbon, 5 1/2"	35.00
Spoon, cream soup, round bowl, 6 3/8"	40.00
Spoon, demitasse, 4 1/4"	20.00
Spoon, fruit, 5 7/8"	35.00
Spoon, iced tea, 8"	40.00
Spoon, infant feeding, 5"	35.00
Spoon, jelly, 6 1/2"	30.00
Spoon, sugar, 5 7/8"	32.00
Spoon, teaspoon, 5 7/8"	20.00
Sugar Tongs, 4"	55.00

Towle, Madeira, Sterling Silver

Butter Serving Knife, FH, 6 7/8"	$32.00
Butter Spreader, FH, 5 3/4"	22.00
Butter Spreader, HH, paddled ST blade, 5 7/8"	25.00
Carving Fork, ST tines, 9 1/8"	50.00
Carving Knife, ST blade, 10 1/8"	50.00
Fork, 7 3/8"	40.00
Fork, 8 1/8"	50.00
Fork, baby, 4 1/4"	32.00
Fork, ice cream, 5 5/8"	40.00
Fork, lemon, 5 3/8"	25.00
Fork, pickle, short handle, 5 7/8"	25.00
Fork, salad, 6 1/2"	32.00
Fork, strawberry, 5 5/8"	32.00
Knife, cheese, ST blade, 7"	40.00
Knife, HH, modern blade, 9"	32.00
Knife, HH, modern blade, 9 7/8"	35.00
Knife, HH, New French blade, 9"	32.00
Ladle, cream sauce, 5 5/8"	32.00
Ladle, gravy, 6 3/4"	70.00
Salad Set, two pieces, plastic bowl	75.00
Server, cheese, ST blade, 6 3/8"	40.00
Server, pie/cake, ST blade, 10 5/8"	50.00
Serving Fork, cold meat, 8 3/8"	70.00
Serving Spoon, casserole, 8 1/4"	100.00
Serving Spoon, tablespoon, 8 1/2"	65.00

Towle, Mary Chilton, Sterling Silver

Bacon Set, two pieces	$80.00
Butter Serving Knife, FH, 7 1/4"	32.00
Carving Fork, ST tines, 8 5/8"	50.00
Carving Knife, ST blade, 9 7/8"	50.00
Carving Set, two pieces, ST blade	100.00
Fork, 7 1/4"	40.00
Fork, 7 3/4"	50.00
Fork, chipped beef, 7 1/2"	70.00
Fork, cocktail, 6"	25.00
Fork, dessert, 5 7/8"	40.00
Fork, lemon, 5 1/4"	25.00
Fork, pickle, long handle, 8"	40.00
Fork, pickle, short handle, 6 1/4"	25.00
Fork, salad, 6 1/4"	35.00
Knife, HH, blunt blade, 9 7/8"	40.00
Knife, HH, Old French blade, 9"	30.00
Ladle, cream sauce, 5 1/2"	35.00
Ladle, cream sauce, 5 3/4"	35.00
Server, pie, SP blade, 9 3/4"	55.00
Serving Spoon, casserole, 9 1/4"	80.00
Serving Spoon, tablespoon, 8 1/4"	60.00
Spoon, bonbon, 4 3/4"	35.00
Spoon, bouillon, round bowl, 5 1/4"	32.00

Spoon, cream soup, round bowl, 6 ½"	40.00
Spoon, demitasse, 4"	20.00
Spoon, fruit, 6"	32.00
Spoon, jelly, 6 ⅞"	25.00
Spoon, preserve, 7 ⅜"	50.00
Spoon, relish, 6 ⅜"	35.00
Spoon, soup, oval bowl, 6 ⅞"	40.00
Spoon, sugar, 5 ⅝"	32.00
Spoon, sugar, 5 ⅞"	32.00
Spoon, teaspoon, 6 ⅛"	22.00
Spoon, teaspoon, 5 o'clock, 5 ¾"	20.00
Sugar Tongs, 3 ¾"	50.00

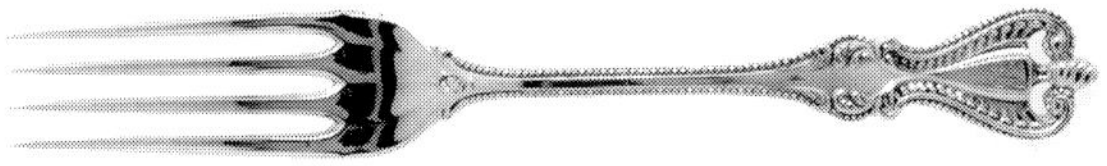

Towle, Old Colonial, Sterling Silver

Butter Spreader, FH, 5 ½"	$30.00
Butter Spreader, FH, 5 ¾"	30.00
Butter Spreader, HH, paddled ST blade, 6"	32.00
Fork, pickle, short handle, 5 ⅞"	35.00
Knife, steak, 8 ⅞"	45.00
Ladle, cream sauce, 6"	50.00
Ladle, gravy, 7 ⅜"	110.00
Server, pie/cake, ST blade, 10 ½"	60.00
Serving Fork, cold meat, 7 ¾"	100.00
Serving Fork, lettuce, 9 ½"	120.00
Spoon, bonbon, 4 ½"	50.00
Spoon, bonbon, 5 ½"	50.00
Spoon, chow chow, 6 ⅜"	50.00
Spoon, cream soup, round bowl, 6"	50.00
Spoon, iced tea, 8"	45.00
Spoon, salt, 2 ⅜"	15.00
Spoon, soup, oval bowl, 7 ⅛"	50.00
Spoon, sugar, 5 ⅞"	35.00
Spoon, teaspoon, 5 ⅝"	22.00
Spoon, teaspoon, 5 o'clock, 5 ⅜"	20.00

Towle, Old Lace, Sterling Silver

Bar Knife, 9"	$30.00
Bowl, bonbon, 7"	160.00
Butter Serving Knife, FH, 7"	35.00
Butter Serving Knife, HH, 6 ⅝"	35.00
Butter Spreader, FH, 5 ⅞"	22.00
Butter Spreader, HH, modern ST blade, 6 ¼"	25.00
Butter Spreader, HH, paddled ST blade, 5 ¾"	25.00
Carving Knife, ST blade, 10 ⅜"	55.00
Carving Set, two pieces, ST blade	110.00
Cheese Pick, 8 ¼"	35.00
Fork, 7 ⅜"	45.00
Fork, 7 ⅞"	65.00
Fork, baby, 4 ¼"	37.00
Fork, cocktail, 5 ¾"	27.00
Fork, ice cream, 5 ½"	40.00
Fork, lemon, 5 ¼"	30.00
Fork, lemon, 5 ½"	30.00
Fork, pickle, short handle, 6"	30.00
Fork, strawberry, 5 ½"	35.00
Knife, cheese, ST blade, 6 ⅞"	40.00
Knife, HH, New French blade, 8 ¾"	35.00
Ladle, cream sauce, 5 ¾"	40.00
Server, cheese, ST blade, 6 ¼"	45.00
Server, lasagna, ST blade, 10 ⅛"	60.00
Server, pie/cake, ST blade, 10 ½"	60.00
Serving Fork, cold meat, 8"	85.00
Serving Spoon, tablespoon, 8 ½"	70.00
Spoon, bonbon, 4 ⅞"	40.00
Spoon, bonbon, 5 ½"	40.00
Spoon, cream soup, round bowl, 6 ½"	35.00
Spoon, demitasse, 4 ¼"	22.00
Spoon, grapefruit, round bowl, 7 ⅛"	40.00
Spoon, iced tea, 8 ⅛"	35.00

Spoon, jelly, 6 3/4″	32.00
Spoon, salt, 2 1/2″	12.00
Spoon, sugar, 6″	40.00
Spoon, teaspoon, 6 1/8″	25.00
Spoon, teaspoon, 5 o'clock, 5 5/8″	22.00
Sugar Tongs, 4″	60.00

Towle, Old Master, Sterling Silver

Bar Knife, 8 7/8″	$35.00
Bowl, vegetable, oval, SP, 13″	40.00
Butter Serving Knife, FH, 6 7/8″	30.00
Butter Serving Knife, HH, 6 7/8″	30.00
Butter Spreader, FH, 5 3/4″	27.00
Butter Spreader, HH, modern ST blade, 6 1/2″	32.00

Photo courtesy of Towle Silversmiths/Syratech Corporation.

Butter Spreader, HH, paddled ST blade, 5 7/8″	32.00
Candlestick, 7 1/4″	150.00
Carving Knife, ST blade, 9 7/8″	50.00
Carving Set, two pieces, ST blade	100.00
Creamer and Sugar, open, mini	300.00
Fork, 7 1/4″	40.00
Fork, 7 3/4″	40.00
Fork, baby, 4 1/8″	40.00
Fork, cocktail, 5 3/4″	25.00
Fork, fish, ST tines, 7 7/8″	40.00
Fork, lemon, 5 1/4″	32.00
Fork, lemon, 5 5/8″	32.00
Fork, pickle, short handle, 5 7/8″	32.00
Fork, salad, 6 3/8″	35.00
Ice Cream Slicer, 13″	300.00
Knife, cheese, ST blade, 7 1/8″	40.00
Knife, HH, modern blade, 8 7/8″	35.00
Knife, HH, modern blade, 9 5/8″	45.00
Knife, HH, New French blade, 8 7/8″	35.00
Knife, HH, New French blade, 9 5/8″	45.00
Knife, steak, 8 1/2″	50.00
Knife, wedding cake, ST blade, 12 1/8″	60.00
Ladle, cream sauce, 5 1/2″	45.00
Ladle, gravy, 6 3/4″	90.00
Ladle, soup, 15 1/8″	230.00
Poultry Shears, 11 1/2″	210.00
Salad Set, two pieces, plastic bowl, 12″	80.00
Scoop, cheese, ST scoop, 8″	35.00
Scoop, coffee, SP scoop, 4″	40.00
Server, cheese, ST blade, 6 1/2″	40.00
Server, macaroni, 10 3/8″	300.00
Server, pasta, ST bowl, 10 1/2″	40.00
Server, pie, ST blade, 9 7/8″	50.00
Server, pie/cake, ST blade, 9 7/8″	50.00
Server, tomato, 7 3/8″	100.00
Serving Fork, cold meat, 8 1/4″	90.00
Serving Spoon, casserole, 9 1/8″	130.00
Serving Spoon, tablespoon, 8 1/2″	85.00
Serving Spoon, tablespoon, pierced, 8 1/2″	100.00
Spoon, baby, straight handle, 4 1/4″	40.00

Spoon, bonbon, 5 $\frac{1}{2}''$	40.00
Spoon, cream soup, round bowl, 6 $\frac{1}{4}''$	45.00
Spoon, demitasse, 4 $\frac{1}{4}''$	25.00
Spoon, iced tea, 7 $\frac{7}{8}''$	40.00
Spoon, jelly, 6 $\frac{3}{8}''$	40.00
Spoon, jelly, 6 $\frac{1}{2}''$	40.00
Spoon, mustard, 5 $\frac{1}{8}''$	40.00
Spoon, soup, oval bowl, 6 $\frac{5}{8}''$	45.00
Spoon, sugar, 5 $\frac{5}{8}''$	30.00
Spoon, sugar, 5 $\frac{7}{8}''$	30.00
Spoon, teaspoon, 6$''$	25.00
Sugar Tongs, 4$''$	55.00
Tea Set, three pieces	2,500.00
Tray, round, SP, 15 $\frac{1}{4}''$	50.00

Serving Spoon, casserole, 8 $\frac{1}{8}''$	120.00
Serving Spoon, tablespoon, 8 $\frac{1}{2}''$	95.00
Spoon, cream soup, round bowl, 6 $\frac{1}{4}''$	50.00
Spoon, demitasse, 4 $\frac{1}{4}''$	30.00
Spoon, iced tea, 7 $\frac{7}{8}''$	45.00
Spoon, soup, oval bowl, 6 $\frac{3}{4}''$	50.00
Spoon, sugar, 6$''$	45.00
Spoon, teaspoon, 6$''$	30.00

Towle, Queen Elizabeth I, Sterling Silver

Butter Serving Knife, HH, 7$''$	$40.00
Cheese Cleaver, ST blade, 7$''$	50.00
Fork, 7 $\frac{3}{8}''$	45.00
Fork, 7 $\frac{7}{8}''$	60.00
Fork, baby, 4 $\frac{1}{8}''$	30.00
Fork, cocktail, 5 $\frac{1}{2}''$	37.00
Fork, lemon, 5 $\frac{1}{8}''$	40.00
Fork, pickle, short handle, 5 $\frac{7}{8}''$	40.00
Fork, salad, 6 $\frac{3}{4}''$	45.00
Fork, youth, 6 $\frac{1}{4}''$	32.00
Knife, bread, ST blade, 15 $\frac{1}{2}''$	75.00
Knife, cheese, ST blade, 7 $\frac{3}{8}''$	50.00
Knife, HH, modern blade, 9 $\frac{5}{8}''$	50.00
Ladle, cream sauce, 5 $\frac{1}{2}''$	50.00
Ladle, gravy, 6 $\frac{7}{8}''$	100.00
Server, fish, ST blade, 11 $\frac{7}{8}''$	50.00
Server, pie/cake, ST blade, 11$''$	50.00
Serving Fork, cold meat, 9 $\frac{1}{4}''$	110.00
Serving Spoon, tablespoon, 8 $\frac{5}{8}''$	90.00
Serving Spoon, tablespoon, pierced, 8 $\frac{5}{8}''$	100.00
Spoon, bonbon, 6$''$	50.00
Spoon, iced tea, 8 $\frac{1}{8}''$	45.00
Spoon, jelly, 6 $\frac{3}{8}''$	50.00
Spoon, soup, oval bowl, 7$''$	50.00

Towle, Old Mirror, Sterling Silver

Butter Serving Knife, FH, 7$''$	$45.00
Butter Spreader, FH, 5 $\frac{3}{4}''$	30.00
Butter Spreader, HH, paddled ST blade, 5 $\frac{3}{4}''$	32.00
Carving Set, two pieces, ST blade	150.00
Fork, 7 $\frac{1}{8}''$	55.00
Fork, 7 $\frac{3}{4}''$	75.00
Fork, cocktail, 5 $\frac{3}{4}''$	35.00
Fork, ice cream, 5 $\frac{3}{4}''$	60.00
Fork, lemon, 5 $\frac{1}{2}''$	35.00
Fork, pickle, short handle, 5 $\frac{7}{8}''$	35.00
Fork, salad, 6 $\frac{3}{8}''$	55.00
Knife, HH, modern blade, 8 $\frac{3}{4}''$	40.00
Knife, HH, New French blade, 8 $\frac{3}{4}''$	40.00
Knife, HH, New French blade, 9 $\frac{3}{4}''$	55.00
Ladle, gravy, 6 $\frac{3}{4}''$	95.00
Server, tomato, 7 $\frac{1}{2}''$	120.00
Serving Fork, cold meat, 7 $\frac{7}{8}''$	100.00

Spoon, teaspoon	30.00
Spoon, teaspoon, 5 o'clock, 6 1/8″	25.00

Towle, Rambler Rose, Sterling Silver

Butter Spreader, FH, 5 7/8″	$25.00
Butter Spreader, HH, modern ST blade, 6 1/8″	27.00
Butter Spreader, HH, paddled ST blade, 5 1/2″	27.00
Butter Spreader, HH, paddled ST blade, 5 3/4″	27.00
Carving Fork, ST tines, 8 1/4″	35.00
Carving Knife, ST blade, 10″	35.00
Fork, 7 3/8″	35.00
Fork, 8″	45.00
Fork, cocktail, 5 3/4″	25.00
Fork, ice cream, 5 3/4″	25.00
Fork, lemon, 5 1/2″	30.00
Fork, pickle, short handle, 6″	30.00
Fork, salad, 6 5/8″	37.00
Knife, cheese, ST blade, 6 3/4″	40.00
Knife, HH, modern blade, 8 5/8″	32.00
Knife, HH, New French blade, 8 5/8″	32.00
Knife, HH, New French blade, 9 1/8″	32.00
Knife, HH, New French blade, 9 1/2″	40.00
Ladle, cream sauce, 5 3/4″	45.00
Ladle, gravy, 6 7/8″	80.00
Server, pie, ST blade, 10 3/8″	45.00
Server, tomato, 7 1/2″	95.00
Serving Fork, cold meat, 7 7/8″	85.00
Serving Spoon, tablespoon, 8 1/2″	80.00
Serving Spoon, tablespoon, pierced, 8 1/2″	95.00
Spoon, bonbon, 5 1/2″	40.00
Spoon, bouillon, round bowl, 5 1/8″	35.00

Spoon, cream soup, round bowl, 6 3/8″	40.00
Spoon, demitasse, 4 1/4″	22.00
Spoon, iced tea, 8 1/8″	35.00
Spoon, jelly, 6 3/4″	40.00
Spoon, salt, 2 1/2″	12.00
Spoon, soup, oval bowl, 6 3/4″	45.00
Spoon, sugar, 5 7/8″	30.00
Spoon, teaspoon, 6″	22.00
Spoon, teaspoon, 5 o'clock, 5 5/8″	20.00
Sugar Tongs, 4″	50.00

Towle, Rose Solitaire, Sterling Silver

Butter Serving Knife, FH, 6 7/8″	$35.00
Butter Serving Knife, HH, 6 3/4″	30.00
Butter Spreader, HH, paddled ST blade, 5 7/8″	30.00
Carving Set, two pieces, ST blade	85.00
Fork, 7 3/8″	40.00
Fork, lemon, 5 1/4″	30.00
Fork, salad	40.00
Knife, HH, modern blade, 9″	32.00
Knife, HH, modern blade, 9 1/2″	45.00
Ladle, cream sauce, 5 3/8″	40.00
Ladle, gravy, 6 1/2″	85.00
Server, pie/cake, ST blade, 10 3/4″	45.00
Serving Fork, cold meat, 9 1/4″	95.00
Serving Spoon, tablespoon, 8 1/2″	80.00
Serving Spoon, tablespoon, pierced, 8 1/2″	90.00
Spoon, bonbon, 5 1/2″	40.00
Spoon, demitasse, 4 1/8″	22.00
Spoon, iced tea, 8″	35.00
Spoon, jelly, 6 1/2″	40.00
Spoon, soup, oval bowl, 6 3/4″	45.00
Spoon, sugar, 5 1/2″	30.00
Spoon, teaspoon, 5 7/8″	22.00

Towle, Silver Flutes, Sterling Silver

Butter Serving Knife, HH, 6 7/8″	$40.00
Butter Spreader, FH, 5 3/4″	25.00
Butter Spreader, HH, paddled ST blade, 5 7/8″	27.00
Carving Set, two pieces, ST blade	130.00
Creamer and Sugar, open, mini	200.00
Fork, 7 3/8″	50.00
Fork, 8″	70.00
Fork, cocktail, 5 3/4″	30.00
Fork, lemon, 5 1/2″	30.00
Fork, pickle, short handle, 6″	30.00
Fork, salad, 6 1/2″	50.00
Fork, youth, 6 1/8″	50.00
Knife, HH, New French blade, 8 7/8″	35.00
Ladle, cream sauce, 5 5/8″	50.00
Ladle, gravy, 6 1/8″	85.00
Ladle, gravy, 7″	85.00
Salad Set, two pieces, plastic bowl	85.00
Server, cheese, ST blade, 6 1/2″	50.00
Server, pie/cake, ST blade, 10 3/8″	70.00
Serving Fork, joint, 11 1/8″	120.00
Serving Fork, salad, wooden tines, 10 3/4″	40.00
Spoon, cream soup, round bowl, 6 1/2″	45.00
Spoon, demitasse, 4 1/4″	22.00
Spoon, iced tea, 8″	40.00
Spoon, jelly, 6 1/2″	35.00
Spoon, sugar, 6″	40.00
Spoon, teaspoon, 6″	25.00
Spoon, youth, 5 3/8″	45.00
Sugar Tongs, 4 1/8″	65.00

Towle, Spanish Provincial, Sterling Silver

Cheese Pick, 8 5/8″	$30.00
Fork, 7 1/2″	45.00
Fork, baby, 4 1/4″	25.00
Fork, cocktail, 5 5/8″	30.00
Fork, fish, ST tines, 8 1/4″	40.00
Fork, lemon, 5 1/2″	30.00
Fork, pickle, short handle, 5 7/8″	30.00
Fork, salad, 6 1/2″	40.00
Knife, cheese, ST blade, 7 1/2″	40.00
Knife, HH, modern blade, 8 3/4″	30.00
Knife, HH, modern blade, 9 1/2″	40.00
Knife, steak, 9 3/8″	40.00
Ladle, cream sauce, 5 5/8″	45.00
Letter Opener, ST blade, 7 3/4″	35.00
Spoon, bonbon, 5 5/8″	40.00
Spoon, infant feeding, 5 1/2″	25.00
Spoon, soup, oval bowl, 6 7/8″	45.00
Spoon, sugar, 6 1/8″	30.00
Spoon, teaspoon	25.00
Spoon, teaspoon, 5 o'clock, 5 1/2″	20.00

STAINLESS

Towle, Beaded Antique, Stainless
(Introduced in 1973)

Butter Serving Knife, HH, 7 1/4″	$12.00
Butter Spreader, HH, modern blade, 6 7/8″	12.00

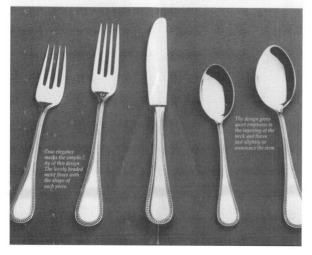

Carving Set, two pieces	55.00
Fork, 8 1/8″	10.00
Fork, salad, 7 1/4″	10.00
Knife, HH, modern blade, 9″	10.00
Knife, steak, 9 1/4″	17.00
Knife, wedding cake, 13 1/4″	30.00
Ladle, gravy, 6 3/4″	15.00
Serving Fork, cold meat, 9 3/8″	15.00
Spoon, soup, oval bowl, 7 1/8″	10.00
Spoon, sugar, 6 1/8″	12.00
Spoon, teaspoon, 6 1/4″	12.00

Towle, Bedford, Stainless

Butter Spreader, FH, 6 3/4″	$12.00
Fork	15.00
Fork, salad	15.00
Knife, New French blade, 8 1/4″	15.00

Ladle, gravy, 6 5/8″	15.00
Serving Fork, cold meat, 9 3/8″	15.00
Serving Spoon, tablespoon, 9 3/8″	20.00
Spoon, sugar, 5 7/8″	12.00
Spoon, teaspoon, 6 1/4″	10.00

Towle, Colonial Plume, Stainless
(Introduced in 1975)

Butter Serving Knife, HH, 7 1/8″	$27.00
Butter Spreader, HH, modern blade, 6 7/8″	25.00
Fork, salad	25.00
Knife	32.00
Ladle, gravy, 7″	37.00
Serving Fork, cold meat, 9 3/8″	40.00
Spoon, soup, oval bowl, 7 1/4″	25.00
Spoon, sugar, 6 1/4″	27.00
Spoon, teaspoon	27.00

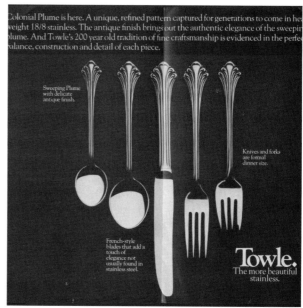

Towle, Design 2, Stainless

Fork, salad	$27.00
Knife	32.00
Ladle, gravy, 6 ½″	37.00
Serving Fork, cold meat, 7 ⅞″	37.00
Serving Spoon, casserole, 7 ¾″	37.00
Spoon, bouillon, round bowl, 5 ½″	25.00
Spoon, sugar, 5 ⅝″	27.00
Spoon, teaspoon	27.00

Towle, London Shell, Stainless
(Introduced in 1977)

Butter Serving Knife, HH, 7″	$15.00
Fork, 8 ⅛″	12.00
Fork, salad, 7 ⅛″	10.00
Knife, HH, modern blade, 9 ⅛″	15.00
Ladle, gravy, 6 ½″	20.00
Ladle, gravy, 7 ¼″	20.00
Serving Fork, cold meat, 8 ⅞″	20.00
Serving Spoon, tablespoon, 8 ¾″	20.00
Serving Spoon, tablespoon, pierced, 8 ¾″	20.00
Spoon, soup, oval bowl, 7 ¼″	10.00
Spoon, sugar, 6 ⅛″	12.00
Spoon, teaspoon, 6 ⅜″	10.00

Towle, Hamilton, Stainless
(Introduced in 1976)

Butter Serving Knife, FH, 6 ⅞″	$22.00
Butter Serving Knife, HH, 7 ⅛″	25.00
Butter Spreader, HH, modern blade, 6 ⅞″	25.00
Fork, 8 ⅛″	22.00
Fork, salad, 7″	17.00
Knife, HH, New French blade, 9 ¼″	25.00
Ladle, gravy, 7 ⅛″	50.00
Serving Fork, cold meat, 8 ⅞″	50.00
Serving Spoon, tablespoon, 8 ⅝″	40.00
Serving Spoon, tablespoon, pierced, 8 ⅝″	40.00
Spoon, soup, oval bowl, 7″	15.00
Spoon, sugar, 6 ¼″	22.00
Spoon, teaspoon, 6 ¼″	20.00

Towle, Magnum, Stainless

Butter Serving Knife, HH	$17.00
Fork	15.00
Fork, salad	12.00
Knife	20.00
Serving Fork, cold meat	25.00
Serving Spoon, tablespoon	25.00
Spoon, soup, oval bowl, 7 ½″	15.00
Spoon, sugar	15.00
Spoon, teaspoon	12.00

Towle, Westchester, Stainless

(Introduced in 1967)

Butter Serving Knife, HH, 7 $^1/_8''$	$35.00
Butter Spreader, HH, modern blade, 6 $^3/_4''$	25.00
Fork, 7 $^5/_8''$	30.00

Fork, 8 $^1/_8''$	30.00
Fork, salad, 6 $^7/_8''$	27.00
Knife, HH, modern blade, 9$''$	32.00
Ladle, gravy, 6 $^7/_8''$	60.00
Serving Fork, cold meat, 9 $^1/_4''$	70.00
Serving Spoon, tablespoon, 8 $^5/_8''$	45.00
Serving Spoon, tablespoon, pierced, 8 $^5/_8''$	50.00
Spoon, iced tea, 7 $^3/_4''$	30.00
Spoon, soup, oval bowl, 6 $^7/_8''$	30.00
Spoon, sugar, 6 $^1/_4''$	35.00
Spoon, teaspoon, 6 $^1/_8''$	25.00

WALLACE SILVERSMITHS

In 1831, Robert Wallace, of Scotch-English descent, was apprenticed to William Mix of Prospect, Connecticut, to learn the art of making Britannia spoons. Two years later, he established his own spoon-making business in a grist mill on Connecticut's Quinnipiac River. During a visit to New York City in 1835, Wallace saw a German (nickel) silver spoon made by Dixon & Sons of Sheffield, England. He purchased the formula from a German chemist for twenty dollars.

Between 1834 and 1849, Wallace made German silver spoons for a variety of firms, including Decan Hall and Hall, Elton & Company. In 1849, he became a partner with J. B. Pomeroy to make German silver spoons for Fred. R. Curtiss Company. The partnership also made Britannia spoons for Hall, Elton & Company and Edgar Atwater.

After a brief, one-year hiatus as a farmer, Robert Wallace formed a ten-year partnership with Samuel Simpsons of Wallingford, Connecticut, in 1855. R. Wallace & Co., the new firm, made German silver flatware and other articles. Shortly thereafter, Issac Lewis, W. W. Lyman, and H. C. Wilcox, partners in the Meriden Britannia Company, joined R. Wallace & Co. When the ten-year contract expired in 1865, Wallace, Simpson, & Co. was organized. Production continued. Wallace had purchased two-thirds of Simpson's shares by 1870, and he acquired the balance in 1871.

R. Wallace & Sons Mfg. Co., established July 17, 1871, brought together Robert, Robert B. and William J., Robert's two sons, and W. J. Leavenworth, Robert's son-in-law. While the company's principal product was German silver spoons, it introduced three sterling flatware patterns—Hawthorne, St. Leon, and The Crown—in 1875.

In July 1875, Robert, his five sons (also including Henry L., George H., and Frank A.), and his two sons-in-law (W. J. Leavenworth and D. E. Morris) formed Wallace Brothers, a partnership that manufactured silver-plated flatware on a cast steel base. The company also made silver-plated hollowware. This independent company was absorbed into R. Wallace & Sons Mfg. Co. in 1879.

The late nineteenth and early twentieth centuries were a time of expansion. New machinery increased the company's mass-production capabilities. The product line expanded to include all types of dresser silver, flatware, and hollowware, in fact, any articles in which silver was a component. Silver-plated flatware was made between 1877 and 1941. Commercial silver-plated flatware production continued until 1953. A line of stainless flatware was also offered. The manufacture of mass-market silver-plated flatware resumed in 1981.

Richard C. Cavette, Amedie J. Germain, David B. Hoover, William Toth, Irving Wahl, and William S. Warren are just some of the famous designers who worked for Wallace Silversmiths. In 1934, Warren created three-dimensional flatware patterns, and Wallace aggressively advertised his "three-dimensional" approach.

R. Wallace & Sons Mfg. Co. purchased the Watson Company of Attleboro, Massachusetts, in 1955, moving its operations to Wallingford one year later. In 1956, R. Wallace & Sons Mfg. Co. changed its name to Wallace Silversmiths. Wallace Silversmiths acquired Tuttle Silver and Smith & Smith, moving both companies' operations to Wallingford.

In 1975, Wallace introduced the Sterling II series, a flatware product that features hollow sterling silver handles and stainless spoon bowls, fork tines, and knife blades. Patterns in the series include Coventry Forge, Grand Venetian, Olympus, Plymouth Colony, and Scarborough. Wallace also created a Remembrance Group of sterling flatware patterns. This group consists of Colonial Fiddle, Dawn Mist, Debutante, Evening Mist, Feather Edge, Feliciana, La Reine, Laramie, Lucerne, Michelle, My Love, Normandie, Royal Rose, Royal Satin, Silver Swirl, Violet, Waltz of Spring, and Washington. The Feliciana pattern, first issued in 1969, was the last pattern in the Remembrance Group.

The Hamilton Watch Company of Lancaster, Pennsylvania, purchased Wallace Silversmiths in 1959. In 1971, it became a division of H.M.W. By 1983, Wallace Silversmiths was a subsidiary of Katy Industries in Elgin, Illinois.

Katy, a large holding company, sold Hamilton Watch and Wallace Silversmiths to Syratech Corporation in East Boston, Massachusetts, in 1986. Today, Wallace Silversmiths offers a complete selection of sterling flatware patterns, as well as sterling and silver-plated accessories, giftware, and hollowware.

**Wallace Silversmiths, French Regency,
Sterling Silver**

Cake Breaker, SP tines, 11″	$65.00
Carving Set, two pieces, ST blade	110.00
Cheese Cleaver, ST blade, 6 ½″	40.00
Fork, 7 ³/₈″	40.00
Fork, 7 ³/₄″	50.00
Fork, cocktail, 5 ½″	27.00
Fork, fish, ST tines, 8 ¼″	40.00

Fork, pickle, short handle, 5 ½″	37.00
Fork, salad, 6 ³/₈″	40.00
Knife, cheese, ST blade, 7 ¹/₈″	40.00
Knife, fish, ST blade, 8 ½″	40.00
Knife, fruit, ST blade, 7″	40.00
Knife, HH, modern blade, 9″	32.00
Ladle, gravy, HH, ST bowl, 8 ¼″	40.00
Pizza Cutter, ST blade, 8″	40.00
Scoop, ice cream, ST bowl, 8″	40.00
Server, fish, ST blade, 11 ⁵/₈″	40.00
Server, lasagna, ST blade, 10″	40.00
Server, pasta, ST bowl, 10 ⁵/₈″	40.00
Serving Fork, salad, ST tines, 11 ½″	40.00
Serving Spoon, dressing, ST bowl, 11 ³/₈″	40.00

Spoon, demitasse, 4 1/8"	25.00
Spoon, iced tea, 7 5/8"	40.00
Spoon, soup, oval bowl, 7"	45.00
Spoon, teaspoon, 6"	27.00

Spoon, sugar, 6 3/4"	50.00
Spoon, teaspoon, 6 5/8"	40.00

Wallace Silversmiths, Grand Colonial, Sterling Silver

Wallace Silversmiths, Golden Aegean Weave, Sterling Silver

Butter Serving Knife, HH, 7 1/2"	$50.00
Butter Spreader, HH, modern ST blade, 6 7/8"	45.00
Cheese Cleaver, ST blade, 7 1/4"	60.00
Fork, 8"	70.00
Fork, cocktail, 6"	50.00
Fork, pickle, short handle, 5 7/8"	55.00
Fork, salad, 6 7/8"	50.00
Knife, cheese, ST blade, 7 1/2"	60.00
Knife, fruit, ST blade, 7 1/2"	50.00
Knife, HH, modern blade, 9 3/8"	50.00
Knife, steak, 9 7/8"	60.00
Knife, wedding cake, ST blade, 13 1/4"	50.00
Ladle, gravy, 6 1/2"	115.00
Ladle, gravy, HH, ST bowl, 8 3/4"	60.00
Pizza Cutter, ST blade, 8 1/2"	60.00
Salad Set, two pieces, ST bowl	120.00
Server, pie/cake, ST blade, 11 3/8"	70.00
Server, pie/cake, ST blade, 11 5/8"	70.00
Serving Spoon, casserole, ST bowl, 11 3/4"	60.00
Serving Spoon, tablespoon, 9"	115.00
Serving Spoon, tablespoon, pierced, 9"	130.00
Spoon, bonbon, 6 3/4"	65.00
Spoon, demitasse, 4 1/2"	35.00
Spoon, iced tea, 8 1/8"	55.00

Bar Knife, 9 1/4"	$40.00
Butter Serving Knife, FH, 6 7/8"	32.00
Butter Spreader, FH, 6"	27.00
Butter Spreader, HH, modern ST blade, 6 1/4"	27.00
Butter Spreader, HH, paddled ST blade, 6 1/8"	27.00
Carving Fork, ST tines, 9 1/2"	55.00
Carving Set, two pieces, ST blade	110.00
Cheese Cleaver, ST blade, 6 5/8"	40.00
Fork, 7 1/4"	40.00
Fork, 7 3/4"	50.00
Fork, baby, 4 1/2"	32.00
Fork, cocktail, 5 5/8"	30.00
Fork, ice cream, 5 1/4"	40.00
Fork, lemon, 5 1/2"	35.00
Fork, pickle, short handle, 5 1/2"	35.00
Fork, salad, 6 3/8"	35.00
Fork, strawberry, 5"	35.00
Fork, youth, 5 3/4"	32.00
Knife, fish, ST blade, 8 5/8"	40.00
Knife, fruit, ST blade, 6 7/8"	40.00
Knife, HH, modern blade, 8 7/8"	32.00
Knife, HH, modern blade, 9 3/4"	45.00
Knife, steak, 9 3/8"	40.00
Knife, youth, 6 3/4"	30.00
Knife, youth, 7 3/8"	30.00
Ladle, cream sauce, 5 1/2"	45.00
Ladle, gravy, 6"	90.00
Ladle, gravy, HH, ST bowl, 8 1/4"	40.00

Pizza Cutter, ST blade, 8″	40.00
Salad Set, two pieces, 9 1/8″	250.00
Salad Set, two pieces,	
plastic bowl, 12 1/2″	70.00
Salt and Pepper Shakers, pair, 4 5/8″	200.00
Scoop, ice cream, ST bowl, 8″	40.00
Server, cheese, ST blade, 6 1/2″	40.00
Server, cranberry, ST bowl, 8 3/4″	40.00
Server, fish, ST blade, 11 5/8″	40.00
Server, lasagna, ST blade, 10″	40.00
Server, pasta, ST bowl, 10 5/8″	40.00
Server, pie, ST blade, 10 3/8″	40.00
Serving Fork, cold meat, 8″	90.00
Serving Fork, salad, ST tines, 11 3/8″	40.00
Serving Spoon, casserole,	
ST bowl, 9 3/4″	45.00
Serving Spoon, tablespoon, 8 5/8″	80.00
Spoon, baby, straight handle, 4 1/2″	32.00
Spoon, bonbon, 5″	45.00
Spoon, bouillon, round bowl, 5 1/2″	40.00
Spoon, cream soup, round bowl, 6″	40.00
Spoon, fruit, 5 7/8″	40.00
Spoon, iced tea, 7 1/2″	40.00
Spoon, jelly, 6 1/4″	40.00
Spoon, soup, oval bowl, 6 7/8″	45.00
Spoon, sugar, shell-shaped bowl, 6″	30.00
Spoon, teaspoon, 6″	25.00

Photo courtesy of Wallace Silversmiths/Syratech Corporation.

Wallace Silversmiths, Grande Baroque, Sterling Silver

Ashtray, SP, 3 1/4″	$15.00
Bar Knife, 9 1/4″	45.00
Bottle Opener, 5 1/4″	60.00
Bowl, bonbon, SP, 8 3/4″	35.00
Butter Curler, SP, 7″	40.00
Butter Dish, covered, round, SP, 7 1/8″	40.00

Butter Pick, 5 1/8″	32.00
Butter Serving Knife, HH, 6 5/8″	40.00
Butter Spreader, FH, 6 3/8″	40.00
Butter Spreader, HH, modern	
ST blade, 6 1/4″	40.00
Carving Fork, ST tines, 9 3/8″	60.00
Carving Set, two pieces, ST blade	120.00
Cheese Cleaver, ST blade, 6 7/8″	45.00
Fork, 7 1/2″	45.00
Fork, baby, 4 1/8″	35.00
Fork, fish, ST tines, 8 3/8″	55.00
Fork, ice cream, 5 1/2″	50.00
Fork, lemon, 5 5/8″	50.00
Fork, pickle, short handle, 5 1/2″	50.00
Fork, salad, 6 1/2″	45.00
Fork, strawberry, 5 1/8″	32.00
Fork, youth, 5 7/8″	40.00
Ice Cream Slicer, 13″	320.00
Ice Tongs, 7 1/4″	240.00
Knife, cheese, ST blade, 7″	45.00

Knife, fish, ST blade, 8 5/8″	55.00		Spoon, iced tea, 7 5/8″	40.00
Knife, HH, modern blade, 8 7/8″	40.00		Spoon, infant feeding, 5 5/8″	40.00
Knife, HH, modern blade, 9 3/4″	55.00		Spoon, jelly, 6 7/8″	60.00
Knife, HH, New French blade, 9 3/8″	40.00		Spoon, soup, oval bowl, 7″	55.00
Knife, steak, 8 3/4″	55.00		Spoon, teaspoon, 6 1/4″	35.00
Knife, wedding cake, ST blade, 12 3/4″	70.00		Spoon, teaspoon, 5 o'clock, 5 3/4″	35.00
Knife, wedding cake, ST blade, 13 1/4″	70.00		Tea Set, three pieces	4,500.00
Ladle, gravy, 6 5/8″	130.00		Tea Set, four pieces, SP	800.00
Ladle, punch, ST bowl, 13″	80.00		Tea Strainer, 7 3/8″	115.00
Salad Set, two pieces, 9 3/8″	400.00		Tray, round, SP, 13 5/8″	70.00
Salad Set, two pieces, ST bowl, 11 1/2″	110.00		Tray, waiter, SP, 28 5/8″	350.00
Salad Tongs, 8 5/8″	400.00			
Scoop, cheese, 6 5/8″	90.00			
Scoop, coffee, SP scoop, 3 7/8″	30.00			
Server, asparagus, 9 7/8″	270.00			
Server, asparagus, hooded, 10 1/4″	470.00			

Wallace Silversmiths, La Reine, Sterling Silver

Server, cranberry, ST bowl, 8 7/8″	55.00		Butter Spreader, FH, 6 1/4″	35.00
Server, lasagna, ST blade, 10″	55.00		Butter Spreader, HH,	
Server, macaroni, 10 5/8″	345.00		paddled ST blade, 6 1/4″	35.00
Server, pasta, ST bowl, 10 3/4″	55.00		Fork, 7″	60.00
Server, pie, ST blade, 10 1/2″	55.00		Fork, 7 1/2″	75.00
Server, pie/cake, ST blade, 11″	55.00		Fork, cocktail, 5 3/4″	37.00
Server, tomato, 8 1/4″	120.00		Fork, salad, 6 1/4″	60.00
Serving Fork, cold meat, 8 1/8″	120.00		Knife, HH, modern blade, 9″	45.00
Serving Fork, cold meat, ST tines, 11″	55.00		Knife, HH, modern blade, 9 5/8″	55.00
Serving Fork, salad, plastic tines, 12 1/2″	50.00		Knife, HH, New French blade, 9 5/8″	55.00
Serving Fork, salad, ST tines, 11 1/2″	55.00		Serving Fork, cold meat, 8 1/2″	110.00
Serving Spoon, casserole, 9 3/8″	200.00		Serving Spoon, tablespoon, 8 1/2″	110.00
Serving Spoon, casserole,			Spoon, cream soup, round bowl, 6″	50.00
shell-shaped ST bowl, 10 1/2″	55.00		Spoon, demitasse, 4 3/8″	30.00
Serving Spoon, dressing,			Spoon, iced tea, 7 3/4″	50.00
ST bowl, 11 1/2″	55.00		Spoon, soup, oval bowl, 7 1/4″	50.00
Serving Spoon, salad, ST bowl, 11 1/2″	55.00		Spoon, sugar, 6 1/8″	50.00
Serving Spoon, tablespoon,			Spoon, teaspoon, 6″	35.00
pierced, 8 3/4″	120.00		Spoon, teaspoon, 5 o'clock, 5 1/2″	30.00
Spoon, baby, straight handle, 4″	35.00			
Spoon, bonbon, 5 3/8″	60.00			
Spoon, cracker, 8 1/4″	130.00			
Spoon, cream soup, round bowl, 6 1/8″	50.00			
Spoon, demitasse, 4 1/8″	32.00			
Spoon, fruit, 6″	50.00			
Spoon, grapefruit, round bowl, 6 3/4″	85.00			

Wallace Silversmiths, Meadow Rose, Sterling Silver

Butter Serving Knife, FH, 6 ¾″	$32.00
Butter Spreader, FH, 5 ¾″	30.00
Butter Spreader, HH, paddled ST blade, 6 ⅛″	30.00
Carving Fork, ST tines, 8 ¾″	55.00
Carving Set, two pieces, large, ST blade	110.00
Carving Set, two pieces, small, ST blade	110.00
Fork, 7 ⅛″	40.00
Fork, 7 ⅜″	40.00
Fork, salad, 6 ¼″	37.00
Knife, HH, modern blade, 8 ¾″	32.00
Knife, HH, modern blade, 9 ⅝″	45.00
Knife, HH, New French blade, 8 ¾″	32.00
Knife, HH, New French blade, 9″	32.00
Knife, youth, 6 ⅝″	30.00
Ladle, gravy, 6 ¼″	95.00
Serving Spoon, tablespoon, 8 ⅜″	90.00
Spoon, cream soup, round bowl, 6 ¼″	45.00
Spoon, demitasse, 4 ¼″	25.00
Spoon, iced tea, 7 ⅜″	40.00
Spoon, relish, 5 ⅞″	45.00
Spoon, sugar, 5 ⅜″	32.00
Spoon, teaspoon, 5 ⅞″	27.00

Wallace Silversmiths, Old Atlanta/Irving, Sterling Silver

Butter Serving Knife, FH, 7″	$32.00
Butter Serving Knife, HH, 6 ⅝″	32.00

Butter Spreader, FH, 6″	30.00
Butter Spreader, HH, modern ST blade, 6 ¼″	30.00
Butter Spreader, HH, paddled ST blade, 6 ⅛″	30.00
Carving Fork, ST tines, 8 ⅝″	55.00
Carving Knife, ST blade, 9 ⅞″	55.00
Carving Set, two pieces, ST blade	110.00
Fork, 7 ⅛″	40.00
Fork, 7 ½″	50.00
Fork, cocktail, 5 ⅞″	27.00
Fork, fish, ST tines, 8 ¼″	40.00
Fork, pickle, short handle, 5 ⅞″	37.00
Fork, salad, 6 ¼″	37.00
Knife, fish, ST blade, 8 ½″	40.00
Knife, fruit, ST blade, 6 ⅞″	40.00
Knife, HH, blunt blade, 9 ½″	45.00
Knife, HH, modern blade, 9″	32.00
Knife, HH, New French blade, 8 ⅝″	32.00
Ladle, cream sauce, 5 ⅝″	45.00
Ladle, gravy, 7 ⅛″	95.00
Salad Set, two pieces	275.00
Server, cheese, SP blade, 6 ¼″	40.00
Server, cheese, ST blade, 6 ½″	40.00
Server, pie/cake, ST blade, 10 ¾″	40.00
Serving Fork, cold meat, 8 ¼″	90.00
Serving Spoon, casserole, 9″	135.00
Serving Spoon, tablespoon, 8 ¼″	90.00
Serving Spoon, tablespoon, pierced, 8″	95.00
Spoon, demitasse, 3 ⅞″	25.00
Spoon, grapefruit, round bowl, 7″	50.00
Spoon, iced tea, 8″	40.00
Spoon, jelly, 6 ¼″	45.00
Spoon, soup, oval bowl, 7 ⅛″	45.00
Spoon, sugar, 6 ⅛″	32.00
Spoon, teaspoon, 6″	27.00
Spoon, teaspoon, 5 o'clock, 5 ⅜″	25.00
Spoon, youth, 5 ⅜″	25.00

Knife, HH, modern blade, 9″ 45.00
Knife, steak, 9 ³/₈″ 55.00
Knife, wedding cake, ST blade, 12 ³/₄″ 80.00
Ladle, soup, ST bowl, 11 ⁷/₈″ 90.00
Server, pie, ST blade, 10 ¹/₂″ 70.00
Server, pie/cake, ST blade, 11 ¹/₄″ 70.00
Serving Spoon, tablespoon, 8 ⁵/₈″ 120.00
Spoon, cream soup, round bowl, 6″ 50.00
Spoon, demitasse, 4″ 32.00
Spoon, jelly, 6 ¹/₂″ 65.00
Spoon, sugar, 6″ 50.00
Spoon, teaspoon, 6″ 40.00

Photo courtesy of Wallace Silversmiths/Syratech Corporation.

Wallace Silversmiths, Rose Point, Sterling Silver

Butter Spreader, FH, 5 ¹/₂″ $30.00
Butter Spreader, HH,
   paddled ST blade, 6 ¹/₄″ 30.00
Carving Set, two pieces, ST blade 115.00
Creamer and Sugar, open, mini 425.00
Fork, 7″ 40.00
Fork, cocktail, 5 ⁵/₈″ 30.00
Fork, lemon, 5 ¹/₂″ 35.00
Fork, strawberry, 5″ 35.00
Knife, fruit, ST blade, 7″ 40.00
Knife, HH, modern blade, 9 ¹/₈″ 35.00
Knife, HH, modern blade, 9 ³/₄″ 50.00
Knife, HH, New French blade, 9 ¹/₈″ 35.00
Knife, steak, 9″ 40.00
Ladle, gravy, 6 ¹/₄″ 90.00
Ladle, soup, 15 ¹/₂″ 270.00
Pitcher, water, 8 ¹/₂″ 1,600.00
Salad Set, two pieces, plastic bowl 90.00
Salt and Pepper Shakers, pair, 4 ³/₄″ 290.00
Server, cheese, SP blade, 6 ¹/₄″ 40.00
Serving Fork, cold meat, 8 ¹/₈″ 95.00
Serving Spoon, tablespoon, 8 ³/₈″ 85.00

Wallace Silversmiths, Romance of the Sea, Sterling Silver

Butter Serving Knife, HH, 6 ⁷/₈″ $50.00
Butter Spreader, HH,
   modern ST blade, 6 ¹/₄″ 40.00
Butter Spreader, HH,
   paddled ST blade, 6 ¹/₄″ 40.00
Carving Fork, ST tines, 9 ¹/₂″ 75.00
Fork, 7 ¹/₄″ 55.00
Fork, fish, ST tines, 8 ³/₈″ 60.00
Fork, lemon, 5 ¹/₂″ 55.00
Fork, pickle, short handle, 5 ¹/₂″ 55.00
Fork, salad, 6 ¹/₂″ 50.00
Knife, cheese, ST blade, 7 ¹/₄″ 60.00
Knife, fruit, ST blade, 7″ 50.00

Photo courtesy of Wallace Silversmiths/Syratech Corporation.

Wallace Silversmiths, Shenandoah, Sterling Silver

Butter Serving Knife, FH, 6 ⁵/₈″	$32.00
Butter Serving Knife, HH, 6 ⁵/₈″	32.00
Butter Spreader, HH,	
modern ST blade, 6 ¹/₄″	30.00
Carving Fork, ST tines, 9 ⁷/₈″	55.00
Carving Set, two pieces, ST blade	110.00
Fork, 7 ³/₈″	40.00
Fork, cocktail, 5 ⁵/₈″	27.00
Fork, fish, ST tines, 8 ¹/₄″	40.00
Fork, salad	37.00
Knife, cheese, ST blade, 7″	40.00
Knife, fish, ST blade, 8 ⁵/₈″	40.00
Knife, HH, modern blade, 9″	32.00
Knife, HH, modern blade, 9 ³/₄″	45.00
Ladle, cream sauce, 5 ⁵/₈″	45.00
Ladle, gravy, 6 ¹/₄″	95.00
Ladle, gravy, HH, ST bowl, 8 ¹/₄″	40.00
Pizza Cutter, ST blade, 8″	40.00
Server, fish, ST blade, 11 ⁵/₈″	40.00
Serving Fork, cold meat, 8″	90.00
Serving Fork, salad, 11 ¹/₂″	135.00
Serving Fork, salad, ST tines, 11 ³/₈″	40.00
Serving Spoon, dressing,	
ST bowl, 11 ¹/₄″	40.00
Serving Spoon, tablespoon, 8 ¹/₂″	90.00
Serving Spoon, tablespoon,	
pierced, 8 ¹/₂″	95.00
Spoon, demitasse, 4 ¹/₈″	25.00
Spoon, iced tea, 7 ³/₄″	40.00
Spoon, soup, oval bowl, 7″	45.00
Spoon, sugar, 6″	32.00
Spoon, teaspoon, 6″	27.00

Serving Spoon, tablespoon,	
pierced, 8 ¹/₄″	100.00
Spoon, cream soup, round bowl, 5 ⁷/₈″	40.00
Spoon, demitasse, 4″	25.00
Spoon, fruit, 6″	40.00
Spoon, iced tea, 7 ¹/₂″	40.00
Spoon, jelly, 6 ³/₈″	40.00
Spoon, mustard, 5 ¹/₄″	40.00
Spoon, soup, oval bowl, 7 ¹/₈″	45.00
Spoon, sugar, 6 ¹/₈″	35.00
Spoon, teaspoon, 6″	25.00
Tea Set, three pieces	3,300.00
Tea Strainer, 7 ¹/₄″	100.00
Water Goblet, 7″	250.00

Wallace Silversmiths, Sir Christopher, Sterling Silver

Butter Serving Knife, HH, 6 5/8″	$40.00
Butter Spreader, FH, 6 3/8″	35.00
Butter Spreader, HH, modern ST blade, 6 1/4″	37.00
Butter Spreader, HH, paddled ST blade, 6″	37.00
Carving Fork, ST tines, 8 7/8″	60.00
Carving Set, two pieces, ST blade	120.00
Food Pusher, 3 3/4″	40.00
Fork, 7 1/4″	45.00
Fork, 7 3/4″	60.00
Fork, cocktail, 5 1/2″	40.00
Fork, fish, ST tines, 7 3/4″	55.00

Photo courtesy of Wallace Silversmiths/Syratech Corporation.

Fork, ice cream, 5 1/2″	50.00
Fork, pickle, short handle, 5 1/2″	50.00
Fork, salad, 6 3/8″	50.00
Fork, strawberry, 4 7/8″	40.00
Fork, youth, 5 3/4″	40.00
Knife, fruit, ST blade, 6 5/8″	45.00
Knife, HH, modern blade, 9 1/8″	40.00
Knife, HH, modern blade, 9 3/4″	50.00
Knife, HH, New French blade, 8 5/8″	40.00
Knife, HH, New French blade, 9 1/8″	40.00
Knife, HH, New French blade, 9 3/4″	50.00
Ladle, cream sauce, 5 5/8″	60.00
Ladle, gravy, 6 3/8″	110.00
Salad Set, two pieces, plastic bowl	110.00
Server, cheese, ST blade, 6 1/2″	50.00
Server, cranberry, ST bowl, 8 1/2″	50.00
Server, lasagna, ST blade, 9 5/8″	55.00
Server, pie/cake, ST blade, 10 3/4″	55.00
Serving Fork, cold meat, 8″	100.00
Serving Spoon, tablespoon, 8 1/2″	95.00
Spoon, bonbon, 5 3/8″	55.00
Spoon, fruit, 6″	50.00
Spoon, iced tea, 7 5/8″	45.00
Spoon, jelly, 6 3/4″	60.00
Spoon, salt, 2 1/2″	17.00
Spoon, sugar, 6″	45.00
Spoon, teaspoon, 6″	35.00

Wallace Silversmiths, Spanish Lace, Sterling Silver

Butter Serving Knife, HH, 7 1/4″	$32.00
Butter Spreader, HH, modern ST blade, 6 3/4″	30.00
Butter Spreader, HH, modern ST blade, 7 1/8″	30.00
Cake Breaker, SP tines, 11 1/4″	65.00
Carving Set, two pieces, ST blade	110.00

Carving Set, three pieces, ST blade	150.00	Carving Fork, ST tines, 8 ³/₄″	60.00
Fork, 7 ⁵/₈″	50.00	Carving Set, two pieces, ST blade	120.00
Fork, cocktail, 5 ⁷/₈″	32.00	Creamer and Sugar, open, mini	600.00
Fork, ice cream, 5 ³/₄″	45.00	Fork, 7 ¹/₈″	40.00
Fork, pickle, short handle, 5 ⁷/₈″	40.00	Fork, 7 ³/₄″	50.00
Fork, salad, 6 ⁵/₈″	40.00	Fork, cocktail, 5 ¹/₂″	30.00
Knife, HH, modern blade, 8 ⁷/₈″	32.00	Fork, lemon, 5 ¹/₂″	35.00
Knife, HH, modern blade, 9 ¹/₄″	32.00	Fork, pickle, short handle, 5 ¹/₂″	37.00
Knife, HH, modern blade, 9 ³/₄″	45.00	Fork, salad, 6 ³/₈″	40.00
Knife, HH, modern blade, 10 ¹/₄″	45.00	Knife, fruit, ST blade, 6 ⁵/₈″	40.00
Ladle, cream sauce, 5 ³/₄″	45.00	Knife, HH, modern blade, 9 ¹/₈″	32.00
Ladle, gravy, 6 ¹/₂″	95.00	Knife, HH, modern blade, 9 ³/₄″	45.00
Salad Set, two pieces, plastic bowl, 12 ¹/₂″	70.00	Knife, youth, 7 ¹/₄″	32.00
Salad Set, two pieces, wooden bowl	70.00	Ladle, cream sauce, 5 ¹/₂″	45.00
Server, cheese, 7″	40.00	Ladle, gravy, 6 ¹/₄″	95.00
Server, pie/cake, ST blade, 11 ¹/₄″	40.00	Pizza Cutter, ST blade, 7 ⁵/₈″	40.00
Serving Fork, cold meat, 8 ¹/₄″	90.00	Plate, sandwich, 10″	200.00
Serving Spoon, tablespoon, 8 ⁵/₈″	90.00	Salt and Pepper Shakers, pair	250.00
Serving Spoon, tablespoon, pierced, 8 ⁵/₈″	95.00	Salt Shaker, 4 ¹/₄″	150.00
Spoon, bonbon, 6 ¹/₄″	45.00	Server, cheese, ST blade, 6 ¹/₂″	40.00
Spoon, demitasse, 4 ¹/₈″	25.00	Server, pie, ST blade, 10″	45.00
Spoon, iced tea, 7 ¹/₂″	40.00	Serving Fork, cold meat, 8 ¹/₈″	95.00
Spoon, soup, oval bowl, 7 ¹/₈″	45.00	Serving Spoon, casserole, 9″	140.00
Spoon, sugar, 6 ¹/₄″	32.00	Serving Spoon, tablespoon, 8 ¹/₂″	90.00
Spoon, teaspoon, 6 ¹/₄″	30.00	Spoon, bonbon, 5 ¹/₂″	45.00
		Spoon, bouillon, round bowl, 5 ¹/₄″	40.00
		Spoon, cream soup, round bowl, 6″	40.00
		Spoon, demitasse, 3 ⁷/₈″	22.00
		Spoon, fruit, 5 ⁷/₈″	40.00
		Spoon, iced tea, 7 ¹/₂″	40.00
		Spoon, jelly, 6 ³/₄″	45.00
		Spoon, soup, oval bowl, 6 ³/₄″	50.00
		Spoon, sugar, 6″	32.00
		Spoon, teaspoon, 6″	25.00
		Spoon, teaspoon, 5 o'clock, 5 ³/₈″	22.00

Wallace Silversmiths, Stradivari, Sterling Silver

Butter Serving Knife, FH, 6 ⁷/₈″	$32.00
Butter Serving Knife, HH, 6 ⁵/₈″	32.00
Butter Spreader, FH, 6″	27.00
Butter Spreader, HH, modern ST blade, 6 ¹/₄″	30.00
Butter Spreader, HH, paddled ST blade, 6″	30.00

Wallace Silversmiths, Violet, Sterling Silver

Butter Spreader, FH, 6 1/8″	$30.00
Carving Set, ST blade	140.00
Fork, 7 1/4″	50.00
Fork, 7 5/8″	60.00
Fork, cocktail, 5 7/8″	32.00
Fork, salad	50.00
Knife, HH, modern blade, 8 7/8″	35.00
Knife, HH, Old French blade, 9 3/8″	35.00
Scoop, ice cream, ST bowl, 7 7/8″	60.00
Server, pie, SP blade, 10 3/8″	65.00
Serving Spoon, casserole, 9 3/8″	120.00
Serving Spoon, casserole, ST bowl, 9″	65.00
Serving Spoon, dressing, ST bowl, 10 5/8″	50.00
Serving Spoon, tablespoon, 8 1/4″	80.00
Spoon, bouillon, round bowl, 5 1/4″	40.00
Spoon, sugar, 6 1/8″	45.00
Spoon, teaspoon	25.00
Spoon, teaspoon, 5 o'clock, 5 3/8″	25.00

Wallace Silversmiths, Waltz of Spring, Sterling Silver

Butter Serving Knife, FH, 7 1/2″	$50.00
Butter Spreader, HH, paddled ST blade, 6″	32.00
Butter Spreader, HH, paddled ST blade, 6 1/4″	32.00
Fork, 7 1/4″	60.00
Fork, 7 3/4″	75.00
Fork, pickle, short handle, 5 5/8″	35.00
Fork, salad	60.00
Knife, HH, modern blade, 9″	55.00
Knife, HH, modern blade, 9 3/4″	45.00
Knife, steak, 9 3/8″	55.00
Ladle, gravy, HH, ST bowl, 8 1/4″	50.00
Server, pie, ST blade, 10 3/8″	85.00
Serving Spoon, tablespoon, 8 1/2″	120.00
Spoon, iced tea, 7 5/8″	50.00
Spoon, sugar, 6 1/4″	50.00
Spoon, teaspoon	35.00

WESTMORLAND STERLING COMPANY

Westmorland Sterling Company in Wallingford, Connecticut, was created by Wearever Aluminum, Inc., and Wallace Silversmiths in 1940. This cooperative effort was a response to the arrival of home selling just prior to the beginning of World War II.

Westmorland sold sterling silver flatware directly to the consumer. Wearever Aluminum developed and implemented the marketing plan. Wallace Silversmiths manufactured five exclusive sterling silver flatware patterns.

Wallace Silversmiths also assumed Westmorland's marketing responsibilities in 1966. The company was reorganized, and a system of franchised dealers was implemented.

Westmorland Sterling Company, George & Martha Washington, Sterling Silver

Butter Serving Knife, FH, 7″	$32.00
Butter Spreader, FH, 6 1/8″	25.00
Carving Fork, ST tines, 9 1/8″	55.00
Fork, 7 1/8″	40.00
Fork, cocktail, 5 5/8″	30.00
Fork, salad, 6″	40.00
Knife, fish, ST blade, 8 1/4″	35.00
Knife, HH, modern blade, 9″	35.00
Knife, HH, modern blade, 9 5/8″	45.00
Knife, HH, New French blade, 8 3/4″	35.00
Ladle, gravy, 7″	80.00
Salad Set, two pieces, plastic bowl, 10 3/4″	70.00
Server, pie, ST blade, 9 3/4″	60.00
Server, tomato, 7 7/8″	80.00
Serving Fork, cold meat, 8 3/8″	80.00

Serving Spoon, tablespoon, 8 1/4″	70.00
Spoon, cream soup, round bowl, 6″	35.00
Spoon, demitasse, 4″	22.00
Spoon, fruit, 6″	32.00
Spoon, iced tea, 7 1/2″	35.00
Spoon, salt, 2 1/2″	15.00
Spoon, soup, oval bowl, 7 1/8″	40.00
Spoon, sugar, 6″	40.00
Sugar Tongs, 4 1/4″	60.00
Sugar Tongs, 4 1/2″	60.00

Westmorland Sterling Company, John & Priscilla, Sterling Silver

Butter Serving Knife, FH, 7 3/8″	$32.00
Butter Spreader, FH, 6 1/8″	25.00
Candelabra, triple light, 7 1/2″	225.00
Carving Fork, ST tines, 9″	55.00
Carving Knife, ST blade, 10 1/4″	55.00

Spoon, demitasse, 4 3/8"	20.00
Spoon, grapefruit, round bowl, 6 7/8"	40.00
Spoon, iced tea, 7 3/4"	35.00
Spoon, soup, oval bowl, 7 1/4"	35.00
Spoon, sugar, 5 7/8"	37.00
Spoon, teaspoon, 6"	25.00
Sugar Tongs, 4 3/8"	60.00

THE TOP FIVE PATTERNS

FEDERAL—

STERLING

GORHAM, FAIRFAX

INTERNATIONAL, MINUET

INTERNATIONAL, PROCESSIONAL

WESTMORLAND, JOHN & PRISCILLA

WHITING, KING ALBERT

Westmorland Sterling Company, Lady Hilton, Sterling Silver

Butter Serving Knife, FH, 6 7/8"	$30.00
Butter Spreader, FH, 5 5/8"	22.00
Butter Spreader, HH, paddled ST blade, 6 1/8"	22.00
Fork, 7 1/4"	45.00
Fork, 7 3/4"	60.00
Fork, baby, 4 3/8"	32.00
Fork, cocktail, 5 1/2"	27.00
Fork, ice cream, 5 1/2"	35.00
Fork, salad, 6 1/8"	32.00
Knife, HH, modern blade, 9 1/8"	30.00
Knife, HH, New French blade, 8 3/4"	30.00
Knife, HH, New French blade, 9 1/2"	45.00
Ladle, gravy, 6 1/2"	75.00
Salad Set, two pieces, plastic bowl	70.00
Server, pie, ST blade, 9 7/8"	60.00
Server, tomato, 7 5/8"	80.00
Serving Spoon, casserole, 8 3/4"	90.00
Serving Spoon, casserole, 9 1/8"	90.00
Serving Spoon, salad, plastic bowl	35.00
Serving Spoon, tablespoon, 8 3/8"	70.00
Serving Spoon, tablespoon, pierced, 8"	75.00
Spoon, cream soup, round bowl, 6"	32.00
Spoon, demitasse, 4 1/4"	20.00
Spoon, fruit, 6 7/8"	35.00

Carving Set, two pieces, ST blade	110.00
Fork, 7 1/4"	45.00
Fork, baby, 4 3/8"	35.00
Fork, cocktail, 5 1/2"	27.00
Fork, ice cream 5 5/8"	35.00
Fork, ice cream 5 3/4"	40.00
Fork, salad, 6 5/8"	32.00
Knife, HH, modern blade, 9"	32.00
Knife, HH, New French blade, 9"	32.00
Ladle, gravy, 6"	80.00
Salad Set, two pieces, plastic bowl	70.00
Server, tomato, 7 5/8"	80.00
Serving Fork, cold meat, 7 3/4"	70.00
Serving Spoon, casserole, 9"	95.00
Serving Spoon, tablespoon, 8 5/8"	70.00
Serving Spoon, tablespoon, pierced, 8 1/2"	80.00
Serving Spoon, tablespoon, pierced, 8 5/8"	80.00
Spoon, cream soup, round bowl, 6 1/8"	35.00

Spoon, grapefruit, round bowl, 6 7/8″	37.00	Fork, 7 1/8″	45.00
Spoon, iced tea, 7 7/8″	32.00	Fork, baby, 4 3/8″	37.00
Spoon, soup, oval bowl, 7 1/4″	32.00	Fork, cocktail, 5 1/2″	30.00
Spoon, sugar, 6″	37.00	Knife, HH, modern blade, 9″	32.00
Spoon, teaspoon, 6″	25.00	Knife, HH, New French blade, 9″	32.00
Sugar Tongs, 4 3/8″	60.00	Ladle, gravy, 6″	80.00
		Salad Set, two pieces, plastic bowl	85.00
		Serving Fork, cold meat, 8″	90.00
		Serving Spoon, salad, plastic bowl, 11″	40.00

Westmorland Sterling Company, Milburn Rose, Sterling Silver

Butter Serving Knife, FH, 7 1/8″	$32.00	Serving Spoon, tablespoon, 8 1/4″	70.00
Butter Spreader, FH, 5 7/8″	25.00	Spoon, baby, straight handle, 4 1/4″	37.00
Butter Spreader, HH, paddled ST blade, 6 1/4″	25.00	Spoon, cream soup, round bowl, 6″	35.00
		Spoon, demitasse, 4 1/8″	20.00
		Spoon, grapefruit, round bowl, 6 7/8″	40.00
		Spoon, iced tea, 7 3/4″	35.00
		Spoon, soup, oval bowl, 7 1/8″	35.00
		Spoon, sugar, 6″	40.00
		Spoon, teaspoon, 6″	25.00

In 1840, Albert T. Tifft and William D. Whiting, who had apprenticed at Draper & Tifft, established Tifft & Whiting in North Attleboro, Massachusetts, to manufacture jewelry.

Like many firms, the company reorganized several times. Whiting bought out Tifft's interest in the firm in 1853, establishing a New York office and introducing ladies' silver combs, hairpins, and small hollowware pieces. In the late 1850s, the firm was known as Whiting, Fressenden & Cowan. It became Whiting & Co. in 1866.

After a fire destroyed the company's plant, it first moved to Newark, New Jersey, and then to Bridgeport, Connecticut. Whiting produced a full line of silverware at its Bridgeport factory. The company was also known for its church silver, trophies, and silver deposit on cut glassware.

William Whiting left Whiting & Co. in the late 1870s and returned to North Attleboro to work with his son, F. W. Whiting, an independent manufacturer. In 1877, F. M. Whiting & Company was created to manufacture silver jewelry and sterling silverware.

Aware that Americans were awed by foreign titles, many of Whiting's flatware patterns were named after European royalty, for example, King Edward, Prince Albert, and Louis XV. Charles Osborne was one of the company's leading designers; his Lily pattern was introduced in 1902.

Whiting fought aggressively to protect its design patents. In the early 1920s, Whiting sued Alvin for a specific design patent infringement involving its Jenny Lind pattern. Designs were closely copied, and although many manufacturers simply looked the other way, Whiting did not. Whiting won, though Alvin appealed.

The Silversmiths Company, a Gorham holding company, acquired an interest in Whiting in the early 1900s. When Gorham reorganized and purchased Silversmiths in 1924, Whiting was acquired as part of the transaction. Manufacturing operations were moved to Providence, Rhode Island, within a year. Gorham continued making pieces using the Whiting trademark.

Whiting Manufacturing Company, King Albert, Sterling Silver

Butter Serving Knife, FH, 6 3/8″	$35.00
Butter Spreader, HH, modern ST blade, 6 1/8″	22.00
Carving Fork, ST tines, 8 1/2″	55.00
Carving Fork, ST tines, 9″	55.00
Carving Knife, ST blade, 9 3/4″	55.00
Carving Set, two pieces, ST blade	110.00
Fork, 7 1/4″	45.00
Fork, 7 7/8″	60.00
Fork, cocktail, 5 3/8″	27.00
Fork, fish, 6 1/4″	45.00
Fork, fruit, ST tines, 6 7/8″	32.00
Fork, lemon, 4 3/4″	30.00
Fork, pickle, short handle, 6″	30.00
Fork, salad, 6 3/8″	32.00
Knife, fruit, ST blade, 8″	32.00
Knife, HH, blunt blade, 9 5/8″	45.00
Knife, HH, New French blade, 9 5/8″	45.00
Knife, HH, Old French blade, 8 5/8″	32.00
Knife, HH, Old French blade, 9 1/8″	32.00
Ladle, cream sauce, 5 1/2″	45.00
Ladle, gravy, 6 1/4″	80.00
Ladle, mayonnaise, 5″	40.00
Server, pie, SP blade, 9 1/2″	60.00
Serving Fork, cold meat, 7 1/4″	70.00
Serving Fork, cold meat, 8 5/8″	80.00

Serving Spoon, tablespoon, 8 3/8″	65.00
Spoon, bonbon, 4 3/8″	40.00
Spoon, bouillon, round bowl, 5 1/8″	30.00
Spoon, demitasse, 4 1/8″	20.00
Spoon, fruit, 5 7/8″	35.00
Spoon, iced tea, 7 3/8″	35.00
Spoon, jelly, 6 5/8″	30.00
Spoon, sugar, 6 1/8″	37.00
Spoon, teaspoon, 5 7/8″	25.00
Spoon, teaspoon, 5 o'clock, 5 1/4″	20.00
Sugar Tongs, 3 1/2″	55.00

Whiting Manufacturing Company, Lily, Sterling Silver

Fork, 6 3/4″	$95.00
Fork, salad, 7″	95.00
Knife, HH, Old French blade, 9 1/4″	70.00
Knife, wedding cake, ST blade, 12 1/2″	150.00
Serving Spoon, tablespoon, 8 1/2″	155.00
Spoon, bouillon, round bowl, 5″	75.00
Spoon, demitasse, 4″	50.00
Spoon, soup, oval bowl, 6 7/8″	70.00
Spoon, sugar, shell-shaped bowl, 5 7/8″	80.00
Spoon, teaspoon, 5 7/8″	60.00
Spoon, teaspoon, 5 o'clock, 5 3/8″	50.00

WMF AKTIENGESELLSCHAFT
(WÜRTTEMBERGISCHE METALLWARENFABRIK)

Daniel Straub, a businessman, and the Schweizer brothers, skilled metal craftsmen, created Metallwarenfabrik Straub & Schweizer in Geislingen, Germany, in 1853. Though in its infancy, the company won a Gold Medal for its silver-plated dining and serving utensils at the 1862 World Exhibition in London. In 1868, Daniel Straub opened a Berlin sales branch.

Straub & Schweizer merged with A. Ritter & Co. of Esslingen in 1880, the new joint stock company named Württembergische Metallwarenfabrik (WMF). At this time, WMF employed close to 500 workers. A galvanic silver-plating process and improved material quality allowed WMF to greatly expand its market. A glassworks and cutting shop was added to the Geislingen site in 1883. The company's distinct initial trademark was designed sometime during the 1880s.

In 1884, WMF established its own medical insurance program. Social benefits included a supporting fund, canteen, and company housing. The company was among the pioneers in producing a magazine for its employees, named *Die Feierstunde* (The Leisure Hour), between 1890 and 1918. Interrupted occasionally and having experienced several name changes, it survives today as *WMF Spiegel (WMF Mirror)*.

In 1892, WMF developed its Perfect Hard Silver Plating process, which strengthens areas of flatware that are particularly prone to wear with a stronger layer of silver. This patented process is continually being refined. In spite of losing many sales branches and manufacturing subsidiaries during World War I, WMF resumed full-scale production of cookware and household articles within a short time after the war ended.

In the 1920s, WMF obtained the sole rights to use Krupp's V 2-A steel to produce tableware and kitchenware. Cromargan® was registered as a trademark for these products. WMF produced the first Cromargan® 18/10 stainless steel cutlery. Today, Cromargan® has become synonymous with 18/10 stainless steel, and its resistance to common food chemicals is equaled only by platinum. Cromargan® is slow to conduct heat; as a result, flatware handles remain cool and comfortable even in hot liquids.

WMF's sales subsidiaries swelled from 24 to 136 between 1933 and 1939. During World War II, the company manufactured armaments. Following the war, its management was relieved by the Allied Powers. A major reorganization of the management, technical, and labor staff occurred. The sales subsidiaries destroyed during the war were rebuilt, and distribution companies were created in the United States, Canada, Holland, Switzerland, Austria, and Italy. Following the war, WMF products were distributed in the United States as William Fraser Silver.

Once the public became familiar with WMF products and the company's logo, the William Fraser Silver name was discontinued.

Demand for Cromargan® cutlery, tableware, and kitchenware greatly increased by the end of the 1950s. Wilhelm Wagenfeld created many of the classic Bauhaus-style WMF products during this period. The hotel program was expanded considerably. In 1955, a factory was opened in Hayingen in the Swabian Jura, for the manufacture of knife blades. In 1966 the factory in Hausham, Upper Bavaria, began producing disposable plastic tableware.

In 1975, WMF established WMF Singapore (Pte.) Ltd., for the production of table cutlery. In 1987, alfi Zitzmann GmbH, in Wertheim, a manufacturer of vacuum jugs, was added to the WMF group, followed one year later by Gebr. Hepp GmbH, in Birkenfield near Pforzheim, a manufacturer of cutlery, tableware, and accessories for the catering industry.

In 1989, WMF entered into partnership with Hutschenreuther AG, Selb, a porcelain manufacturer. Today, WMF manufactures an extensive range of products, in particular, tableware and kitchenware for private use as well as for the catering industry. Distribution is achieved through the company's own sales branches, the specialist trade, department stores, and major mail-order firms. WMF has distributing companies in Canada, Europe, and the United States.

WMF, Line, Stainless, "WMF" backstamp

Bowl, bonbon, 5"	$30.00
Butter Spreader	15.00
Egg Cup, 3 3/4"	15.00
Egg Cup and Spoon, 3 3/4"	22.00
Fork	15.00
Fork, cocktail	15.00
Fork, pastry, 6 1/4"	12.00
Fork, salad	15.00
Knife	25.00
Knife, dessert, 8"	15.00
Ladle, gravy	40.00
Napkin Holder, 4 7/8"	22.00
Platter, oval, 22"	165.00
Serving Fork	30.00
Serving Fork, cold meat	20.00
Serving Spoon	30.00

Serving Spoon, tablespoon	20.00
Spoon, demitasse, 5"	12.00
Spoon, iced tea	15.00
Spoon, soup, oval bowl	15.00
Spoon, teaspoon	12.00
Spoon, teaspoon, 5 o'clock, 5 3/4"	15.00
Tray, escargot, 6"	30.00
Tray, waiter, 20 1/4"	160.00
Tumbler, 4 1/4"	17.00

WMF, Line, Stainless, "WMF Cromargan Germany" backstamp

Butter Spreader, FH, 6 3/8"	$15.00
Fork	15.00
Fork, cocktail	15.00
Fork, pastry, 6 1/4"	12.00
Fork, salad, 7 1/4"	15.00

Knife	25.00	Serving Spoon, tablespoon	27.00
Knife, dessert, 8″	15.00	Serving Spoon, tablespoon, pierced	27.00
Ladle, gravy	40.00	Spoon, demitasse, 5″	15.00
Serving Fork	30.00	Spoon, iced tea	17.00
Serving Fork, cold meat, 7 ½″	20.00	Spoon, soup, oval bowl	17.00
Serving Spoon	30.00	Spoon, sugar	20.00
Serving Spoon, tablespoon, 7 ⅝″	20.00	Spoon, teaspoon	17.00
Spoon, demitasse, 5″	12.00		
Spoon, iced tea, 8 ½″	15.00		
Spoon, soup, oval bowl	15.00		
Spoon, teaspoon	12.00		
Spoon, teaspoon, 5 o'clock, 5 ¾″	15.00		

WMF, Pilgrim, Stainless

Butter Spreader	$17.00
Fork	17.00
Fork, cocktail	17.00
Fork, salad	17.00
Knife, HH, modern blade, 8 ⅜″	22.00
Ladle, gravy	45.00
Ladle, soup	60.00
Serving Fork	35.00
Serving Spoon	35.00
Serving Spoon, round bowl	37.00

III

APPENDIX:
THE TOP PATTERNS

Top 25 Flatware Patterns (Alphabetically)

Buttercup by Gorham
Candlelight by Towle
Chantilly by Gorham
Classic Rose by Reed & Barton
Coronation by Oneida/Heirloom
Daffodil by International
Damask Rose by Oneida/Heirloom
Eternally Yours by International
Fairfax by Gorham
First Love by International
Francis I by Reed & Barton
French Provincial by Towle
Grande Baroque by Wallace
Joan of Arc by International
King Richard by Towle
Old Master by Towle
Prelude by International
Remembrance by International
Repoussé by Kirk Stieff
Rondo by Gorham
Rose Point by Wallace
Royal Danish by International
Shelley by Oneida/Heirloom
Strasbourg by Gorham
Venetia by Oneida/Heirloom

Top 26–50 Flatware Patterns (Alphabetically)

American Colonial by Oneida/Heirloom
Camellia by Gorham
Chateau Rose by Gorham
Chippendale by Towle
Eloquence by Lunt
English Gadroon by Gorham
Etruscan by Gorham
Flair by International
George & Martha Washington by Westmorland
Greenbrier by Gorham
Heritage by International
King Edward by Gorham
Lasting Rose by Oneida/Heirloom
Lyric by Gorham
Melrose by Gorham
Modern Victorian by Lunt
Mozart by Oneida/Heirloom
Nouveau by Gorham
Old Colonial by Towle
Old Maryland by Kirk Stieff
Queen's Fancy by International
Rambler Rose by Towle
Silver Flutes by Towle
Spring Glory by International
Tara by Reed & Barton

Top 51–100 Flatware Patterns (Alphabetically)

Act II by Oneida/Heirloom
Adoration by International
Beaded Antique by Towle
Burgundy by Reed & Barton
Capistrano by Oneida/Heirloom
Castle Rose by Royal Crest
Colonial Plume by Towle
Danish Princess by International
Design 2 by Towle
1810 by International
Eighteenth Century by Reed & Barton
Fontana by Towle
French Renaissance by Reed & Barton
Georgian Rose by Reed & Barton
Grand Colonial by Wallace
Juilliard by Oneida/Heirloom
Lady Hamilton by Oneida/Heirloom
Lily by Whiting Division
London Shell by Towle
Louis XIV by Towle
Madeira by Towle
Marlborough by Reed & Barton
Michelangelo by Oneida/Heirloom
Milburn Rose by Westmorland
Morning Star by Oneida/Heirloom
My Rose by Oneida/Heirloom
Old Lace by Towle
Old Mirror by Towle
Paul Revere by Oneida/Heirloom
Pilgrim by Fraser, William
Reflection by International
Regency by Reed & Barton
Rose by Kirk Stieff
Rose Solitaire by Towle
Savannah by Reed & Barton
Sea Rose by Gorham
Silver Sculpture by Reed & Barton
Sir Christopher by Wallace
South Seas by Oneida/Heirloom
Stieff Rose by Kirk Stieff
Stradivari by Wallace
Tennyson by Oneida/Heirloom
Today by International
Toujours by Oneida/Heirloom
Twin Star by Oneida/Heirloom
Vintage by International
White Orchid by Oneida/Heirloom
Wild Rose by International
William & Mary by Lunt
Will 'O' Wisp by Oneida/Heirloom

Bibliography

General References

Chefetz, Sheila. *Antiques for the Table: A Complete Guide to Dining Room Accessories for Collecting and Entertaining.* New York: Viking Studio Books, 1993.

Langford, Joel. *Silver: A Practical Guide to Collecting Silverware and Identifying Hallmarks.* Secaucus, N.J.: Chartwell Books, 1991.

Rainwater, Dorothy T. *Encyclopedia of American Silver Manufacturers.* 3d ed., rev. West Chester, Penn.: Schiffer Publishing, 1986.

Rainwater, Dorothy T., and H. Ivan. *American Silverplate.* West Chester, Penn.: Schiffer Publishing, 1988.

Romero, Christie. *Warman's Jewelry.* Radnor, Penn.: Wallace-Homestead, 1995.

Pattern Identification, Form, and Reference Books

Davis, Fredna Harris, and Kenneth K. Deibel. *Silver Plated Flatware Patterns.* 2d ed. Dallas, Tex.: Bluebonnet Press, 1981.

Dolan, Maryanne. *1830's–1990's American Sterling Silver Flatware: A Collector's Identification & Value Guide.* Florence, Ala.: Books Americana, 1993.

Gluck, Nancy. *The Grosvenor Pattern of Silverplate.* Norwalk, Conn.: Silver Season, 1996.

Gluck, Nancy. *The Vintage Pattern of Silverplated Flatware.* Norwalk, Conn.: Silver Season, 1995.

Hagan, Tere. *Silverplated Flatware.* 4th ed., rev. Paducah, Ky.: Collector Books, 1990.

Jeweler's Circular—Keystone Sterling Flatware Pattern Index. 2d ed. Radnor, Penn.: Chilton, 1989.

Osterberg, Richard. *Sterling Silver Flatware for Dining Elegance.* Atglen, Penn.: Schiffer Publishing, 1994.

Replacements, Ltd. *Stainless Steel Flatware Identification Guide.* Greensboro, N.C.: Replacements, Ltd., n.d.

Pattern Index

REPLACEMENTS, LTD.

The World's Largest Retailer of Discontinued and Active China, Crystal, Flatware and Collectibles

In 1981, Bob Page, an accountant-turned-flea-marketer, founded Replacements, Ltd. Since then, the company's growth and success can only be described as phenomenal.

Today, Replacements, Ltd. locates hard-to-find pieces in over 80,000 patterns - some of which have not been produced for more than 100 years. Now serving over 2 million customers, with an inventory of 4 million pieces, they mail up to 250,000 inventory listings weekly to customers seeking additional pieces in their patterns.

The concept for Replacements, Ltd. originated in the late 1970's when Page, then an auditor for the state of North Carolina, started spending his weekends combing flea markets buying china and crystal. Before long, he was filling requests from customers to find pieces they could not locate.

"I was buying and selling pieces primarily as a diversion," Page explains. "Back when I was an auditor, no one was ever happy to see me. And, quite frankly, I wasn't thrilled about being there either."

Page began placing small ads in shelter publications and started building a file of potential customers. Soon, his inventory outgrew his attic, where he had been storing the pieces, and it was time to make a change. "I reached the point where I was spending more time with dishes than auditing," Page says. "I'd be up until one or two o'clock in the morning. Finally, I took the big step: I quit my auditing job and hired one part-time assistant. Today I'm having so much fun, I often have to remind myself what day of the week it is!"

Replacements, Ltd. continued to grow quickly. In fact, in 1986, Inc. Magazine ranked Replacements, Ltd. 81st on its list of fastest-growing independently-owned companies in the U.S. "Our growth has been incredible," says Page, who was named 1991 North Carolina Entrepreneur of the Year. "I had no idea of the potential when I started out."

Clear standards of high quality merchandise and the highest possible levels of customer service are the cornerstones of the business, resulting in a shopping experience unparalleled in today's marketplace. Page also attributes much of the success of Replacements, Ltd. to a network of nearly 1,500 dedicated suppliers from all around the U.S. The company currently employs about 500 people in an expanded 225,000 square foot facility (the size of four football fields).

Another major contributor to the company's fast growth and top-level customer service is the extensive computer system used to keep track of the inventory. This state-of-the-art system also maintains customer files, including requests for specific pieces in their patterns. It is maintained by a full-time staff of over 20 people and is constantly upgraded to ensure customers receive the information they desire quickly and accurately.

For those who are unsure of the name and/or manufacturer

Greensboro, North Carolina Facility

Some of the 50,000 shelves in the 225,000 square foot warehouse

of their patterns, Replacements, Ltd. also offers a free pattern identification service. In addition, numerous books and publications focusing on pattern identification have been published by Replacements, Ltd. for both suppliers and individuals.

Replacements, Ltd. receives countless phone calls and letters from its many satisfied customers. Some need to replace broken or lost items while others want to supplement the sets they have had for years. A constant in the varied subjects customers write about is their long and fruitless search - a search that ended when they learned what Replacements, Ltd. could offer. "Since many patterns are family heirlooms that have been handed down from generation to generation, most customers are sentimental about replacing broken or missing pieces," Page says. "It's a great feeling to help our customers replace pieces in their patterns and to be able to see their satisfaction. Like our logo says - *we replace the irreplaceable.*"

Another growing area that Replacements, Ltd. has developed for its customers is the collectibles market. The company now offers a wide range of collectibles from companies such as Bing and

Grondahl, Royal Copenhagen, Boehm, Hummel, Lladro and many more. "It was a natural progression of our business," says Page, "and something our customers had been requesting."

The Replacements, Ltd. Showroom and Museum in Greensboro, NC is a 12,000 square-foot retail facility located in front of the massive warehouse. It is decorated with turn of the century hand-carved showcases, 20-foot ceilings and classic chandeliers. Inside, one can view an incredibly varied selection of merchandise - from figurines, mugs and ornaments to the china, crystal and flatware that made the company famous.

The fascinating Replacements, Ltd. Museum, adjacent to the retail Showroom, is the home for over 2,000 rare and unusual pieces that Page has collected over the years. It includes a special section dedicated to one of Page's first loves - early 20th century glass from companies like Tiffin, Fostoria, Heisey, Imperial and Cambridge.

FOR MORE INFORMATION

• Call **1-800-REPLACE** (1-800-737-5223 from 8 am to 10 pm Eastern Time, 7 days a week)

• Write to: 1089 Knox Road, PO Box 26029 Greensboro, NC 27420

• Fax: 910-697-3100

• Visit the Replacements, Ltd. Showroom and Museum, at exit 132 off I-85/40 in Greensboro, NC. The Showroom and Museum are open 7 days a week, from 8 am to 9 pm.

A view of Replacements' 12,000 square foot Showroom

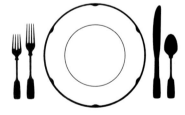

REPLACEMENTS, LTD.
"We Replace The Irreplaceable"

1-800-REPLACE (1-800-737-5223)